Taoist Inner Alchemy

TAOIST INNER ALCHEMY

Master Huang Yuanji's Guide
to the Way of Meditation

GE GUOLONG

Translated by Mattias Daly

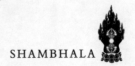

SHAMBHALA

Shambhala Publications, Inc.
2129 13th Street
Boulder, Colorado 80302
www.shambhala.com

Cover art: Landscape of the four seasons in the styles of old masters, Wei Zhike, 1635.
Gift of J. T. Tai, 1968, Metropolitan Museum of Art, 68.195.
Cover design: Jamie Tipton
Interior design: Kate E. White

9 8 7 6 5 4 3 2 1

First Edition
Printed in the United States of America

Shambhala Publications makes every effort to print on acid-free, recycled paper.
Shambhala Publications is distributed worldwide by Penguin Random House, Inc.,
and its subsidiaries.

LIBRARY OF CONGRESS CATALOGING-IN-PUBLICATION DATA
Names: Goulong, Ge, author. | Daly, Mattias, translator.
Title: Taoist inner alchemy: Master Huang Yuanji's guide to the way of meditation /
Ge Guolong; translated by Mattias Daly.
Description: First edition. | Boulder: Shambhala, [2024] | Includes bibliographical
references. |
Identifiers: LCCN 2023014759 | ISBN 9781645472124 (trade paperback)
Subjects: LCSH: Yuanji, Huang | Taoism.
Classification: LCC BL1900.A2 G67 2024 | DDC 299.5/14435—dc23/eng/20230818
LC record available at https://lccn.loc.gov/2023014759

Contents

Contents

Author's Introduction

Taoism's classic texts are extremely numerous. With so many other ancient writings to choose from, why base a book on discussions of ten chapters from Huang Yuanji's *The Oral Record of the Hall of Joyous Teaching*? I chose to do so because, both in terms of its contents and its manner of presentation, Huang Yuanji's book is unique. The reasons I believe this deserve a brief explanation.

The classic writings of Taoism can be divided into numerous categories. One of those categories is books created through planchette writing; these are books that were received through communication with the spiritual realm. Many internal alchemy writings dating to the Ming and Qing dynasties were transmitted from Ancestor Lü Dongbin in this way. Books of this sort were not penned by specific individuals, but rather came about through communication between people of this world and beings existing in formlessness. Sometimes their contents are not especially clear, and they have a "stream of consciousness" quality to them.

Another category of books was written by ancient scholars who researched Taoism deeply. Reading huge numbers of books, they became profoundly versed in Taoist thought. Their knowledge allowed them to write "classics" of their own, as well as to pen commentaries on various important texts. The books they wrote were strong on theory and presented ideas quite systematically. However, these writers did not necessarily go deeply into Taoist practice. Often, they were members of the literati whose intellectual cultivation allowed them to write eloquently about things they had not in fact directly experienced. These scholastic commentators on the Tao are sometimes likened to people who write books on military strategy without having experienced combat.

A third category of Taoist books contain the words of highly accomplished Taoist adepts; some were written by these masters themselves, and others by people who collected their sayings. The knowledge presented in these books comes from people who personally experienced Taoist practice, instead of those who thought about or imagined it. Moreover, compared with the aforementioned books that came about by using planchette writing to communicate with the heavenly realms, these books come across as more down to earth. They can serve as guides for actual practice. In my opinion, their ability to assist readers with their cultivation makes them incredibly valuable.

Yet another category of Taoist books consists of books of poetry and verses written by earlier masters. Titles in this category include voluminous works of poetry by the ancestral founders of the Complete Reality school of Taoism, as well as Zhang Boduan's *Awakening to Reality*. These writings are so full of coded symbols that one can study them for a very long time without gaining a clear idea of what they are meant to express. So much skill is required for one to be able to decipher these collections of verse that they sometimes feel aloof and vague.

The Oral Record of the Hall of Joyous Teaching happens to be a book with none of the shortcomings of the categories listed above. Its greatest merit lies in the fact that this book consists of transcripts of Huang Yuanji's discourses, taken down by his disciples. From what they recorded, it is clear to see that Huang was not just an authentic Taoist cultivator, but one who had reached quite a high level of realization. Many of the most important classics from different religions were also records of oral teachings given by great masters. Because the words such books contain came from the mouths of accomplished adepts, their very existence is capable of lending power to those who encounter them. Moreover, because these teachers were actual practitioners, the words they spoke were based in real experience, not imagination or academic knowledge.

The *Oral Record* presents profound information in a simple manner. Although its time period means that it was written in classical Chinese, Huang Yuanji was clearly teaching in the colloquial language of the day, yielding a text that is quite accessible and easy to understand. However, even though the book is written in a plain manner, there is nothing shallow about its contents. It contains teachings on the entire process of Taoist inner alchemy cultivation, ranging from building a foundation to the highest levels of practice. It also includes authentic explanations of fundamental theories as well as methods needed to actually start walking the path. In other words, this is a text that equally emphasizes both theory and practice.

Some books are heavily pitched toward theory, but they give little insight into how one should actually practice. Other books place a lot of emphasis on the particulars of practice, to the point that they are essentially step-by-step training manuals. Such manuals do not take the reader deeply into the principles upon which practice is based. It is crucial for those of us with an interest in internal alchemy to keep in mind that Taoism's principles and its practices must be learned side by side in order for there to be any hope of success.

If one only has an idea of cultivation as a defined system of practices but does not thoroughly understand the principles that inform cultivation, then one will practice as though blind, because one will have no idea where one is supposed to be going. Practice without a clear sense of destination becomes mechanical, and it will not allow one to enter into the higher stages. This is because Taoist cultivation cannot be brought to fruition through mechanistic processes. What is required for real accomplishment is an elevated level of consciousness and self-awareness. Of course, if one merely nods along knowingly with the above warning, without engaging in any actual practice, then one will be just like the ancient literati who did nothing but probe into all kinds of theories. Filling one's head with new things to think about will not bring one any closer to the path.

In terms of both theory and practical instructions, the teachings in the *Oral Record* are very comprehensive. The book reveals a wealth of critical cultivation instructions in an open, unguarded manner. These instructions were revealed in the context of the needs of the disciples Huang Yuanji was addressing when he taught, making them highly applicable in real situations. For this reason, I wrote another book, *A Modern Interpretation of Taoist Alchemy: Explaining "The Oral*

Record of the Hall of Joyous Teaching," which organizes, explains, and distills the contents of all 142 discourses in Huang Yuanji's original work.

Each chapter in the book you are holding is based upon a lecture I gave on one of Huang Yuanji's discourses in the *Oral Record*. These ten lectures had to fit into the space of five evenings, so there was no way to try and look at the *Oral Record* in its entirety. Instead, each night I discussed two representative chapters from Huang's book. While my lectures only touched upon a small fraction of the *Oral Record*'s contents, they still encompass all of the key themes in Huang Yuanji's teachings.

That said, this book is not meant to simply be an explication of ten discourses from the *Oral Record*. Rather, the book is a multifaceted look at the ideological system underpinning internal alchemy, meant to explain this aspect of Taoism in a way that is accessible to modern readers. This means that, beyond containing an analysis of Huang Yuanji's discourse, each chapter connects to the general themes of internal alchemy, while also including some of the fruits of my own research and cultivation practice. Thus, this book simultaneously presents the marrow of *The Oral Record of the Hall of Joyous Teaching*, the basic structure of internal alchemy theory, and the essential considerations of Taoist philosophy and practice. I chose the ten discourses that begin each chapter precisely because they are excellent starting points for our journey toward understanding internal alchemy's core teachings.

—GE GUOLONG

Translator's Introduction

I was first given a book of Huang Yuanji's teachings in 2012 by Liu Yuanhui, a Taoist nun in the Complete Reality order who is abbess of the Three Purities monastery in the foothills of the Changbai mountains in Jilin Province in northeast China. The heavy tome was somewhat beyond me, both in terms of my knowledge of Taoist inner alchemy theory as well as my own meditation practice, but I hung on to it, occasionally flipping through its hundreds of pages in search of a foothold. Five years later, while on a three-week winter retreat at the monastery, I tried my hand at translating the opening chapters of *The Oral Record of the Hall of Joyous Teaching*, which constituted the first half of the book Abbess Liu had given me (the second half comprised Huang Yuanji's exegesis of Lao-tzu's *Tao Te Ching* and a small number of stand-alone internal alchemy teachings in the forms of essays and poems). My main reason for doing this was simply to deepen my own engagement with the text by rendering it in my native tongue—and also to have something to do between meditation sessions, owl-accompanied walks in the frozen woods, and near-daily snow-shoveling sessions.

By the time I left the monastery to return to Beijing, I had finished translating the first four or five chapters of the book (out of, oh, two hundred fifty or so), and was getting a feel for putting the semi-vernacular, semi-literary language Huang Yuanji used as he taught his students into English. Still, it never really crossed my mind that these translations might warrant publication. Even though Huang Yuanji's way of discussing internal alchemy was nothing like what is found in the arcane, symbolism-laden writings of the Tang, Song, and Jin-Yuan periods, he certainly wasn't speaking anything remotely like "plain

English." His teachings still needed to be unpacked for anybody not already "in the door" to actually get anything from them, and I certainly wasn't willing or qualified to try and translate two hundred essays *and* write commentaries on them.

I put the translations out of mind until the summer of 2017, when, as I was packing up my apartment in Beijing, I came across the copy of Ge Guolong's *Ten Discourses on Taoist Alchemy* I purchased in Shanghai in 2010, *way* before I could make heads or tails of its contents. Cracking open Ge's now-dusty book a second time, I suddenly realized it was a series of lectures based around ten of Huang Yuanji's teachings. Not only that, it included all of the chapters I'd already translated, and, since Ge was speaking to an audience of laypeople in Hong Kong as he lectured, he expanded upon the chapters' contents in a way that made them accessible to an audience of modern people steeped neither in classical literary Chinese, nor the core Taoist (and Buddhist and Confucian) ideas underlying internal alchemy. Having by then lived in China for a decade, during which time I sought out numerous Taoist and Buddhist teachers, I reread Ge's book voraciously. I came away convinced that his book could provide a bridge between modern readers of English and a form of a Taoist practice that began to be codified in highly recondite writings during the late Tang dynasty.

In the autumn of that year I visited Ge Guolong in his apartment in the suburbs north of Beijing to propose translating the book into English. Offering his support, he reminded me that Taoist teachings are useless unless put into practice, and he placed special emphasis on the close relationship between Taoist alchemy and Chan Buddhism (an emphasis that closely echoed Abbess Liu's oft-repeated exhortations not to mistakenly conclude that these two traditions seek disparate ends). Over the course of the following four years, I tackled the book's ten chapters whenever lulls in my work and graduate studies presented themselves. I completed the final three chapters in a whirlwind during Taiwan's summer lockdown in 2021, in no small part thanks to the help I received from dozens of people who generously donated to support a project that took many hundreds of hours to complete.

HUANG YUANJI AND HIS TEACHINGS

Each chapter in this volume begins with the text of a discourse delivered by a wandering Taoist teacher called Huang Yuanji during the late Qing dynasty (1644–1911). Given his influence and temporal proximity, surprisingly little is known about this Taoist adept. His date of birth is unknown, but according to the foreword he wrote for his commentaries on the *Tao Te Ching*, those were first published in 1884, suggesting he was born sometime in the early to mid-nineteenth century. A colophon to the same text, written by one of his disciples, states that Huang hailed from Fengcheng in Jiangxi Province in southeast China, an area known for a high concentration of well-off, highly educated families. However, there are no written traces of Huang Yuanji's life in his hometown. All of his known activities as a teacher took place in Sichuan, a province in China's southwest that received large numbers of migrants from the southeast during the nineteenth century, and which had a lively scene of Taoist masters offering public teachings and publishing voluminous works that were publicly available. According to Taiwanese scholar Lee Li-Liang's comprehensive research into Huang Yuanji's background, a foreword to a rare version of his *Tao Te Ching* commentaries records that he taught in Fushun in Sichuan Province at a school called the Hall of Joyous Teaching between 1874 and 1883; however, Lee also cites other records documenting a period of teaching that lasted for over ten years. Huang delivered teachings orally. His disciples transcribed them as he spoke, eventually publishing them in three volumes: *The Oral Record of the Hall of Joyous Teaching, The Essential Meaning of the Tao Te Ching,* and *The Key to the Gate of Taoism.*

Huang's background in Taoism is not recorded, although he mentioned to his students that he searched arduously for more than ten years before receiving internal alchemy teachings. According to his foreword to *The Essential Meaning of the Tao Te Ching,* he arrived in Sichuan to traverse its famous mountains (both Mount Qingcheng and Mount Emei are major draws for religious pilgrims coming to Sichuan) and to visit "friends in the Tao." Eventually he came across the community of cultivators, both male and female, at the Hall of Joyous Teaching in Fushun. Originally he simply arrived as an unknown traveler and listened to the teacher who was lecturing without revealing himself. Finding this teacher to be a cultivator of substance, Huang engaged him or her in conversation. Evidently his own achievement quickly became clear enough to the school's community that he was invited to remain there and teach.

Huang Yuanji's death is shrouded in even more mystery than his life. Publications directly connected to his time in Sichuan were all written before his passing, and if any of his direct students left writings behind recounting how Huang Yuanji ultimately departed from their midst, those writings have not survived to the present day. One recounting, found in a book published in Taiwan in 1966, claims that in 1884 Huang gathered his students in the Hall of Joyous Teaching, formally disbanded the school, and then exited the building in his students' company. Thereupon he ascended into the sky in full view of his disciples, many of whom tearfully lamented that they had not studied harder while they still had the chance. Adding to the sense of mystery, rumors of Huang's having briefly reappeared in various places in Taiwan and China in recent years are occasionally passed around the Taoist community. To this day, his works remain in publication and are known to many if not most Chinese-speaking inner alchemy enthusiasts.

Huang Yuanji unambiguously taught his students Taoist inner alchemy, but like many in his day (and indeed like many of the early adepts who established the tradition), he clearly believed that esoteric forms of Confucian and Buddhist cultivation included practices comparable to, if not ultimately equivalent to, internal alchemy. As such he borrowed liberally from Buddhist and Confucian sources to flesh out his teachings, both at the exoteric and esoteric levels. Huang Yuanji's teachings do refer to terms many people consider to be integral to Taoist alchemy, such as the *dantian*, the *ren-du* meridians running up the back and down the front of the body, and, relatedly, the "microcosmic orbit" and "macrocosmic orbit." However, aside from the dantian (which appears in approximately one-sixth of *The Oral Record of the Hall of Joyous Teaching*'s chapters), these concepts are actually mentioned very sparingly. Every Taoist practitioner I have met who considers Huang Yuanji as a spiritual forebear emphasizes that all movements of qi through the body's meridians in internal alchemy practice should take place naturally, without the interference of intention and thought. This may be one reason that the qi meridians are seldom mentioned in Huang's teachings. Moreover, it has been pointed out to me that not all of Huang's mentions of the dantian necessarily relate to any of the three locations in the body described in huge amounts of modern Taoist, qigong, *neigong*, and internal martial arts literature. Instead, in Huang Yuanji's usage, the dantian, or "field of elixir," may actually be an oblique reference to the "mysterious pass," which is introduced in detail in chapter 3 of this book, or to "true intent," which is discussed in chapters 4 and 10. Precedent for such an interpretation exists in ancient alchemical texts dating to the Song dynasty.

The particulars of Huang Yuanji's practical instructions are too obscure to flesh out in this introduction, in part because we cannot be sure which living practitioners, if any, know exactly what Huang Yuanji taught and practiced behind closed doors, and also because living practitioners of internal alchemy methods tracing back to Huang Yuanji have themselves not made their methods public. Up through the present day, it remains the norm for Taoist alchemy's practical instructions to be reserved for private teachings given face-to-face, often one-on-one, after lengthy periods of observation between students and teachers. Vows of secrecy and discretion remain the norm, and permission to teach is seldom if ever granted to students who have not already reached a high level of training. This is in no small part because it is well understood in Taoism that powerful meditation practices can produce side effects, imbalances, and even illnesses. It is therefore not considered wise or compassionate to transmit teachings to anybody one is not fully prepared to give ongoing guidance to. Huang Yuanji and Ge Guolong do not depart from tradition in this book, and neither do I. As such, despite the penetrating insights into Taoist alchemy that these ten chapters offer, they cannot be used as a practice manual.

What can be said is that Huang Yuanji's teachings belong to the "highest order" of inner alchemy. As is explained in the pages that follow, teachings of this sort make almost exclusive use of "prior heaven" aspects of the mind, the human body, and the universe as a whole; they also center upon the practice of wu wei. Because Huang Yuanji taught internal alchemy in this vein, this book's contents diverge distinctly from the many qigong and neigong practices that involve specific instructions pertaining to bodily postures, physical movements, ways of breathing, and methods of moving or gathering qi in the body via the power of the mind. Huang's teachings center instead upon getting the ever-active human mind out of the way of that which has the potential to unfold naturally. For this reason, some aspects of these teachings recall the writings of Chan (Zen) Buddhism and Dzogchen. Nevertheless, integral Taoist concepts such as yin-yang, *jing-qi-shen*, wu wei, nonexistence, and the Tao itself remain central. While Huang Yuanji goes so far as to venture that what Shakyamuni Buddha practiced was none other than a form of internal alchemy, this book is not simply "Chan in Taoist robes." Its core philosophies clearly reflect a tradition whose roots trace back to the same wellspring that produced the *Book of Changes*, *The Yellow Emperor's Inner Classic*, the *Tao Te Ching*, and other works predating the flourishing of Buddhism on Chinese soil.

NOTES ON THE TRANSLATION

I have generally used the Hanyu Pinyin system of transliteration in this book, except in the case of characters that start with the letter *x* in Pinyin, as they are hard to pronounce and grating on the eye. These words instead begin with *hs*, which points closely to their Mandarin pronunciation. Thus, the word *hsing*, which appears constantly in this work, is actually listed in most contemporary Chinese-English dictionaries under *xing*. I use the Wade-Giles "Taoism" instead of "Daoism" because I think it looks prettier and is still generally more familiar. (For the sake of clarity, that's a soft *t*, just like the one in *water* in Philly. If you don't know what that means, guess you better go visit the City of Brotherly Love, and you might as well get yaself a cheese steak while you at it!) Out of fondness, I also call Laozi and Zhuangzi by the versions of their names I was first acquainted with, Lao-tzu and Chuang-tzu. How exactly should they be pronounced? Who knows. All we can say for sure is that the languages they spoke sounded as dissimilar to standard Beijing Mandarin as Taiwanese, Cantonese, Hakka, and Shanghainese all do today (all five of these modern "dialects" are mutually unintelligible).

As these chapters all derive from lightly edited lecture transcripts, there are sections in the original where it is clear that Ge Guolong was "thinking aloud," jumping between trains of thought, or repeating himself. In order to make the final product more readable I did my best to tighten up the language of these parts of the text. Otherwise, I did not drastically alter the original contents, but I did make countless tiny tweaks that seemed necessary in order to put Ge's thoughts into intelligible English. As I did so, I drew upon my experience as an interpreter (including in settings in China where philosophy or spiritual and energetic practices were being discussed), and tried to imagine myself interpreting Ge Guolong's lectures in person, before an audience of people whose primary reason for attending the lectures was to deepen their spiritual lives. While Ge and I are both academics, we are also both practitioners. His original lectures and my translations are geared toward informing practice, not scholarly research.

I am indebted to the many Taoist and Buddhist teachers whose years of mentoring and patiently answering endless questions made it possible for me to translate this book. Peter Moy, Abbess Liu Yuanhui, and Sun Ch'ang-Lu have all shared countless precious teachings and insights with me, allowing me to peer into the world of inner alchemy as more than a curious outsider. Professor Ge Guolong has my deep gratitude for entrusting me with this project, as does Red Pine, who kept wind at my sails from beginning to end. Excellent instruction from the faculty of National Taiwan University's Graduate Institute of Chinese Literature allowed me to gain proficiency reading and translating classical Chinese; I am especially grateful for the guidance and encouragement of my MA thesis advisor, Professor Lin Yung-Sheng. I also thank Professor Hsieh Tsung-Hui of the Department of Chinese at National Taiwan Normal University for opening the door to rigorous academic research into Taoism's classical writings—scholastic pursuits can easily become a path leading away from the kinds of insights that are necessary for Taoist practice, but at the same time, proficiency in reading, interpreting, and contextualizing classic texts is a necessity in internal alchemy. I am grateful for the many nameless contributors to digital databases such as CBETA, CText, Daoinfo, Home in Mists, Kanseki Repository, Taolibrary, and Wikisource, as well as the search-engine designers whose work allows the modern scholar to enjoy easy access to rare and obscure writings that was unimaginable a generation ago. Having said that, I hasten to add that absolutely no AI or machine-assisted translation was used in the creation of this book.

Special thanks go to Beth Frankl for seeing promise in this project and welcoming it to Shambhala Publications' roster, as well as to Stephan Downes and John Golebiewski for patiently taking care of the details. I thank Cannon Labrie and Susan Barnett for their editorial review. Additionally, I could not have completed this translation without the generous, trusting support of the many people who made donations via GoFundMe. They are Omran Alshasmi, Thomas Campbell, Chevy Chen, Tom M. Chen, Ryan Crocombe, Margaret Daly-Denton, Catherine Despeux, Arik Dobson, Bill Engst, Isaac Epstein, Laurence Gallacier-Raphenon, Alessandra Guarino, Oscar Idelji-Tehrani, Daniel Jacob, Matt James, Bobby Kasik, Gregory Kulevich, Elaine Lai, Brenda Loew, Zhibo Lu, Bryan McMahon, Stella Miller, Thomas Morillon, Felix Niland, Tracy Peck, Bill Porter, Saish Prabhu, Harry Prest, Liz Rose, Toby Rush, Tim Sibbald, Michael Smith, PJ Sneeringer, Pierce Suen, Evelyn J. Thompson, Minh Truong, Matthew Tye, Danny van Deelen, Tomas Waldegren, and Andy Wallace, in addition to many other anonymous parties. Oh oh oh, and you know I ain't forget: thanks are very much due to my family and friends, particularly for putting up with this weirdo in their midst. And 'thout a doubt, shout out to the Lizards Crew. *Grâsz Grütz!*

—MATTIAS DALY
Taipei, Taiwan
111th year of the Republic of China

Taoist Inner Alchemy

無上因緣

UNSURPASSED DESTINY

Humans are born between heaven and earth. Aside from the great Way of the golden elixir and the work of turning around and returning, all the vast varieties of endlessly enjoyable glories and riches are nothing but objects of delusion. With ordinary people who do not know the Tao, revelry, sex, property, and profit are their pursuits. What they proclaim as their own reapings and surpluses come only because in past lives they cultivated merit and gained goodness, which in this life they benefit from most grandly.

Who knows that through excessive enjoyment and use jing *and* shen *vanish and scatter? When their ends come, not only do people return emptyhanded, but furthermore their true qi of heaven, earth, and self also vanishes, disappearing back to nonexistence. This is what the Supreme Sovereign called "heaven, earth, and the myriad things stealing my primordial qi."*

Though one may know prosperity, high position, and beautiful scenery, and though one may be emperor, king, general, or minister, if one does not know how to restore one's hsing *and establish one's* ming, *then one will only deepen the dissipation of one's real primordial qi day by day, without a speck of benefit to one's real self. Thus, toiling for wealth and rank is far worse than finding contentment in poverty and low status.*

The ancients said, "In this world, if you do not cultivate Tao and de, *it is as though you've entered a mountain of treasure but come back emptyhanded." These words are true and not false.*

While teaching throughout the region of Shu, I have seen how, if the common people are not laboring in devotion to wealth, prestige, scholarly honor, and official rank, then they are galloping passionately after liquor, sex, money, and anger. This fills my heart with pity. Yet, though I am of a heart to save them, they do not know how to reverse course. Yet more, not only are they unwilling to receive salvation, instead they click their tongues with words of annoyance, saying my Way is fanciful and bizarre. Alas! With people such as these, although I am full of compassionate intent, there is nothing I can do!

Ask yourselves, in today's world, are most people's consciences not buried and neglected? It is just that people do not ask themselves: During a single kalpa, how many human lives can one attain? Days and nights fly by in the blink of an eye, and then it is the twilight of your life. How do you know that your wealth and prestige in this life will not become poverty and lowliness in the next? How do you know that while today you are a person, you will not return to the world as livestock?

The ancients said: "A human body is rarely attained, the Middle Kingdom is difficult to be born in, and the Great Tao is seldom encountered." Given that you have obtained a human body, had the luck to be born in the Middle Kingdom, and moreover have heard the correct doctrine, you must have unexcelled predestined affinity. Compared with all the emperors, kings, ministers, and generals, who enjoy themselves today but are dead tomorrow, and whose reincarnations are unbearably wretched, are your circumstances not infinitely superior?

Henceforth, if you concertedly cultivate, even if you do not become an immortal or a sage, when you return to the world for rebirth, you will still be a person with root. This, too, is good fortune. Moreover, for the convening of this assembly, the heavens above have especially bestowed grace, allowing completion of cultivation in this kalpa. All of you who meet with this good luck, make great efforts to make progress. Do not fear difficulty, and do not avoid hardship. If you make vows on the grounds of morality, and concentrate your heart on meritorious deeds, then how could heaven's spiritual immortals all be so ignorant and deaf as to fail to see and hear you? The only fear is that people are unwilling to put their hearts into it. Worry not that the heavenly deities will not silently protect and guide you.

This world's ways are chaotic, and human hearts are dim and confused. Ordinary people believe that this era and this land are dangerous. But among superior people who have the Tao, instead there is the belief that being here is great good fortune. Why is that? Suppose that one's circumstances were unremarkable, that one did not undergo tortures or experience dashed hopes, would one not just be smoothly passing through? Who, then, would be willing to turn his or her heart toward the Tao, to set his or her will on seeking the mysterious? Only with these thousands of trials and myriad tribulations, with things not as one wishes them, with nobody taking one's side, will one realize that the ways of the dusty world just bring fatigue and worry, not holding a single benefit.

Therefore, be indifferent to fame and wealth and concentrate on being yourselves; be weary of the human world and make oaths to cultivate clarity. Though in this life you may not become an immortal, still you will have climbed onto the steps of the way to transcendence. Supposing you reincarnate in the world as a human, will heaven's deities willingly abandon you in order to seek out another? Thus did the ancients say, "Spiritual immortals are born of spiritual immortal seeds—ordinary people do not just up and transcend for no reason!"

I will speak again on today's chance meeting. Nowadays, people studying the Tao are countless. But how many are able to obtain an unreservedly clear explanation of the true, eternal, incomprehensible Tao's complete essence and vast function? Only you, who follow my discourses, which have not a thread or speck of omission that would cause you to plummet into the study of side paths. Contemplate what an opportunity this is! This is enough to show the heavenly deities' love for those on the path, and that they are especially generous toward you.

Yet, beginning with your entry into the Way, you will time and again be scraped across the grindstone, passing through wind and waves. In the eyes of onlookers, people who study Tao seem not to carry heaven's protection, and to instead encounter numerous terrors. Little do others know that to suffer a round of slander and criticism is to advance by a fraction in Tao and de; that to pass through a round of tempering is to grow by a fraction in jing and shen. Moreover, bad habits rooted in former lives are eliminated by this; prior sins and coming retributions are mended by this. It is just like a person soiled by filthy sludge, being once cleansed; or like jade or gold hidden within stone, going through the forge, and then beginning to scintillate.

This Tao of attaining both felicity and wisdom is not found in settling into a smooth and steady life. Rather, it is found in passing through perils *and hardships. Students, do not lose restraint because of others' words, nor have the least flinching of will. In my view, you are all truly the stuff of spiritual immortals, not like those who drag through the mud and water, here hoping for spiritual immortality, there pining for riches and rank, two notions muddled in a single heart.*

■ ■ ■

Why start this book by offering this particular discourse of Huang Yuanji's, out of hundreds that he gave? Well, if one embarks upon any of Taoism's cultivation paths, or if one enters into any religion's inner teachings on spirituality, there will always be a question of destiny—a question of what factors enabled one to pass through the entrance to these teachings. There are all kinds of people in the world, some who have no religious beliefs at all, some who believe in Christianity, some who believe in Buddhism, some who believe in Taoism, and so on. All people have predestined affinities, some of which may lead them toward certain religions, or lead them to enter a path of self-cultivation. Speaking from the standpoint of Taoist internal alchemy, a person must have predestined affinity with this tradition in order to have the opportunity to put its teachings into practice. Thus, whenever a master first introduces students to Taoism, he or she will always emphasize this important issue.

The first aspect of destined affinity that we will discuss is really a matter of the worldview and life outlook that a person might establish in response to a simple question: Why would anybody need or want to cultivate the Tao? To best answer this question, we can borrow ideas from Buddhism's Four Noble Truths, which are a very succinct summary of the Buddhist worldview.

The Four Noble Truths are examinations of four observations: (1) that there is suffering in life; (2) that suffering is brought about through cause and effect; (3) that suffering can be brought to an end; and, (4) that there is a way to lead to the cessation of suffering. These four observations contain a general evaluation of the actual circumstances of human life. When Buddhism says "there is suffering," its point is that there exists suffering in each and every person's life—nobody is exempted. In his discourse above, much as though he was introducing

Buddhism's first noble truth, Huang Yuanji draws our attention to suffering, as well as to the things that people seek to obtain in life. In the end, Huang concludes that worldly pursuits are meaningless. He does this because any Taoist teacher who wishes to transmit the knowledge of Taoist cultivation and encourage students to actually practice must explain what a real human life is. This means pointing out what is of real value in life, and what is of false value, as well as what things have meaning, and what is meaningless. Buddhism holds that if one wishes to embark upon the Buddhist path, the first thing one needs to do is recognize that suffering is an intrinsic part of human life. The same recognition is required for those who wish to cultivate the Tao.

Naturally, some people might respond to the above by saying, "I think human life is really very joyous. I don't think life is bitter at all, so does that mean I don't need to cultivate the Way?" Buddhism's answer to this question is that, while one may think that one's life is free of suffering, the conditions of one's life will inevitably change. If a person really and truly feels that he or she actually lives without suffering, and is eternally happy, then that person indeed has no need of cultivation—if this person is not already a buddha, then he or she is probably a Taoist immortal! But in real life there is always suffering, starting with the most obvious sufferings associated with birth, aging, sickness, and death. Furthermore, each person ultimately faces a fundamental form of suffering, what Buddhism calls "the suffering of impermanence."

One might think, "right now everything for me is perfectly satisfactory, my career's great, and I'm very happy." But good fortune is unreliable, and it does not last forever. A person's happiness rests upon a constellation of conditions in the world, and these conditions are themselves impermanent. There is nothing in life that can permanently serve as a fallback. Not only are external conditions ephemeral and changeable, our bodies, too, are impermanent. Our flesh-and-blood bodies only survive for a very limited amount of time in this world. Thus, though we chase after all manner of things and indeed feel great joy when we obtain some of them, our happiness can be gone in an instant. Suffering comes the very moment the conditions that our happiness relies upon to exist disappear. In this world, suffering and joy are two opposites that give birth to one another.

Most people go through life bounding along after their desires, but the fulfillment of desires is incapable of creating true satisfaction, because desires themselves are infinite. There is simply no end point for desire. Even if one is making money, one never really makes enough—it is clear that no amount of money is sufficient to buy lasting contentment. Furthermore, no matter how much money one makes, in the end it is really just a number at the bank. One's bank balance does not actually have all that much to do with one's life, because the real needs of the human body are finite. How much food one can eat, how many clothes one can wear, how many homes one can actually occupy—the quantities are actually quite tiny.

■ ■ ■

Suffering can come at any time, and its source can be internal or external. In the heat of summer, one can barely resist stripping off layers of clothing. Feeling unbearably hot is a form of suffering that we usually associate with the weather, but our psychological states can also create the same discomfort, irrespective of the external environment. When our minds become anxious, we might burn with "inner" heat, for example. That said, while sages may be keen to remind us that suffering may always be just around the corner, we should be careful not to conclude that religions have a negative, pessimistic view of human life. Actually, recognizing the problems inherent in human life is precisely what brings opportunities for resolving them, and can lead us down a path to a higher and more ideal level of existence. Naturally, if we do not even recognize the problems besetting us, then we will remain incapable of finding ways to solve them.

Some needs have to be promptly satisfied, such as when we remove clothing when hot or eat when hungry. Needs like this, which are in the moment, originate with our bodies. Unlike these needs, which are mostly physical, desires are psychological. They stem from our habits of making comparisons and from our imaginations. Because we never succeed at fully satisfying our psychological desires, they end up becoming a root cause of human suffering.

All people seek happiness—few are those truly willing to pass their days in torment. Yet, in reality, the majority of people in our world still manage to spend much of their lives in varying degrees and depths of suffering. Why is this? Speaking from the perspective of Taoist cultivation, it is due to a lack of the type of wisdom that is needed to resolve suffering. Having what we call wisdom means being able to see the true face of a situation. Our suffering comes precisely because we often cannot see things as they really are, and so we act in violation of the reality of our circumstances, desperately fighting to occupy and own things that are fundamentally impermanent. The desire to permanently possess that which cannot last creates our suffering. However, if we can recognize that this world is at its base impermanent, then we will break the habit of trying to rule it, and the suffering brought about by attachment to desire will dissipate.

■ ■ ■

Of course, one can own a great many things, but at root, anything one might possess can be compared to clothing. Just as draping oneself with either beautiful or ragged garments will not change one's body, adorning oneself with different possessions will not actually affect one's real life. As for what actually counts as "real life," this is a central question pursued by all religions. The entire process of cultivation is a search for an answer.

It is not only that the objects of the external world can never be more than pieces of clothing accessorizing our lives. If we look at things from the standpoint of cultivation, then we can go a step further in our examination, at which point we will discover that even our bodies are like clothes. My body is mine, and I live within it, but the answer to "who am I?" is definitely not "this body," and that means there is a fundamental difference between "me" and "my body." When we walk yet another step forward in our inner observation, we discover that we are not our thoughts, either. Our thoughts constantly come and go. Within each of us there are countless different thoughts swirling around, so which one of them is really "me?" Similarly, we have all manner of emotions and sensations, but these sensations can be bitter one moment, and then joyous the next. Since they are in constant flux, none of them can be the real "me."

Our problem is precisely that we identify with all these things. At a very surficial level, we identify externally with our homes and automobiles. Moving a little bit deeper, we identify with and cling to our flesh-and-blood bodies. Moving yet deeper, we attach to our goodness, our badness, our beauty, our ugliness—our distinctions and our experiences. The most fundamental attachment comes from seeing our thoughts as ourselves—I have a thought and then I identify with this thought. For example, a person might speak ill of me, leading me to unwaveringly take these words to heart, whereas in actual fact these words do not influence my real life at all. They have no relationship to my real life.

Identifying with the external layers of self prevents us from discovering the true, root reality of our existence. In other words, we never discover the "real me." This "real me" can also be called "fundamental nature," or "original face." It can also be called other things—"soul" is fine, too. You can use different names to refer to it, but none of these names is it. Knowing these names definitely does not equate with having real self-knowledge, which is something that each person must search for and discover within. Using Taoism's vocabulary, each person has a prior-heaven original nature that comes from within the Tao and is in harmony with the Tao. However, during our post-heaven lives, we forget our prior-heaven natures, and then we end up identifying with our multifarious post-heaven selves. Cultivating Tao means returning to our true selves—it means going back into the Tao. In later discourses we will unpack the meaning of this idea in detail.

■ ■ ■

No matter which religion a cultivation system belongs to, it will have a set of answers to big questions such as these: What is human life? Where do our problems lie? What was the initial cause of these problems? What are the methods and paths that solve our problems? What is the ultimate destination we aim to arrive at? These are the questions that Buddhism's Four Noble Truths address. We can also see the formulation of Buddhism's four truths on "suffering, the causes of suffering, the extinction of suffering, and the path" as reflective of a model that is common to other religions. All religions speak of these four issues as they offer basic assessments and explanations of human life, and as they explain what type of path one should walk in order to find the proverbial garden, the realm of liberation.

In the view of most religions, having the destiny to encounter the theories and practices of cultivation is very rare. In actuality, a vast many people pass their entire lives in busyness and hardship. They fundamentally lack the time to contemplate the above questions. After living lives of haste and exhaustion, they simply return to dust, and then it is too late to become aware of the problems religions seek to answer. This is why Huang Yuanji's message to his disciples is essentially, "this opportunity to hear the true methods for cultivating Tao from a real master who can explain them to you is extraordinarily rare."

Huang also tells his students, "a human body is rarely attained." The idea that a human body is difficult to obtain originally comes from Buddhism. In Buddhism's eyes, humanity is but one part of the wheel of transmigration—after death, in accordance with the force of one's accumulated karma, a person will be reborn in one of the "six paths," which include gods, demigods, humans, animals, hungry ghosts, and prisoners of the hells. It is extremely rare to take rebirth as a human being, because the karma one creates can easily force one to transmigrate into the lower three paths of animals, denizens of hell, and hungry ghosts. It is very difficult to be liberated from the pervasive suffering of these lower three paths. Because there are both suffering and joy as well as loss and gain in the human world, it is seen as being in the middle, in between the realms of hellish hardship and heavenly pleasure. Because a human can rise upward or fall downward with relative ease, being human is seen as a potential opportunity. One reason that having a human life is especially advantageous is that, in the realm of humans, one may experience the extraordinary conditions necessary to study Buddhism or Taoism. The point that Huang Yuanji strenuously hopes to convey to his students is that having the opportunity to hear tell of the Dharma and the Tao signifies that a person has precious, karmically destined affinity.

Affinity is not something that is said to come easily. Buddhist sutras frequently state that in billions of kalpas of reincarnation ("kalpa" is a Sanskrit word for a unit of time that measures nearly seventeen million years) it is difficult to encounter even a single opportunity to live a human life. Furthermore, if one has not long, long ago planted the seeds of wisdom, then one will not get the opportunity to hear rare teachings while one is alive in the human world. Instead, one will simply pass one's days in muddled confusion, ignorant of the meaning of life.

■ ■ ■

As precious as destined affinity is, even a person who has it will still encounter all sorts of adversity in the process of cultivating the Tao. In the "dusty world" there are all types of difficulties that must be faced. Huang Yuanji encourages his students not to be discouraged, as it is precisely because we suffer that we feel inspired to truly figure out what human life is about, to cherish our destined affinity with Taoist cultivation, and to take adversities and turn them into opportunities to cultivate. In Taoism, any setback or crisis can be used as an opportunity to closely examine human life.

For example, a large portion of people who walk religious paths were led there by illness. If one consistently enjoys good health, one might not devote much thought to the questions we are discussing. But when one suffers through a bout of serious illness, and sees with one's own eyes how many people in the hospital cannot be certain of waking up tomorrow, certain questions suddenly become unavoidable: "What is life, and where is it taking me? What lies beyond death, and what remains after I die? If death is total annihilation, is there any meaning to everything I've done in my life? What *is* human life?"

To truly step into religion is to live one's life in pursuit of answers—religion is not about simply believing. Belief is something that comes cheap. We can decide to believe or disbelieve in something, but if we do not understand it, then the belief is only skin-deep. The real key lies in making detailed examinations. For instance, some people say, "all objects and phenomena are made from matter, so after death there is nothing at all; a person's death is like snuffing out a candle. Religions, souls, whatever—it's all superstition." Yet, since among the living there is nobody who died and came back, then those who proclaim with absolute certainty that there is nothing after death are themselves superstitious, as there is no way for them to personally verify their conclusions. The questions raised in this chapter need thorough inquiry and exploration. At deep levels of cultivation, truly religious individuals prove for themselves that there is eternal life. They say that life is never extinguished, neither comes nor goes, and exists eternally. We ordinary people suffer because we are ignorant of our real lives, and instead identify with our false, external lives.

To simply decide that the explanations offered by various religions are all superstitious is to indulge in enormous superstition. In Taoism, there is no simple question of belief or disbelief. The Taoist tradition is a systematic set of theories and practices. Inasmuch as it is a religion, it is one that each practitioner must personally verify. Taoist inner alchemy is quite unique, in that it is not a set of dogmas and strictures that asks people to just offer their belief and call it a day. Internal alchemy practice is meant to let people answer the following questions: Where do the universe and life come from, and where are they going? What is the way to return to our roots and origins? How do we go back to simplicity and truth? In response to these questions, Taoism presents a formula for studying wisdom. Even if one does not believe in Taoism, one can still use its methods and experience realizations. Thus one might say that Taoism is a type of body-mind experiment, one that can allow us to physically and mentally experience different states of being. By experiencing this process firsthand, one gradually comes to appreciate the meaning of life.

■ ■ ■

Now that we have touched on the broad themes in Huang Yuanji's first discourse, let's take a closer look at the text. Huang begins, "Humans are born between heaven and earth. Aside from the great Way of the golden elixir and the work of turning around and returning, all the vast varieties of endlessly enjoyable glories and riches are nothing but objects of delusion." These opening sentences speak to the plight of our human lives. During our lives, we do indeed experience all sorts of enjoyments. The potential pleasures that wealth and status can bring are endless, and so people pursue them desperately. But if one sees them through eyes of wisdom, or through the eyes of the Tao, then all of these things appear as objects of delusion. They are illusory, just like the stuff of children's games. One can create a toy and give it to a child, who will become totally consumed playing games with it, but the games are fundamentally unreal, and at any moment they might come to an end.

During the massive 2008 earthquake in Sichuan Province, countless lives vanished like smoke and ashes in the wind. Among those who were crushed during the earthquake, there were certainly many who enjoyed prestige and wealth. Would they have predicted that something like that could really happen to them? Of course, this is an extreme example, but even if one never witnesses a massive disaster, one's grip on life is never less tenuous than it was for the people wiped out in the 2008 earthquake. Our positions and our riches are all illusory and impermanent. There is no way to guarantee we will not lose them while we are still here, and there is no way to take them with us when we go.

So in the worldview of cultivators there exists a standard for assessing the value of things. It revolves around the question of whether or not we can take them with us when we die. Buddhism's answer is found in the phrase, "Of all your myriad possessions, you can take none when you go. Only your karma goes with you." There is nothing you can take with you when you pass away: not your house, nor all the money stored in your bank account. The only thing you will leave with is your karma. Your karma comprises the seeds planted in your psyche by everything you have ever done and thought. These residual seeds follow along with you, acting as the latent force of karma.

Taoist cultivators hold that the product of Taoist alchemy is also something of real, eternal value—it goes with a person when he or she leaves the world. Internal alchemy is also called "the Great Way of the Golden Elixir." The practice of inner alchemy is sometimes referred to as "the skill of returning." These two terms summarize the meaning of Taoist alchemical cultivation. Very early on, the term "golden elixir" referred to something that ancient practitioners of "external" alchemy aimed to produce from physical substances. But in inner alchemy, "golden elixir" is a metaphorical term that implies an alchemical technique that unfolds entirely within one's being. This "gold" is unrelated to the physical gold that alchemists of yore hoped to obtain by transmuting worthless metals. Rather, it is a symbol for something that is extracted and purified from within our lives. By virtue of being alive, we all already possess a low-grade version of the elixir (which, in alchemy, is also called "medicine"). Through cultivation, we can refine it until it becomes extremely sublime. Jing, qi, and shen are the three great forms this medicine takes in our beings. They are refined through persistent use of the skill of returning, such that jing is refined into qi, qi is refined into shen, and shen is refined into emptiness, until emptiness merges with the Tao. The above terms contain the systematic work of cultivation in a nutshell. The meaning of each of them is explained in detail throughout this book.

■ ■ ■

"Returning" is a core idea in internal alchemy. Taoism holds that our life paths are capable of going in two directions. The first of these directions is *confluent*. It entails going "with the current," and refers to the direction that people normally follow. The confluent direction is one of outflow, of dispersal, and of jing being exhausted as shen runs wild. It is the direction along which we chase after our externalized desires. The second direction is *countercurrent*. This is the way of coming back, of moving inward, of going deeper, and of going from coarseness to refinement. It is the direction that cleaves closer to the origin, layer by layer. Having countercurrent skill means being able to walk in this direction to return to the Tao, and to go toward one's real life. The words "confluent" and "countercurrent" sum up the directional principle in Taoist self-refinement.

Huang Yuanji's next lines read: "With ordinary people who do not know the Tao, revelry, sex, property, and profit are their pursuits. What they proclaim as their own reapings and surpluses come only because in past lives they cultivated merit and gained goodness, which in this life they benefit from most grandly.

"Who knows that through excessive enjoyment and use, jing and shen vanish and scatter? When their ends come, not only do people return empty-handed, but furthermore their true qi of heaven, earth, and self also vanishes, disappearing back to nonexistence."

"Ordinary people who do not know the Tao" refers to everyday, worldly people. To one degree or another, most of us see some combination of partying, sex, money, power, property, rank, and fame as valuable and worth devoting a lifetime to chasing after. People were no different in Huang Yuanji's time, and they too devoted their days to these things. If they succeeded in attaining them, making their families rich and living in comfort along the way, then owing to the beliefs that were common in China in that era, they often concluded that they were simply reaping the fruits of good karma from past lives, which they were very happy to spend their days enjoying in the current life. But, according to Huang Yuanji, what they had not figured out about the enjoyment of worldly pleasures is that, just when one thinks one has gotten a leg up, one is actually worse off, as one is actively dissipating one's jing and shen.

Herein lies a very important problem. Because of our lack of wisdom, we often have only a vague sense of what is of real value and what is of illusory value. An obvious example of this problem can be seen in our diets. We might think that being able to afford haute cuisine means we finally made it to the good life, but is it really good for us to fill our stomachs with meat and fish and other "fine" foods? Upon reflection, we all know that eating too much rich food can harm us, not only physically, but also by slowing down our minds. Similarly, think about having the luxury to spend all day watching movies and TV shows. We might start out thinking that watching screens endlessly will make us happy, but just as Lao-tzu warned when he wrote that "the five colors blind one's eyes," after one has watched hours of television, one's spirit goes bounding off in all directions, one gets scatterbrained, and insomnia comes in place of sleep at night. One's head feels dizzy and swollen after a day glued to screens.

Often enough, people with money do not exactly live happily. The pleasures their money can buy certainly look enjoyable, but they can easily become sources of harm in a person's life. From a certain angle, one can argue that poorer people are capable of living more happily than the rich, because having fewer toys can result in living more simply. It is possible to be quite happy just drinking a beer, munching on peanuts, and sitting by the road. The rich have enough money to be able to eat whatever they want, but time and again, when faced with a mountain of imported delicacies on the dining table, they find themselves thinking, "ugh, I haven't the appetite for all that, I'd rather just eat some veggies." Good fortune is relative, and it should be partaken of with wisdom.

Of course, strictly speaking, the economic and material conditions brought about by success, fame, and wealth are not intrinsically bad, and they can sometimes be boons to Taoist cultivation. If one has money, then one has no need to fret about cash, and can rigorously cultivate instead. Money is not innately evil, but if one is not skilled at using it, it becomes evil. So what Huang Yuanji is saying here is that if one does not use one's resources wisely, then they will slowly erode that which is really essential and valuable in life: jing, qi, and shen. Moreover, if worldly delights dominate one's entire existence, then one simply will not have the time and energy needed to explore life's fundamental realities.

■ ■ ■

Huang Yuanji continues the above train of thought by saying, "This is what the Supreme Sovereign called 'heaven, earth, and the myriad things stealing my primordial qi.'" Here, the "Supreme Sovereign" refers to Lao-tzu, because in the Taoist religion Lao-tzu has an honorific title, the Great Supreme Ancient Sovereign. The line Huang quotes does not come directly from the *Tao Te Ching*, but it paraphrases its meaning. Huang Yuanji did not deliver lectures in the same way that one would write an essay, by faithfully quoting the original texts line by line. Instead he sometimes paraphrased general ideas. "Heaven, earth, and the myriad things" refers to all the wealth and possessions we own, which then abscond with our primordial qi. This does not mean heaven, earth, and the myriad things literally steal from us. The word "theft" only refers to what seems to happen from our perspective, because it seems like heaven, earth, and everything between them steal our primordial qi from us as we go through life chasing after our desires.

Luckily, according to Taoist teachings, we can also "steal" from heaven, earth, and the myriad things. Thus, within the word "theft" is implicit another important bidirectional concept in Taoism. Yes, the myriad things steal from humanity, but humans can also steal from the myriad things. What this means is that when one meditates and enters into such a tranquil state that one dissolves into the unity of heaven, earth, and all things, the energy of all of these thing will begin to gather and concentrate within one's own body. In this case, the Taoist practitioner, too, is stealing. This result can only occur because humans are intrinsically interconnected with the world. We are not and never have been independent of and separated from the world around us.

Huang Yuanji's next words are: "Though one may know prosperity, high position, and beautiful scenery, and though one may be emperor, king, general, or minister, if one does not know how to restore one's *hsing* and establish one's *ming*, then one will only deepen the dissipation of one's real primordial qi day by day, without a speck of benefit to one's real self. Thus, toiling for wealth and rank is far worse than finding contentment in poverty and low status."

This paragraph connects directly to what Huang said above, and it continues to speak of the two paths lives can go down. One path has us chasing after glory, riches, and power that lie beyond ourselves. In terms of our real lives, these things are external and extraneous. Not only are they irrelevant to real life, they lead to the destruction and depletion of that which is real within us. When one is entranced by prestige and wealth, one places one's entire life in their servitude.

This way of living is backward. Many people live their whole lives in service of their goals. We see this in politicians who want to occupy ever-more powerful offices, or people who already struck it rich but want to earn even more money. If one lives in order to gain power or make money, one lives as power or money's servant. To cultivators of Tao, real life is the only thing of great importance. Success, fame, money, and power in and of themselves bring no meaning to our lives. Instead, they exhaust and disperse our real, primordial qi. To a person who understands what real life is, there is no meaning in that. Thus, Huang Yuanji points out how glory and wealth can actually torment people, while lives of poverty can in fact lead us to a sort of mental freedom. Of course, this point is relative, too. If a poor person is not content, then he or she will be deeply envious of the rich. One cannot say that a life of poverty is a good thing; if one does not have wisdom and a more elevated view, or is too poor to look after oneself, then not being well off quickly becomes an obstacle.

■ ■ ■

Huang Yuanji's next words are: "The ancients said, 'In this world, if you do not cultivate Tao and *de*, it is as though you've entered a mountain of treasure but come back empty-handed.' These words are true and not false."

Once again, Huang reminds us that, while we need to recognize that many of the things we pursue and aspire to in life are meaningless, at the same time, we need to know how to search for a life imbued with value. The cultivation of Tao and de is what Taoism also calls the paired cultivation of hsing and ming. The entire process of Taoist cultivation is one of seeking our real lives in order to return to the Tao. If we do not cultivate Tao and de, then after having this rare opportunity to live as a human, we will die with nothing to show for it, just like having visited a treasure mountain but coming home empty handed. In order to drive home that the above maxim is rich with reason and not in the least bit misleading, right after quoting it, Huang Yuanji says, "these words are true and not false." He then continues:

"While teaching throughout the region of Shu, I have seen how, if the common people are not laboring in devotion to wealth, prestige, scholarly honor, and official rank, then they are galloping passionately after liquor, sex, money, and anger. This fills my heart with pity. Yet, though I am of a heart to save them, they do not know how to reverse course."

Huang Yuanji traveled from Fengcheng in Jiangxi Province to numerous locations in Sichuan Province, which is sometimes called Shu, to give Dharma talks and transmit the Tao. While on the road, he witnessed how countless worldly people were either striving after riches, fame, and success, or else spending their time in taverns and brothels, swirling about in a mix of liquor, sex, profiteering, and anger. Seeing their inability to comprehend the great Tao caused compassion to well up in his heart. Truly achieved masters of Taoist cultivation wish to save all sentient beings. They explain the classic teachings and expound the Dharma. Their hearts are filled with mercy, or what

Buddhism commonly speaks of as compassion. Buddhism says that one can only become a buddha when one is at once self-awakened and capable of awakening others. After people achieve the great Tao, they arrive at the stage of ultimate liberation. Even so, while they themselves are free, realized adepts take pity on those who are lost to the world and unaware of the true meaning of life, and try to devise means of helping them, lest they miss the chance to cultivate. The lost and confused are not always appreciative of help, though, and thus Huang Yuanji laments, "Yet, though I am of a heart to save them, they do not know how to reverse course." He is saying that he took the role of Taoist master, teaching the methods of cultivation in order to help save sentient beings from their torment, and yet most people simply do not listen. Still attached to their ways of living, they cannot see that they are already lost, much less turn back to find their way.

"Yet more," Huang says, "not only are they unwilling to receive salvation, instead they click their tongues with words of annoyance, saying my Way is fanciful and bizarre." Not only did the people of Shu refuse to listen, but they also gossiped about how this teacher Huang seemed to be a bit of a weirdo. "What's he doing sitting there and meditating all day? It's absolutely pointless. The only things we want in life are a bit of money and glamour, best enjoyed under the glow of red lanterns shining on emerald liquor. Why would we want to go and cultivate the lonely and boring Tao?" Some people would have coldly mocked Huang, grumbling, "You say you've got all these high achievements, so are you here to fool me out of my money? What exactly is it you're trying to cheat me out of?" Spiritual teachers have met with the same sort of reaction since ancient times, and not much has changed today.

Huang Yuanji then heaves a sigh and says, "Alas! With people such as these, although I am full of compassionate intent, there is nothing I can do!" What he means is that, despite his pity and his willingness to help, with people who do not have the destiny to cultivate, there is little that can be done for them. There is a well-known saying in Buddhism, "the Buddha cannot save people who lack affinity." It contains an important message: cultivating Tao to the point that we feel very good about ourselves and then embarking on a mission of constantly trying to help other people is actually a mistake. The wish to help others can turn into harassment if the importance of destined affinity is ignored. One reason this chapter so heavily emphasizes "unsurpassed destiny" is that, if we pay no heed to this question, and instead try to help others in a forceful manner, we will just end up aggravating them. It is a bit like waking up while the person next to us is still sound asleep and enjoying a lovely dream. If we cannot resist the urge to shake the person to rouse him or her out of dreamland, we are guaranteed to quickly find a very unhappy face scowling back at us.

■ ■ ■

Neither Buddhist nor Taoist teachers claim that there is an omnipotent ruler capable of emancipating people or forcing them to be this way or that way. Instead, teachers closely observe whether or not a potential student has affinity, and then if they feel they are capable of helping a person, they will try as hard as they can to do so. But they cannot decide for others whether or not they want to walk this road, nor can they compel people to cultivate.

In the absence of a divine ruler who can determine people's fates, Taoist cultivation must be understood as a form of self-awakening. Self-awakening is the elevation of the quality of one's own consciousness. This is not something that can be forced upon or given to a person from without. One's own real life is not an addition to what one already is. Certain "great masters" tell people that if they give them a sum of money, they will bestow them liberation in return. As soon as one hears this one should recognize it as charlatanry, because liberation is impossible to give others. Whatever can be given is just a thing, and if things can be given, they can be taken away, too. If a so-called master was able to give the gift of "liberation" today, then tomorrow, the moment he or she stopped receiving a disciple's offerings and obeisance, he or she could take it right back. In such scenarios, whatever it is that changes hands is not real liberation. Spirituality based upon transactions, material or otherwise, is a racket, pure and simple.

The lineages in Taoism that focus on internal alchemy maintain that disciples must become self-reliant in order to cultivate. A master can transmit principles and methods, but a master cannot put them into use on behalf of a student. This is why, in effect, Huang Yuanji instructs his disciples to turn their thoughts inward and ask themselves, "Do I want to seek real life? Do I really want to learn what is of true value in human life? Do I want a meaningful life?"

Huang's actual words are: "Ask yourselves, in today's world, are most people's consciences not buried and neglected? It is just that people do not ask themselves: During a single kalpa, how many human lives can one attain? Days and nights fly by in the blink of an eye, and then it is the twilight of your life." Here, too, Huang turns our gaze toward the plight inherent in human existence. When he says "in today's world," he is of course referring to the people of Qing dynasty China, but today we are just the same. Submerged in the glitz of the world and its dissolute excitements, a great many human minds end up drowning in material desires. Just like us, many people in Huang Yuanji's day lived their whole lives in service of things that are irrelevant to real life, never fully understanding how rare and difficult it is simply to incarnate as a human being, nor reflecting upon the ephemerality of human life. Even if a person lives for a whole century, that is just a fleeting moment compared to the endless river of time—we are gone in the blink of an eye. If we think back to when we were small, it is painfully obvious that the innocence of childhood turned into young adulthood with incredible speed, with the transition to old age looming close behind. How long does a human really have? If we sincerely contemplate this question, many things become easy to let go of, and there is no more need for clinging and scheming.

■ ■ ■

Huang Yuanji goes on to say: "How do you know that your wealth and prestige in this life will not become poverty and lowliness in the next? How do you know that while today you are a person, you will not return to the world as livestock? The ancients said: 'A human body is rarely attained, the Middle Kingdom is difficult to be born in, and the Great Tao is seldom encountered.' Given that you have obtained a human body, had the luck to be born in the Middle Kingdom, and moreover have heard the correct doctrine, you must have unexcelled predestined affinity."

The above paragraph alights directly upon the theme of this entire chapter. Its message is that even if we are living well and our conditions are excellent, we still need to stop and think: In this life we are humans, but what will we be in the next life? None of us know! When the ancients said "a human life is rare," they meant that it is extremely difficult to incarnate as a human. The phrase "the Middle Kingdom is difficult to be born into" comes from Buddhism, and originally meant India. Madhyadesa, or central north India, where Buddhism was born, was sometimes translated as "Middle Kingdom" in ancient Chinese. While Huang Yuanji was teaching Taoism, he casually borrowed the term without adhering to any strict definition. Here he is not necessarily even referring to China, but rather expressing that it is an extraordinarily precious thing to live anywhere where one can find a teacher who transmits the Tao and expounds the Dharma. Having such an opportunity is "unsurpassed destiny."

When experienced religious teachers expound upon the classics, they often emphasize the preciousness of destined affinity in order to develop respect for the teachings in their students and disciples' minds. This is so that students will not see the path as a trifling thing that people might as well do without, or as a diversion that is only as good as the amusement it delivers. Instead of taking it seriously, some people see cultivation as something to dabble in after dinner. But if there is to be any hope of real achievement, the opportunity to cultivate cannot be treated lightly, or else it will slip by.

Huang Yuanji offers his students encouragement by telling them that, having obtained a human birth *and* hearing the words of the Dharma, they are better off than royalty and aristocrats. He says, "Compared with all the emperors, kings, ministers, and generals, who enjoy themselves today but are dead tomorrow, and whose reincarnations are unbearably wretched, are your circumstances not infinitely superior?" Huang contrasts people who hear of the Tao or the Dharma and then go on to cultivate with emperors and kings, and he says that practitioners' karmic conditions are a hundred million times better than those of royalty.

This idea comes to most people as a surprise. Usually we think that there is some great value in being a powerful ruler, but in reality, the power any leader enjoys disappears just as suddenly as it came, and then there is no telling where such a person will end up when the present life comes to its end. After a person comes into glory and wealth, his or her opportunities to create negative karma multiply commensurately. If a person who possesses power, rank, fame, or wealth is controlled by greed, it is unlikely that he or she will avoid creating negative karma. Doing so is what destines a person to plummet downward on the wheel of transmigration in the next life. Contrast this with a Taoist cultivator who might be quite poor in this life, but, because he or she knows the teachings, is able to practice and improve the quality of his or her life. Such a person's state of mind in this life and destination in the next are certainly immeasurably better than those of most kings and rulers.

Everything in the discourse at the start of this chapter stresses the importance of transforming one's value system. In his role as a Taoist teacher, Huang Yuanji explains why typical pursuits are meaningless and how a life of cultivating the Way becomes a source of meaning. There is a limit to the progress that can be made in Taoist cultivation by those who do not internalize its underlying values. If Taoist practice is just an adornment upon a life otherwise spent wholeheartedly chasing worldly things, it will not lead to any real achievements. In a word, it is impossible to develop wisdom strong enough to overcome the force of one's accumulated karma by just listening to the occasional Taoist lecture or meditating every now and then.

Taoist cultivation is not a simple question of techniques. One does not just learn how to sit and meditate or how to do a certain practice and then call it a day. Simply doing a certain practice is not enough to bring about accomplishment, because the Taoist path involves altering one's lifestyle and elevating the plane on which one lives. If one does not turn a major corner with one's patterns of thinking, worldview, and outlook on life, then Taoist practices actually have no way of helping one make much progress along the path. At its most basic, Taoism requires one to enter into a state of tranquility. If one cannot put down the stuff of the dusty world, and instead spends the whole day mired in thoughts of one's mundane affairs, the tranquility that is required to actually experience the unfolding of the Taoist path will never come. Thus, while at first glance it may seem that Huang Yuanji's above discourse is devoid of any lessons on internal alchemy, in fact, it is high-level guidance for the refinement of one's heart and one's thoughts.

Earlier I spoke about how we cannot take anything we own with us when we pass away. However, according to Taoist teachings, our achievements in cultivation can be taken with us. This is why it is thought that many people who end up studying Taoism actually came into the world with a root in the tradition that they inherited from their previous existences—they did not end up walking the practitioner's path out of the blue. With people who have no destined affinity with the Tao, no matter how hard one tries to explain the teachings to them, it is all but impossible to make an impression. On the other hand, even though some predestined cultivators start out their lives lost in the world, after somebody points out the way for them, they suddenly wake up and say, "ah-ha, *this* is how things really are!" Sometimes such people even quickly enter a fairly advanced stage of practice. This can only happen when a person has inherited a root in cultivation that was built up over numerous lifetimes of practice. This is why Huang Yuanji says, "Henceforth, if you concertedly cultivate, even if you do not become an immortal or a sage, when you return to the world for rebirth, you will still be a person with root. This, too, is good fortune." Even if his disciples did not become immortals or buddhas in this lifetime, were they to return to the world again as humans, they would bring their roots with them, which is certainly something to celebrate.

■ ■ ■

The next paragraph reads, "Moreover, for the convening of this assembly, the heavens above have especially bestowed grace, allowing completion of cultivation in this kalpa. All of you who meet with this good luck, make great efforts to make progress. Do not fear difficulty, and do not avoid hardship. If you make vows on the grounds of morality, and concentrate your heart on meritorious deeds, then how could heaven's spiritual immortals all be so ignorant and deaf as to fail to see and hear you? The only fear is that people are unwilling to put their hearts into it. Worry not that the heavenly deities will not silently protect and guide you."

This paragraph raises another important issue, that of heavenly assistance and grace. Huang Yuanji says that the heavens granted special grace for the "Dharma assembly" where he taught the Tao, as though the deities above devoted special dispensation allowing the students present to reach liberation within a single kalpa. Normally it is said that it takes many kalpas to finish cultivating the Way (one Buddhist doctrine states that it requires three immeasurably long kalpas to arrive at buddhahood), so such heavenly providence presents a shining opportunity. Huang means that if his students were extraordinarily diligent in their cultivation of Tao and de, the spiritual immortals in the heavenly realms would surely not be deaf and indifferent to their efforts. In essence, Huang is telling his students, "Deities see everything you do, and they will help you. Fear only you yourselves not practicing sincerely."

It is important to discuss the concept of deities in Taoism. Spirits and deities are of great importance to all religions—without them one cannot construct a religion. However, there are many different ways in which spirits and deities are conceptualized. Christians speak of God as being the one and only god. This God is not so much a personified deity as he is the highest and most original existence in the universe, and thus is it that he can only be one, not many. To Christians, their God is the one and only true god, whereas the deities worshipped by other religions are all falsehoods, unworthy of being spoken of in the same breath as their God. In a certain sense this argument is correct, because specific deities cannot be viewed as on par with the supreme force governing the universe. Thus, the true god is not a concrete personage or anthropomorphic deity with a specifiable form and appearance.

Speaking from Taoism's perspective, God is Tao. Put another way, that which is the source of all gods' godhood is Tao. This means that the spirit that exists at the same level as the Tao itself is one. There cannot be two, because the Tao is the sole root, center, and origin of the entire universe and all that exists. What Taoists imply when they say "Tao" is akin to what philosophers might call "a supreme noumenal existence."

The next layer of deities includes actual incarnations of the Tao, or personified gods who incarnated on our planet. Jesus, for example, is seen by Christians as the Son of God, or a personification of God who came to earth. Similarly, according to Taoist lore, there have been numerous instances in different eras when ancestral teachers who were actually incarnations or embodiments of the highest spirit walked the earth. But, in addition to having a pantheon with deities who are understood as being emanations of the Tao, Taoism also identifies deities who are people who achieved a high-level existential state. In fact, deities of this sort bear no essential difference from you or me, as Taoism holds that through cultivation, training, and the accumulation of merit, a human being can become a spiritual immortal. Christianity maintains that a person cannot become a deity, because humans and God are eternally distinct. The deities of Taoism, however, are not akin to the Christian God. Becoming a spiritual immortal really means liberating one's real life. After inner alchemy training reaches the highest stage, a practitioner lives a deity's existence. The adept is then capable of residing any place in the universe, or in "the heavens above," which is not a specific location, but what could be described as a "different" space and time, or a different dimension.

So, according to Taoist teachings, while humans cannot be gods in the sense of acting as supreme rulers of the universe, they are able to become spiritual immortals. They do so by returning to the Tao. This means becoming inseparable from the Tao, such that they blend into and become one with it. It is because we all come from and ultimately revert to the Tao that Taoism says adepts can return to the Tao and start anew as spiritual immortals. Having spiritual immortality does not imply having lordship over the cosmos, but it does point toward a very high level of existence, implicit in which are powers that allow for a high degree of freedom and self-determination.

In the realms liberated beings occupy, they are able to keep an eye on the human world. If, for instance, a person became a spiritual immortal via Taoist cultivation, then this figure might be especially prone to looking after other people who practice Taoism. Similarly, if a man or a woman became a buddha or bodhisattva by cultivating Buddhism, then this being might pay special attention to Buddhist practitioners. These are not so much questions of preference as of affinity. On every path, there are many who walked to achievement long before us. Thus, some of those heavenly deities who made their accomplishments through the practice of inner alchemy might have somehow told Huang Yuanji, "We are going to specially look out for your students. If they cultivate, then we will take care of them."

Nevertheless, as we have already discussed, there is no spiritual immortal who can confer anything that comes from beyond ourselves in order to make us directly achieve immortality or buddhahood. The support or help that deities can give us is something that we must personally respond to and act upon in order to benefit from it. That which is within us and that which comes from outside us must unite as one. Philosophy speaks of internal causes and external causes; each person's commitment to cultivation is the initial cause as well as the indispensable root of achievement, but this commitment also requires external conditions to come to fruition. Heavenly deities have more refined wisdom and intelligence than we do, and with these they can help look after us. Huang Yuanji's message is that if, on the path of a Taoist practitioner, a person encounters setbacks and barriers, spiritual immortals can help from the sidelines. But this is nothing like what one hears from the leaders of cults who claim, "Whoever I wish to liberate will be liberated, and whoever I don't want to liberate will never be free." The power to decide such things is no one's to possess.

■ ■ ■

Huang Yuanji proceeds, saying: "This world's ways are chaotic and human hearts are dim and confused. Ordinary people believe that this era and this land are dangerous. But among superior people who have the Tao, instead there is the belief that being here is great good fortune. Why is that? Suppose that one's circumstances were unremarkable, that one did not undergo tortures or experience dashed hopes, would one not just be smoothly passing through? Who, then, would be willing to turn his or her heart toward the Tao, to set his or her will on seeking the mysterious? Only with these thousands of trials and myriad tribulations, with things not as one wishes them, with nobody taking one's side, will one realize that the ways of the dusty world just bring fatigue and worry, not holding a single benefit. Therefore, be indifferent to fame and wealth, and concentrate on being yourselves; be weary of the human world and make oaths to cultivate clarity."

Here, Huang Yuanji is probing the question of what counts as circumstances favorable to Taoist practice. We may find ourselves living in a world of decadent morals and social confusion, where people's minds have become chaotic in response to their surroundings. Everybody around us might seem to be chasing fame and money, doing terrible things to sate their desires, and living lives of brutal competition. In such an era the average person is liable to sigh, "Agh, these conditions are terrible, there are hardly any good opportunities to speak of." But to a person with real mettle who possesses knowledge of the Tao—to a true cultivator—such circumstances can appear favorable, if not outright fortuitous.

Why would a Taoist teacher like Huang Yuanji see the world in such a light? The reason is that if a person's path in life is free of setbacks and bumps along the road, then there may be no impetus to think deeply on the meaning of life, and precious decades can easily be frittered away. Sometimes the setbacks and hardships in an otherwise unremarkable life are really opportunities in disguise. Many people's entries into religion are caused by abnormal life situations. Suffering major setbacks gets people to suddenly see new meanings in their lives, things that require real exploration. Everybody has moments of crisis that can prompt introspection. If we take advantage of them, they can cause the germination of conditions that lead us to the Tao.

Any hardship or misfortune can be transformed into a boon to cultivation. Buddhism has a maxim, "turn suffering into enlightenment." It implies that our difficulties can become fuel for arousing "bodhi," which is a Sanskrit term for awakening. Some people live uneventful lives that seem to be very nice, but from the standpoint of cultivation, there is nothing particularly valuable about a life in which one does little more than pass the days. On the other hand, some people experience plenty of suffering and hardship, and these things lead them to really experience and contemplate life. Their struggles may inspire their creativity and open new horizons for them. For Taoist practitioners, wisdom is the necessary ingredient if there is to be hope of transmuting misfortune into felicity. This means that if, after passing through the hardships inherent in worldly existence, one begins to cast one's gaze beyond goals like accumulating money and making a name for oneself, one has a real chance of truly seeking Tao.

Huang Yuanji continues, "Though in this life you may not become an immortal, still you will have climbed onto the steps of the way to transcendence. Supposing you reincarnate in the world as a human, will heaven's deities willingly abandon you in order to seek out another? Thus did the ancients say, 'Spiritual immortals are born of spiritual immortal seeds—ordinary people do not just up and transcend for no reason!'" We have already mentioned the kind of situation Huang Yuanji is speaking about here. If a person accomplishes some of the stages of inner alchemy in the present life—even if he or she does not achieve spiritual immortality before passing away—then should this person be reborn in the human world, he or she will carry latent affinity for Taoist practice into the next life. Naturally, the masters of this tradition would not abandon such a person in his or her next life in favor of somebody with no affinity at all. After all, those who have a foundation are much easier to teach!

Huang's next lines are, "I will speak again on today's chance meeting. Nowadays, people studying the Tao are countless. But how many are able to obtain an unreservedly clear explanation of the true, eternal, incomprehensible Tao's complete essence and vast function?" His point is that in any era there are bound to be numerous students of Tao, but those whose practice leads to real progress and accomplishment are always a small minority. This is largely because the search for a true master is extremely difficult, and most people fail to meet one. Unfortunately, many Taoist teachers have one-sided views and incomplete understandings. Invariably, a teacher who is yet to awaken to the magnitude and power of the Tao in its entirety possesses only partial knowledge of the path.

Some teachers, for example, turn the cultivation of Taoism and inner alchemy into something mystical, as though it was like learning magic spells. "Long ago," they say, "my master transmitted a secret oral instruction to me. All the secrets are contained within just eight Chinese characters. Do you want to know this precious eight-character formula? It has been guarded for centuries, but I can see it is your destiny to learn the ways of the immortals. So, for a mere twenty thousand dollars, the secret can be yours!" However, if one actually pays up, then after the eight characters are bestowed with an air of grand mystique, what does one discover? The sentence was not even a secret to begin with, and lots of books on alchemy already put it out there for anyone to see—it might even be right here in this book! Alas, cultivating the Tao is never as simple as obtaining some secret code or formula.

A complete course of Taoist study moves from theory to practice. However, some people only understand the theory without knowing how to practice, and some people with a bit of practical experience eschew the theory, saying that it is just for scholars and researchers who never actually train—sitting and meditating every day is the "real Tao," they say. But if a person just meditates on this and that, without having any knowledge base, most likely he or she will mistake various sensations and reactions in the body for realization, instead of awakening to the true Tao. Some teachers use health as the criterion for measuring progress. If my health is so great that my cheeks are as rosy as a child's, does that mean I have attained the Tao? Does a glowing countenance really equate to spiritual achievement? Not necessarily. I might be healthy today, but I could go into decline tomorrow, because the physical body is always subject to change. If one has not truly experienced the Tao and arrived at the stage where one's mind does not waver, then there is nothing reliable about any changes that might occur in the body, even if they yield strong qi or great health.

■ ■ ■

As I said above, *The Oral Record of the Hall of Joyous Teaching* is a rare and complete teaching, delivered by a teacher who is clearly very sure of himself. Huang Yuanji practically spells out to his students, "I am transmitting a complete and eminently practical corpus of Taoist teachings. I am prepared to explain all of its components, from the lofty to the basic, including both hsing practices and ming practices. It is all here." It has always been exceedingly uncommon for the Tao to be taught in this way. Huang asks a question that sounds almost rhetorical: "How many are able to obtain an unreservedly clear explanation of the true, eternal, incomprehensible Tao's complete essence and vast function?" But he answers it in concrete terms when he says, "Only you, who follow my discourses, which have not a thread or speck of omission that would cause you to plummet into the study of side paths. Contemplate what an opportunity this is!" Here, Huang Yuanji is promising his students that he will make a complete transmission, without the omission of even a single word, nor the presence of any skewed or partial understandings.

Emphasizing the rarity of such an opportunity, Huang Yuanji continues, "This is enough to show the heavenly deities' love for those on the path, and that they are especially generous toward you. Yet, beginning with your entry into the Way, you will time and again be scraped across the grindstone, passing through wind and waves. In the eyes of onlookers, people who study Tao seem not to carry heaven's protection, and to instead encounter numerous terrors. Little do others know that to suffer a round of slander and criticism is to advance by a fraction in Tao and de; that to pass through a round of tempering is to grow by a fraction in jing and shen."

Huang Yuanji assures his students that they will be afforded protection by Taoist deities, and that he will unreservedly instruct them on the essence and workings of the Tao. But he realizes that this promise gives rise to a question, which is, why will there be some students who, after embarking upon the Taoist path, still encounter numerous trials and hardships? Why, if practitioners are afforded the grace of the deities, would any of them still need to pass through multiple tumultuous lifetimes as human beings? The answer is that there is no teaching that states that as soon as a person begins to practice Taoism, he or she will encounter nothing but smooth sailing from then on. On the contrary, a newly minted practitioner might end up passing through more tribulations than he or she ever did before. People who are not clear on this point might think, "What is this? I'm already cultivating, why should I still have to encounter any more frustrations? I'm a Taoist, only good things should come to me, I couldn't possibly be faced with any more setbacks!" But that simply is not the way things go.

While we are treading the long path of Taoist cultivation, sometimes when we are making progress it looks more like we are sliding backward. That is why there is a saying in Chinese, "big improvements can appear to be steps backward; big declines can at first seem like improvements." We might encounter situations where the people in our lives speak ill of us, slander us, or even attack us. When they do so, they are actually giving us opportunities to temper and refine ourselves. In the long run, being forced through such trials actually improves our moral fiber as well as our spirits.

There is a passage in the *Diamond Sutra* that says that if, after hearing the sutra, one is slandered or attacked by other people, one should view these attacks as the fruition and dissolution of the negative karma accumulated throughout countless previous lifetimes. With the passing of each instance of conflict, one's karmic burden lightens, and as a result, one makes more progress along the path. Huang Yuanji's above statement relates to this teaching on karma. We all carry karmic burdens composed of everything we have done in the past. Carrying karmic debts is a bit like owing money to the bank—it is impossible to truly relax until our debts have been repaid. It is the challenges and ordeals we experience that allow us to repay the karmic debts we created in the past. Real progress in Taoist cultivation will only come to us if we endure this process of dissolving and transforming karmic burdens.

■ ■ ■

Huang Yuanji devotes quite a few lines to driving home his point about the importance of dissolving karma. He says, "Even more, bad habits rooted in former lives are eliminated by this; prior sins and coming retributions are mended by this. It is just like a person soiled by filthy sludge, being once cleansed; or like jade or gold hidden within stone, going through the forge, and then beginning to scintillate." In the first analogy here, carrying karmic burdens is akin to being covered in mud; weathering the ablutions of hardship is like a purifying shower for our bodies and minds. In the second analogy, it is as though our real lives are the gold trapped within the ore of karma. With each round of smelting, layers of dross are thrown off, until the glimmer of real gold is revealed.

The text then reads, "This Tao of attaining both felicity and wisdom is not found in settling into a smooth and steady life. Rather, it is found in passing through perils and hardships. Students, do not lose restraint because of others' words, nor have the least flinching of will." Huang Yuanji means that passing through difficulties with equanimity is actually a way of cultivating both good fortune and wisdom. The foundation for Taoist cultivation must be based upon two types of bedrock, one made of the good fortune that comes as a result of selfless deeds, and the other made of wisdom. Fortunateness is intimately related to our karma, because, as we lighten our karmic loads, we gradually find ourselves rewarded with felicitous circumstances in life. In the context of the teaching Huang Yuanji is offering here, wisdom denotes the mind's original state of being. As we progress in our practice, we become more and more able to experience the nature of our mind, which is rooted in Tao. By this, we gain access to liberation.

In sum, hardship provides circumstances that allow us to put Taoist teachings into practice. We do so by acting virtuously when we face difficulties and by looking upon them with the wisdom that comes from our hearts' original natures. We must remember that progress in Taoist cultivation can actually come more easily to those who experience a gamut of life challenges than it does to those whose lives are smooth and uneventful. We must also heed Huang Yuanji's advice and be sure not to let our wills shrink when people around us express their uninformed opinions about the path.

■ ■ ■

The above discourse closes with these words: "In my view, you are all truly the stuff of spiritual immortals, not like those who drag through the mud and water, here hoping for spiritual immortality, there pining for riches and rank, two notions muddled in a single heart." Huang ends his teaching with words of encouragement for his students, reminding them that they have truly embarked on the journey toward realizing the Tao. They have already set themselves apart from people who muddle about in the swamps of indecision, hoping to study the Way of spiritual immortals in this moment and then desiring fame and fortune in the next. People who cultivate single-mindedly, Huang says, are on a totally different plane from those whose hearts are battle-grounds for contradictory callings.

This whole chapter tells us that, in order to cultivate the Tao, one must solidify one's will, cherish one's opportunities, and determine which things in life are truly valuable. Only by so doing will one be able to cultivate wholeheartedly and see the path to its conclusion.

明心見性

ILLUMINATING YOUR MIND
TO SEE YOUR NATURE

I shall point out the truth and significance of illuminating mind to see its fundamental nature. The prior-heaven mind is fundamental nature. The fundamental nature of prior heaven is empty, nonexistent primordial qi. In short, it is emptiness, that is all. Humans, beginning from birth, are bound by temperament, obscured by lust and desire, and entwined in love and affection. Consequently, our minds have long been not empty.

Qi follows the orders of the mind, and jing is in service of shen. Galloping and chasing, wantonly roaming, they are dissipated and squandered until nearly gone. This is where students set about starting the work, and thus do we place such value on concentrating shen and harmonizing the breath. For shen not concentrated will scatter, and, when it is scattered, wandering thoughts and delusions continuously arise. How then could it gather in one place to take command of refining the elixir? Only when it is concentrated is shen unified. When unified, it is empty.

Our minds' emptiness is the hsing originally endowed by heaven. Beyond us, the emptiness of the void is unborn, empty, nonexistent hsing.

Breathing not harmonized is abandoned. When breathing is abandoned, then the viscera within and the flesh and skin without are but a whorl of flighty, impatiently moving qi. If one hoped to concentrate and gather qi into oneness in order for it to be the foundation for fostering ming—alas, it would be difficult. Only through regularity can there be balance. From balance comes harmony. Our bodies' harmony is the ming we receive from heaven and earth after we are born. The unified qi of the vast harmony is the unborn ming suspended between heaven and earth. The latter is real hsing and real ming—the hsing and ming that are integrated without distinction with heaven, earth, humanity, and things. These are also the hsing and ming that spiritual immortals attain to become what they are.

To you students who wish to restore ming and return to the root in order to reach the place where shen transmutes: there is no other way to cultivate, there is only concentrating shen to make it tranquil, and harmonizing the breath to make it even. Do not forget the breath, do not assist it. Be neither quick nor slow. Only do this: let mind, shen, qi, and breath all enter into an emptiness that is supreme, a tranquility that is deep. But this is not contrived emptiness. It is self-such emptiness. The heavens, earth, ghosts, deities, people, and all things come from this same source. Thus, it is also not an emptiness that is absent of substance.

Only when shen is fully empty will the clear and harmonious qi of heaven and earth naturally seek refuge in one another. That humans may join with heaven and earth, assist in transformation and creation, change inexhaustibly, and be unfathomably marvelous, is due to the emptiness of shen and the breath responding to the qi of the universe's own emptiness, causing it to enter us. That is why, within this emptiness, there is substance.

Gradually concentrate and gather. Of their own accord, body and mind within and without will attain the adamantine, strong, centered, rightened, pure, absolute, essential state. It is only by seeing hsing in this manner that true hsing will appear.

How is mind illuminated? Only when empty is it numinous. When numinous, it is illuminated. In a mind illuminated, the multitudinous principles are all complete, and the myriad phenomena are wholly encompassed.

When an illuminated mind has yet to move, it is vast and mighty, without knowledge and without knowing. This is called "thoughts not arising within, thoughts not entering from without." It is just awareness, brilliant and penetrating. In a single principle's midst are immersed all phenomena, each embraced. This is attainment.

When the illuminated mind comes into contact with things, it moves. Sensing, it thereupon responds. Encountering roundness, it becomes rounded.

Yielding to angularity, it becomes angled. Vivacious and uninhibited, its un-fathomability is like that of a swimming dragon.

It is said: "In tranquility there is primordial shen, in movement there is true intent." Primordial shen and true intent are one and the same; there is nothing more to their distinction than stillness and motion. We have also heard the ancients state: "A mind without hsing has no sovereign; hsing without mind has nothing to support it." Thus, mind carries hsing, and hsing unifies mind. From this we know that the mind's heights, its brilliance, its expansiveness and immensity, and its inexhaustible marvelousness are all the measure of hsing. Enlightening this real mind is to illuminate hsing.

Before hsing enters the human body, it swirls in clear space as primordial qi. Once it descends into the human body, it is primordial shen. The key is that both are empty and nonexistent. You students who are just getting started, first lay down your minds and let them be full of life. Entrust everything to the silent heavens and wander on the surface of ultimate emptiness. You will begin to be able to subdue the lead and mercury within your body, and to steal the primordial yang of heaven and earth that lies beyond you. In time, shen will naturally concentrate and breathing naturally harmonize. You will only feel a single point of shen breath in your dantian, gurgling, surging, flowing, and eddying, as though extant, and as though naught.

Now, keep watch on it. Place awareness upon it. Be much like a cat stalking a mouse, or a rabbit who has encountered an eagle, single-mindedly gazing and examining, not allowing your mind to wander. Just as you are, sensing what is within and responding to what is without, be aware of heaven and earth's primordial qi coursing through the interior and exterior of your body, without ever coming to rest. When hsing skill arrives here, then ming work is naturally easy.

The other world's mountain sprites and water spirits can change into human form; their ming skill is said to be exquisite. Yet, when coming to view and savor our world, they see the desirable and become desirous, they see the fearsome and become afraid, and they even do unkind, unjust, dishonest, and disgraceful things. That they ultimately suffer punishment or execution and cannot escape is entirely because they shirked on the work of refining hsing. When, as teacher, I instruct people that they must treat illuminating mind to see hsing as the primary task, I speak precisely of this. Do you all understand this, or not?

■ ■ ■

I did not choose the ten discourses from Huang Yuanji's *The Oral Record of the Hall of Joyous Teaching* that appear in this book at random—they are interrelated and work in concert with one another. Huang's lectures approach alchemy from different angles and, taken as a whole, present a system of practice. Exploring these ten discourses allows us to distill a basic summary of the process of refining the internal elixir as well as to encounter all of the major principles of Taoist cultivation.

"Illuminating Your Mind to See Your Nature" appears as the second discourse because the work the chapter title describes is Taoist alchemy's most central component. In fact, speaking more broadly, it represents the centerpiece of all the different types of training in the entire corpus of Taoist cultivation. I am of the opinion that although there are different schools, lineages, and paths of true Taoist practice, they all revolve around this nucleus. Thus, if one were to ignore this core teaching, then one could not be on the correct path. This is why practicing without illuminating the mind is described in terms such as walking along corrupted routes, following crooked roads, entering side doors, or treading left-hand paths. If a teacher is speaking of the true, correct path—the Great Tao—then his or her teachings will most definitely contain this central point that is common to all branches of Taoism. The fact that all different schools and lineages eventually speak of illuminating mind and seeing original nature is not simply a matter of who influenced whom. Rather, it is a matter of the truth of life and the universe—of what reality fundamentally is. The reality of each of our true lives is the same, and thus, this teaching is pervasive.

Consider how Chinese Buddhism was inherited from India, a place that has had its own cultivation traditions since ancient times. After Shakyamuni founded the Buddhist tradition, it was transplanted to China. Taoism is China's own native religion, and, like Buddhism, it too is a tradition that comes from antiquity. One cannot say that Taoism came into being because of Buddhism's influence, just as one cannot say that Buddhism was born of the influence of Taoist philosophy or religion. They both descend from different origins. Nevertheless, from the Song and Ming dynasties onward, despite the fact that the three schools of Confucianism, Buddhism, and Taoism had all developed independently of each other, many great masters began to emphasize that "the three teachings are one." This included Huang Yuanji, who espoused the oneness of the three teachings when he taught the Tao. Sometimes he drew upon certain ideas from Confucians or cited the Confucian *Four Books* in order to flesh out his own ideas, and he of course quoted Buddhist ideas, most notably those of Chan Buddhism.

This melding of the three schools into one reflects the blending and exchange that took place at the level of cultural interaction, but it also reflects deeper intrinsic compatibility. This blending occurred a bit like the way people with distinct cultural backgrounds or worldviews can suddenly meet and get along so well that they feel like kindred spirits. Mutual understanding can arise like this because, at the end of the day, the predicaments all humans face are quite similar. Similarly, because many of the key issues cultivators from different traditions are concerned with are the same, they are often able to find common ground without having had any prior encounters. Due to the intrinsic compatibility of traditions devoted to understanding reality, when different traditions' representatives start to mingle there will always be mutual influence. It is as though they quickly discover, "I can use your vocabulary to explain my way, and you can use my vocabulary to explain yours. The true, eternal Way that transcends language itself seems to be the same thing for both of us."

Lao-tzu's first declaration in the *Tao Te Ching* was, "Any way that is called 'the Tao' is not the eternal Tao." With language we can do no more than attempt to attach footnotes to Great Way, which remains beyond words no matter what we say about it. No explanation or expression will ever suffice to represent the Tao, as its ultimate truth lies beyond conception and is therefore ineffable. This is the reason why various traditions' modes of verbally pointing in the direction of the Tao can come across as very different, while those things at their core that transcend language are completely identical.

I have a personal interest in many different philosophical schools and religions. I do not just research Taoism, but Buddhism, as well. I am also interested in some of the masters of New Age religions. After studying and experiencing their teachings, I have usually been able to find areas of intrinsic compatibility. These areas of overlap are found in the realm of methods for cultivating the mind in order to trigger an awakening to its fundamental nature—precisely the issue this chapter is devoted to.

"Illuminating the mind to see one's nature" was originally a term from Chan Buddhism, which describes the ultimate purpose of Chan practice. Chan is described in Buddhism as being "a separate transmission beyond the sutras, not established in words, which directly points out the human mind, so that one can see one's mind's nature and become a buddha." In short, Chan is not something that can be found inside of words. Being beyond language, the function of its teachings is to directly point toward the mind in order to create the conditions for one to see the Tao and directly experience one's own buddha nature. This process is encapsulated in a pithy saying: "Seeing your mind's nature, you become a buddha."

Taoist alchemists also speak of illuminating the mind to see original nature, which can be written as *hsing*. Taoists' understanding of this process is interconnected with Chan teachings and does not contradict them. However, Taoism's points of emphasis, the angles from which it approaches this work, and the ways in which it expresses its goals can be quite different from Buddhism's.

■ ■ ■

It is well known that Taoist alchemists speak of simultaneously cultivating hsing (original nature) and ming (life essence). People who have not looked deeply into these teachings sometimes reflexively react to them by saying, "but isn't illuminating the mind to see one's nature a Buddhist thing? It doesn't have anything to do with Taoist alchemists." Such statements are skewed. Taoists most definitely do emphasize illuminating the mind in order to see original nature, and doing so definitely does not contradict the cultivation of ming. The two are not opposed. In the broad framework of simultaneous hsing and ming cultivation, illuminating the mind to see one's nature occupies the nucleus of hsing practice.

When inner alchemists talk about illuminating the mind to see original nature, they root their discussions within the framework of simultaneously cultivating hsing and ming. Hsing and ming are so fundamentally connected and integrated that, at the highest and most comprehensive level, there is no distinction between the two. They are unified. Because the Tao itself transcends all distinctions between hsing and ming, authentic hsing cultivation includes ming, and authentic ming cultivation cannot be separated from hsing. Thus it is that illuminating the mind to see its nature is not merely the nucleus of hsing cultivation it lies at the center of both hsing and ming cultivation. This is why Huang Yuanji takes such pains to stress that illuminating the mind to see one's nature is the root of all practice.

■ ■ ■

What exactly is meant by illuminating one's mind to see one's nature? We can try using various terms or theories to explain it, but regardless of what is said, if all one sees are words, then words are all one will ever get. Illuminating the mind is done by shedding light upon the interior of one's heart, not by illuminating a manuscript. One must pierce through the words in these teachings in order to reverse one's perspective and observe one's own mind. This is what leads to locating one's own hsing and realizing one's own fundamental nature. The real experience of illuminating the mind and recognizing original nature is too subtle and profound to be approximated linguistically.

Despite the limitations of language, we can still compare the words left behind by accomplished Taoist cultivators with our own experiences of the mind's original nature. As you read through Huang Yuanji's discourses, you should connect with your own inner nature as best you can, so as to develop a feeling for his meaning. Do not focus solely on the words and the subject matter in these chapters. Instead, allow your mind to resonate with what is written here. This is the way to get this book to actually help you illuminate your mind to see your nature, instead of just giving you an intellectual understanding of the theories and lore related to Taoist practice.

A discussion of the concept of "illuminating the mind" might start with a very basic question: What is mind? But actually, it may be best if I do not make a stringent effort to explain or define mind, because everybody already knows what it is. After all, our minds never stop working all day long. A very simplistic explanation for what the mind is is thought. The word "mind" can be conceived as representing the totality of our mental activity, while the word "thought" refers to individual instances of mental activity.

That we are humans is because we have minds, and not simply because we have bodies. There is a short story in *Chuang-tzu* in which a sow suddenly dies. At first her piglets do not realize that their mother has passed away, and they continue happily suckling at her teats for milk. But the instant they realize she is dead they run away from her body in fear. Is it that these piglets do not love their mother? Of course they love her, but now they realize that the sow's corpse is no longer their mother. With the core—the sow's mind—no longer present, her body is no more than a carcass. To the piglets it is incapable of representing "mother." Nobody feels love for a cadaver, even that which belonged to a loved one. At essence, what we love are one another's hearts, not one another's bodies.

Buddhism teaches that all people have buddha nature, which means that all humans have an independent, sentient mind. However, the minds of most people are unawakened. In Buddhist terms, to have an "unawakened" mind means to remain bound to the habits of reification and objectification. Our minds are home to an endless stream of discrete objects of attachment that we think and worry about. At a certain level, our minds are filled with thoughts of external things: our businesses, careers, rent and mortgages, car payments, work responsibilities, and so on. At a somewhat deeper level, our minds get caught up in our bodily sensations, and they get focused on the act of thinking itself. All of us are aware of a huge spectrum of phenomena, but there always remains one crucial thing our minds are unaware of: the mind itself. To have a mind that cannot truly see itself is to be without self-knowledge.

This is a point that is worth soberly reflecting upon for a moment. We all know countless facts, and we are all capable of thinking about a huge variety of complicated matters, but do we actually know our own selves? If we have actually tasted self-knowledge, is it something that is present for us at all times and all places? If your honest answer is, "I always know myself, no matter where I am and what's happening," then congratulations! You are already at least halfway to being a spiritual immortal, and you certainly do not need to hear any more teachings about this.

For the rest of us, it is necessary to practice, in order to discover firsthand that the fundamental essence of our minds is the same as the Tao. Hsing, or original nature, is fundamentally sentient, brilliant, vast, and immeasurable. Our basic nature is as expansive as the empty sky and just as free of attachment and obstruction. However, despite being of this essential nature, our unawakened minds can be seized by one object or phenomenon after another, eventually becoming trapped by thought.

If we reflect upon our lives, it is possible to discover that we were each formed by the multitude of emotions, ideas, and thoughts in our minds, and yet this all took place without us ever having been conscious of the basic essence of the mind itself. The mind's "basic essence," which is another way of saying hsing, refers to what the mind was before it became tethered to conditions or yoked to this or that object or phenomenon. To find the way back to this uncontrived, primeval state is—to use the terminology of Chan Buddhism—to find one's "original face." This is to lay eyes upon hsing, our original state of being.

■ ■ ■

Observe yourself for a moment. What is your mind before a thought is born—when there is no thinking and nothing to attach your attention to?

If, in the moment between thoughts, you find that your mind is not occupied by thoughts, but is aware of its own being, then your mind is self-aware. Self-awareness is the nucleus of Taoist cultivation.

Because we almost never "turn around" and observe ourselves, we do not know ourselves. Instead, we only know the endless stream of things arising one after another. If we conceive of consciousness and sentience as rays of the mind's light, it is as though our minds never turn their light back inward to shine upon themselves. These rays of light only ever radiate outward. On the Taoist path, the mind's self-awareness or lack thereof ends up becoming a critical matter.

Where lies the import in "having awareness?" We all already have direct experience of the answer to this question. For instance, while I am delivering a lecture, I might move my hands in dramatic gesticulations while my mind is entirely focused on the topic that I am lecturing about. When this happens, my hands' movements are "unconscious." Conversely, if I place my awareness upon my hands and then consciously move them around, the feeling will be entirely different, and I will know exactly what my hands are doing. Typically, because our awareness is constantly scattering in a thousand different directions, it never "turns around" and becomes conscious of its own presence. Much of the time, our minds barely even turn around enough for us to maintain consciousness of our personal, physical presence, much as in the example above, when I gesticulate without even knowing what my hands are doing. If we barely notice our bodies, then so much further are we from illuminating our own minds with our awareness, and so much further are we from glimpsing our minds' nature. We are capable of being conscious of many, many things, but the subjects of our consciousness are in flux all day long. It is little wonder that our minds end up so messy and disordered that they lack any center or place of return.

Our minds innately contain tremendous energy, latent potential, and wisdom. However, because we let our minds be scattered by endless trivia, including the countless self-centered ideas arising all day long, our minds are incapable of finding unity and harmony. Disunity and disharmony sap the mind of its energy and inherent wisdom.

The biggest problem most of us have is that our minds are locked in an unending dance of chaotic thinking. Of course, there are some times when our minds are not flitting about, but those times generally only come when we are sound asleep. Most of the day we alternate between fantasies and discursive thinking. In the rare moments when we are not thinking about anything at all, we are asleep, and therefore totally unaware. To put it in stark terms, to be a normal human being is to have a mind with only two modes of functioning: mental tumult and unconscious oblivion.

Some people might read the above paragraphs and retort, "but my mind is perfectly lucid. I'm not asleep right now and I certainly don't have any scattered thoughts!" Most people who would react in this way do have minds full of scattered thoughts—they just have not yet discovered that this is so. They have relatively "coarse" minds, which means that they have not yet finely observed themselves. As soon as one really observes oneself, one will be startled to realize that the mind is always taking off and landing, always thinking, first of one thing, then another.

Even when we are dreaming we are still thinking, and our dreams are often continuations of whatever it was we were worrying about during the day. Sleep is not true rest. If one wants to truly rest, one must illuminate one's mind and encounter one's original nature. One must discover the mind's original appearance before one can be the master of one's own mind. However, be careful not to conclude that adepts who have illuminated their minds and revealed their natures do not think. They do, but their manner of thinking takes on a new character, because their mastery of the mind allows them to think consciously and deliberately. Accomplished adepts think if need be, but whenever the need to think is gone, then they can stop their mental activity and enter into states of samadhi.

■ ■ ■

One of the ways the word "hsing" can be understood is as "mind nature." The word "mind" usually points to something of a dynamic and transitory character, but "hsing" is a reference to the mind's unchanging prior-heaven qualities, which come from and correspond with their original source, the Tao. Another way of putting this is that hsing is the same as Tao. Therefore, within humans, the Tao manifests as our hsing. To illuminate one's mind is to comprehend the mind's actual condition; to see hsing, or nature, is to see the original appearance of one's mind. When one sees the mind for what it truly is, one's original nature manifests. In ancient Chinese, "to see" and "to manifest" were both written with the same character, but this does not mean that when one "sees hsing" one sees something appear before one's eyes. Rather, "with one's mind's eye" one obtains insight into the mind's nature.

"Illuminating mind" and "seeing hsing" are two separate but related concepts. To see hsing is to see the mind's essential prior-heaven nature. Before the mind's fundamental nature is apparent to us, our minds are deluded and full of chaotic thoughts. Illuminating the mind with awareness is thus necessary, both so that we can recognize and become familiar with our minds in their deluded states and so that we will know the mind in its awakened state. Genuine illumination of the mind is a prerequisite to revealing its nature.

What does actually mean to "see" the mind's nature? Who sees it? These questions might be best answered with a question. Suppose one day I had a particularly good meditation session, and I seemed to see something special appear while I was meditating. If I concluded that what I saw was *my* original nature, then the question arises: Just who was it who saw my nature? The point of this question is that anything that one can see is, by definition, not one's fundamental nature. This is to say that one's original nature, one's hsing, is not a subjective thing that can be witnessed. The reason for this is that hsing is the very part of each person that does the seeing. Because it is hsing that sees, hsing logically cannot be any thing that is seen. Therefore, all subjective phenomena that can be seen, felt, or known are most definitely not original nature.

When Taoists say that one must "see one's nature" that does not mean that there exists something out there for practitioners to behold. That which we call "seeing nature" actually refers to hsing spontaneously emerging or manifesting. Because hsing is the ultimate subject, it reveals itself to itself. Figuratively speaking, it is as though original nature's rays of light illuminate its own being—that is what is meant by "seeing one's nature." In this analogy, those rays of light represent one's awareness—they are illumination that comes from one's living consciousness.

Each person's fundamental nature has always existed. When cultivating hsing, nothing new is created. Hsing is not something anybody ever lost. Rather, it gets forgotten. In practice, we need to call it back into wakefulness and get it to elucidate itself with its own light. When this happens, the mind's nature is revealed.

All we have done so far is talk about the principles of illuminating the mind to see its nature. If one wishes to accomplish this task, one needs to practice in order to gain true comprehension. One must go inward, turning one's observant-ness upon one's own mind so as to experience its real, original essence.

■ ■ ■

When illuminating the mind to reveal its nature is discussed in inner alchemy, it is defined in a unique way that uses the word "empty" as a descriptor. The Taoist notion of "mind nature" is generally fairly compatible with Buddhism and Confucianism in the way they talk about mind nature. However, sometimes Taoists completely eschew words like "mind" and "hsing," and instead cut directly to talking about "emptiness." This happens when they talk about "returning to emptiness," "refining the shen to return to emptiness," or "returning to emptiness and entering the Tao." This idea of emptiness comes directly from a line in the *Tao Te Ching*, where Lao-tzu instructs, "arrive at an emptiness supreme, hold to a tranquility deep." Lao-tzu's instruction is for practitioners to be empty to the utmost degree while maintaining a state of placid serenity.

In such a context, "emptiness" can be thought of as an allusion or symbol for original nature. As beginning students of Tao, we do not know what our original nature is, so we can only use metaphors to try and imagine what it might be. As the word "emptiness" is understood in Taoist cultivation, it describes borderless-ness and boundlessness; it is limitlessness and endlessness. One cannot grab ahold of emptiness, nor can one turn it into an object. It is the background of all objects' and all phenomena's existence; it is a field. It is within emptiness, which presents no obstacles, that the unfathomable marvels of existence exist. It is amid emptiness that all objects and phenomena come into being and transform, and yet none of them add to or diminish emptiness itself. Emptiness is what "is because it is." It was never created, and it has always existed.

It needs to be said that emptiness is not some deathly stillness, nor is it synonymous with obliteration. Within emptiness there are all the "marvelous workings" of the universe. It is none other than emptiness that gives all objects and phenomena ground in which to develop and evolve. In Taoist practice, when one truly enters into the realm of emptiness, one actually experiences fulfillment and energetic transformation. Amid emptiness, one unites with the Tao, supported by totality. Because the Tao is a limitless, all-encompassing "field being," a person who has merged with emptiness also connects to the heavens, the earth, and the ten thousand things. This is why emptiness receives extraordinary emphasis in the study of inner alchemy.

In order to try and understand this intellectually, imagine being lost in the chaos of thinking. Thoughts swirls like clouds in the sky on a windy day, endlessly coming and going, ceaselessly changing shape and appearance. In such an image, one's original nature can be represented by the emptiness of the sky, which remains unchanged no matter what the wind and clouds do. Illuminating the mind means knowing that one's thoughts are coming and going like clouds in the sky but not being affected by them. When one understands the nature of one's mind, one no longer identifies with thoughts; one sheds the belief that thoughts are "me" and therefore loses the habit of bounding off in whatever direction thoughts pull one in.

Seeing one's nature is experiencing the "empty sky" that is the essence of one's mind. To see one's nature is to realize that one's "original appearance" is just like the emptiness that is the sky. From the standpoint of the mind's nature, thoughts come and go just as clouds do, but they cannot get in the way of emptiness, nor can they destroy it. Of course, if heavy clouds of discursive thought become too thick, then they can still cover the entire sky. And yet, when this happens, even though the sky's emptiness is no longer evident, it is still there, just as always. This is the reason there is fundamentally no need for anybody to go and create anything in Taoist practice. One merely need remove the obstacles and occlusions that prevent the sky-like state from being apparent. Revealing emptiness is all that needs to be done.

To take the above analogy a step further, the "light rays" of original nature's wisdom can be compared with sunlight. When storm clouds of scattered thought become too plentiful, sunlight gets blotted out, and only darkness remains. This is when one's mental realm becomes gloomy and grim. However, by giving rise to observant wisdom and consciously shining light on whatever passes through the mind, one can break through the dark clouds, allowing bright skies to return. When one does this, it is not that one creates the "sunlight" of awareness. Rather, one consciously makes use of something that has always been there but seldom comes into play—because most of us are unaware of its presence.

In this chapter's discourse, after providing a cursory explanation of the meaning of illuminating mind to see hsing, Huang Yuanji then introduces some basic techniques.

Simply reading the above theories may not be enough to make one feel confident that they can be understood. This is why having a very solid practice to use is indispensable. Although relying upon a practice cannot guarantee that one will illuminate the mind and see one's nature, having a concrete technique is still the most expedient way to get started. Some Taoist cultivators overemphasize "methodless-ness," arguing that methods in and of themselves are attachments that limit and delude people. Such practitioners stress that the only thing that needs to be done is to directly enter into the Tao. This is an extreme position, and those who hold it have nothing to offer those who wish to directly enter the Tao but find themselves unable to do so. One always needs an expedient pathway. Pathways are incapable of directly causing people to illuminate their minds and reveal hsing, but they can create favorable circumstances. The realm of essential nature does not need to be created (nor can it be created), but the beginning practices of cultivation can help people break through the dark clouds of obscuration in the mind so hsing may more easily become manifest. The initial methods of Taoist inner alchemy are called "concentrating shen, regulating breath." These four words are a formula for our practice.

There is nothing to worry about if, after wading through this chapter's theoretical portions, you feel like your head is full of murky water and you do not really understand what you just read. When you have time, find a place to become quiet. You can sit cross-legged or you can even stand; just choose a posture that you find easy, balanced, and relaxed. That is when you will be best able to do the work of concentrating your shen and regulating your breath.

What does "concentrating shen" entail? Our states of mind are unstable. We often latch on to our countless concerns, first thinking of this, then of that. When that happens, the mind needs to become concentrated and collected—we must retrieve shen. In order to "retrieve" the mind, if one is a person who has already illuminated mind and glimpsed its nature, then one can simply return the mind to itself. But if one still does not know how to do that, one can make use of an expedient method wherein one intentionally places the mind on a specific object of meditation. The method presented in this chapter is to place the mind upon one's own body, so that body and mind become one.

Even though there is big a difference between our bodies and our essential natures, the distance between them is relatively close—your body is much closer to what you really are than the distant concerns of success, fame, wealth, or your career. It is much closer to your essential nature than thoughts like, "in the future I'm going to accomplish this or that, and then people will see me in such and such light." The thought that one possesses a body, while tainted with delusion, is nevertheless much closer to reality than most other delusions. That is why we first learn to gather our minds by letting them rest upon our bodies. When we do this, shen will return to the physical body, instead of going bounding off wherever thoughts take it.

Our bodies have lots of different parts, so one might wonder, where exactly should shen return to? Sensing one's body in its totality is sufficient to unite body and mind. Practically speaking, this means feeling the inside of your body. Each of us has a body, but we are usually insensate of our bodies. Simply by returning our mental awareness to our bodies, we cause body and mind to become one.

■ ■ ■

If one finds it difficult to fathom what it means to feel the body in its totality and wishes to find an even simpler method of retrieving the mind, one can focus on letting regularity come to one's breathing. Doing so allows one to place one's mind upon the breath. Breathing acts like a bridge that connects our minds to our bodies. Gathering the mind upon the breath is an extremely efficacious and widely used practice; many traditions, including those of Indian yoga and Chan Buddhism, emphasize "uniting mind and breath." It is an excellent expedient that can be a gate to entering samadhi.

We have no way of controlling how the organs in our bodies function, nor can we control our blood flow and blood pressure. And yet, up to a certain extent, we do have active control over our breathing. Inasmuch as we can actively regulate it, the breath is unique among physiological functions. This is part of the reason that practitioners of inner alchemy often use an analogy that compares the human body to a furnace, in which consciousness is akin to the furnace's fire, while the breath is like the furnace's bellows. The profound tool of breathing can be used to "fan the fire," making it grow or subside.

How does one get started in letting regularity come to the breath? One should not try to control one's breathing. Rather, one should *let* it naturally become deeper, longer, and more even. People's breathing is typically short and shallow. However, when the mind is balanced and quiet, breathing naturally deepens. Body and mind can unite upon the breath, meaning that breathing can allow one to naturally and deeply experience the connection of body and mind. Furthermore, when one observes one's breathing, one's mind has a place to settle. As one's mind returns to the here and now, tumultuous thinking will cease, and one will stop ruminating about the past and future.

Practicing using the breath has another subtle but profound implication, which is that your breathing always takes place in the present. Can a person breathe somewhere other than here and now? Can a person announce that today he or she will do some extra breathing in order to get tomorrow's breathing out of the way? Impossible. A person cannot go back in time and make up for past breaths, either. The breath is always in the present, so when one observes one's breathing, one necessarily returns to the here and now with each breath right as it is taking place. Doing this tethers the mind. Our so-called monkeys of mind and horses of thought are very hard to tether, because they are long habituated to romping around discursively. When we make use of breathing as a practical expedient, we let the mind become stable and calm, as though we gave it a post to tether itself to amid the chaos. This can be accomplished simply by using our minds to feel and experience our breathing. We need only to tranquilly accompany our breaths.

■ ■ ■

Because habits of constantly thinking and engaging in delusion are second nature for most of us, we will inevitably discover that it is impossible to completely "unite mind and breath" when we first try to practice. As we attempt to meditate, most of us will notice an unending cascade of scattered thoughts. When this happens, the answer is *not* to struggle or go to war with discursive thinking or to start worrying to ourselves, "argh, why am I *still* giving rise to thoughts?" As soon as we start to think like that, we give birth to yet another new thought! Errant thoughts that occur during meditation are nothing to be afraid of at first, but if we start to struggle with them, then things might actually get a bit scary, because it soon becomes evident that it is impossible to defeat a thought. We might say to ourselves, "I don't want a single thought to be born—I just want to settle down," but the stronger our desire for calm becomes, the more calmness eludes us. So, we have to remember not to fret about discursive thoughts or delusions of the mind. We must also recall that thoughts are bound by their very nature to come, but also to go. Thoughts cannot linger indefinitely.

Paradoxically, our minds are not actually full of thoughts in any real sense. Take a look and see. When we really go searching within to try and locate our own thoughts, we will not find even one. The wandering Indian monk Bodhidharma transmitted Chan Buddhism to China. Famously, when he instructed his disciple Hui Ke to find his mind, after much effort Hui Ke could only declare, "I am searching for my mind, but it is impossible to find it!" The implication of this story is that, if we sincerely search for thoughts, we soon learn that we are incapable of truly locating them. This is because thoughts are not objects. They have no substance or form, and the moment we start to look for them, we find only emptiness. Observantly searching for thoughts is the real way to conquer them.

Once we realize that our thoughts do not exist as discrete entities, we have no more reason to try to fight against discursive mental activity. The most important thing is to be knowingly aware of our thoughts as they arise. Thoughts are no more real for people who do not cultivate the Tao than they are for people who have this realization, but most people do not know how to place knowing awareness upon their thoughts. Instead, they treat their thoughts as though they were something real. This is why it is possible for people to end up perpetually at odds with their thoughts, as they arise one after another without any break. When we know, through directly observing them, that our thoughts are fundamentally empty and insubstantial, then the impulse to try and control them disappears.

Once we have learned not to concern ourselves with our thoughts, we just return to our breathing. By applying ourselves to continually observing the breath, gradually we become able to enter into a state of serene tranquility, or samadhi. We enter into samadhi because doing so creates conditions that are favorable for illuminating the mind and revealing its nature.

■ ■ ■

Inner alchemy needs to be explained in modern terms, but not simply so that we can have an academic discussion about its concepts or its historical and cultural background. My hope is that elucidating the authentic spirit of inner alchemy will enable people to personally experience this practice in their own bodies and minds. These chapters are not merely meant as an exploration of ideas. Rather, I hope that people will treat the act of reading this book as an opportunity to engage in practice, just as I treat the writing of it as an aspect of my self-cultivation.

Genuine practice has to be fully integrated with daily life. Merging life with practice is what Chan Buddhists call "knocking everything into one." We should not think that practice is something one only does at a special, designated time each day. Similarly, practice is not successful if one only feels peace of mind while one is sitting in meditation. Instead, one has to learn how to maintain a state of practice that is present no matter what one is doing with one's time. That said, learning to do that is a long process that starts with using techniques like the ones presented in this chapter. Below are simple instructions for getting started:

First of all, align your body, so that your whole body is upright and relaxed. Try as best you can to straighten your back, as you do not want to be crooked or twisted. Relaxation does not mean going limp or slouching—it means having relaxed naturalness. You can begin by relaxing your head, starting at the crown, and then slowly becoming conscious of each part of your head as it relaxes. Relax your eyes, your nose, your mouth, and your neck, and then begin to relax downward from your shoulders. Relaxation implies letting each and every cell naturally return to its place, but do not be anxious to try and figure out how that is done. Just relax, observing your body's interior, letting it relax along with the exterior. It is important to let this process of relaxing and observing your body continue all the way down into your legs and feet, because people typically seldom place their awareness upon their bodies, and that is where you need your awareness to be if you are to observe your breath.

Once you have relaxed your body, simply return your attention to your breath. Steadily observe your breathing with your mind.

As thoughts arise, remember: everything you thought and did today has already passed. Let the things of the past remain in the past. Do not bring them into the present. As for what will come tomorrow, deal with it then. There is no need for you to contemplate the future right now. Right now, there is nothing you need to do other than to be in a state of tranquil quiescence. Simply continuing to observe your breath, or continuing to read this book, is enough. Do not worry about anything else. All of us already spend plenty of time worrying about our lives. There is no need, in this precious moment, to think yet again about any of the issues of the world.

■ ■ ■

We already looked at what it means to illuminate the mind to reveal original nature, so beginning here we will look at the text of Huang Yuanji's teaching. Huang lays out the theme of his discourse in this chapter by saying, "I shall point out the truth and significance of illuminating mind to see its fundamental nature." He then explains what the mind's fundamental nature, or hsing, is: "The prior-heaven mind is fundamental nature. The fundamental nature of prior heaven is empty, nonexistent primordial qi. In short, it is emptiness, that is all."

The terms "mind" and "fundamental nature of mind" (the latter being hsing) both actually refer to the same thing, but they describe it from different perspectives, with different points of emphasis. Each of us only has one real life, so it is not accurate to think that over here is one's mind, and over there is the mind's essential nature—they are inseparable. However, the word "hsing" strictly refers to the transcendent state that comes from the prior-heaven nature of the Tao. The meaning of the word "mind," on the other hand, is more inclusive. It can imply both the prior-heaven, original state of the mind *as well as* the later-heaven mind. In other words, "mind" is a term that can refer to both the chaotic, mixed up thoughts running through the mind, as well as the mind's fundamental essence.

When mingling with Taoist or Buddhist cultivators, one often hears that "the mind is no other than hsing." This statement is not inaccurate, but when reading phrases like this, it is crucial to be clear on which definition of the word "mind" is being used. In the case of this phrase, "mind" refers to prior-heaven mind, which is the same as hsing. The statement "the mind is no other than hsing" refers to the mind's state before it develops into a tainted, later-heaven condition. In our later-heaven lives, because our minds get clogged up by our excessive attachments, they stop settling down and returning inward into their own being. Our minds lose the ability to revert to their prior-heaven original appearance, and we live fully in the state of later-heaven thinking. Once that happens, we have to learn how to withdraw from the confusion of our later-heaven minds and return to our minds' prior-heaven essence. That is the way to find hsing, the fundamental nature of mind.

Huang Yuanji uses the word "empty" to describe original nature and primordial qi because emptiness is on par with the Tao. It is thus a word that describes the nature of the Tao. The most important characteristic of primordial qi is that it is empty. The distinctions that define later heaven have yet to arise within that which is empty, so within primordial qi, one actually finds neither shen nor qi. All that is there is just empty essence.

■ ■ ■

Huang Yuanji's next sentences read: "Humans, beginning from birth, are bound by temperament, obscured by lust and desire, and entwined in love and affection. Consequently, our minds have long been not empty. Qi follows the orders of the mind, and jing is in service of shen. Galloping and chasing, wantonly roaming, they are dissipated and squandered until nearly gone. This is where students set about starting the work, and thus do we place such value on concentrating shen and harmonizing the breath."

We just discussed how prior-heaven mind, or prior-heaven hsing, is emptiness. That we need to cultivate is simply because, once we come into later-heaven life, we are no longer in the prior-heaven state. Our later-heaven minds, being bound by our temperaments, obscured by our desires, and entangled by our ardor, are not empty. They chase outward after the objects of passion, desire, infatuation, and love, and in turn transform our character.

What is character? In terms of the Chinese pictographs making up this word, 氣質, it can be understood as describing the quality of our qi. All people have qi, which is the profound and subtle energy of life itself. However, the quality of different people's qi is not the same. Qi's quality is affected by the mind, so just as people's minds are different, so too is their qi. If a person's mind is clear and serene, so too will be his or her qi. If a person's mind is polluted, this individual will have polluted qi. In Chinese culture, the word "qi" is imbued with such extraordinary depths of meaning that it can encompass anything. Its usages are incredibly broad, and when it is connected to other words, a wealth of meaning is created.

When Huang Yuanji says of qi that it "follows the orders of the mind," he means that our minds and our qi are intimately connected. So, for instance, if one tends to be irritable, one's qi will show the influence of this mentality. Huang also says "jing is in service of shen." Jing is one of the so-called trio of treasures that is jing, qi, and shen; it can be understood as the material essences underlying our biological existence. Jing, like qi, is also yoked to shen. Thus, if the activity of one's shen is hectic, jing will follow it in acting chaotically and its natural functions will be negatively influenced.

The consequence of the way in which most of us lead our later-heaven lives is that we have preponderances of deluded thoughts, our mental activity is often frenzied and randomly discursive, and our minds are prone to chasing after external phenomena. Our unruly mental activity causes our jing and qi—the essences and energies of life—to get frittered away. Such are the circumstances of later-heaven life.

Because of how our later-heaven human lives tend to unfold, when students who wish to cultivate the Tao ask where they should begin, the answer is usually that they should start with concentrating shen and harmonizing breath. This is necessary because, if one's shen is not focused it will inevitably scatter, flitting here and there, and going off on limitless flights of fancy. It is impossible for a shen that habitually behaves like that to concentrate into oneness, so as to become the unified center that presides over the refining of the elixir. If one lacks a unified mental center, original nature will not reveal itself, and therefore the metaphorical "leader" will not be in command. If hsing is not present to act as the "leader," there will be nothing to coordinate and guide one's alchemical practice, and one's jing and shen will simply disperse in any direction they can.

■ ■ ■

In order to cultivate the Tao, one's mind must have a unified center. It is precisely this center that we normal people lack. Each of us has an "I," and we constantly declare "I am this, I am that." However, this "I" is not actually a single, unified thing. Rather, each person's "I" is really a huge heap of "I's." "I" is a crowd; at different times and places, different I's come out to perform.

This proliferation of "I's" in our minds is a bit like the personnel in a company. If the leader of the company—the one who is responsible for guiding the rest of the personnel—is absent at major meetings, the employees will all start jumping on stage and make pronouncements of their own. Lacking any oversight, each employee can claim he or she is the boss of the company and start giving orders, making decisions, and signing contracts with other companies. The big problem is, since these employees are not actually the boss, once a new contract is signed and the person who made the decision steps off the stage, an entirely different "I" can take over and tear up the contract, declaring, "This contract is void, I never agreed to it! Anyway, I've got a better idea!" Bedlam reigns throughout so many people's lives because their "I's" all seem to sign totally contradictory agreements, hold differing opinions, make conflicting plans, and think altogether differently about life.

As long as the real leader remains absent, our lives will continue to be hectic, so it is incumbent upon us to find this central figure and let it take charge. This is the only way for there to be unity in the guidance of our proverbial company. To cultivators, unity of mind is extremely important. All of the employees passing themselves off as the boss need to return to their rightful positions and cease making decisions in lieu of their employer. Once the boss has returned and the employees stay at their posts, the company will, as a single entity, be able to conduct business smoothly and efficiently.

The reason concentrating shen is such a crucial practice is that this is what allows the mind to behave as a single entity, instead of a throng of conflicting "I's." When shen is concentrated, shen is one. When the boss returns, the chaotic hubbub of "I's" becomes empty. This is what it means to exist as a single entity. Once empty, one returns to the original nature that is given to each person by the universe. In our present lives, this prior-heaven "boss" is hsing, the innate essence of our minds. Before our present lives, in our origins in ultimate emptiness before we were born, the core of our being was the empty essential nature that exists before life takes shape.

■ ■ ■

This is a good place for our discussion of the principles of concentrating shen to segue into the practice of harmonizing the breath. A person's shen and qi are intimately linked. If shen is disordered, one's breath will correspondingly be irregular. To align the breath is to imbue it with awareness, rhythm, and regularity, so that breathing becomes harmonious. If one does not align the breath, it will be choppy and uneven. Breathing unevenly influences the qi of one's body. When one's qi loses harmony, one's internal organs and even one's skin and flesh are affected. When qi lacks harmony, it functions without the unity that is needed as a basis for establishing "real life." Thus, in practice, Taoists align their breathing both to achieve equanimity of mind as well as to bring harmony to their qi.

When Taoist adepts introduce the principles of cultivation, they always discuss shen and qi together. If shen is discussed first, the topic of qi is broached immediately afterward. In the same way, discourses on hsing must be followed by explanations of ming. Shen and qi come part and parcel with one another, as do hsing and ming. This is why, in this discourse, Huang Yuanji first speaks about empty, original, prior-heaven hsing, and then focuses on the ming that humans receive from heaven and earth. In this discourse, Huang uses the concept of qi to explain ming. His core point is that when harmony returns to our bodies, we restore "real life." "Real life" refers to what ming fundamentally is. Huang Yuanji describes it as "the unified qi of the vast harmony, unborn and suspended between heaven and earth."

In his discourse in this chapter, whenever Huang Yuanji talks about the paired concepts of shen and qi or hsing and ming, he is referring to "real hsing" and "real ming." The implications of the word "real" here is that those of us who do not understand how to cultivate the Tao all live with "distorted hsing" and "distorted ming." Using the above analogy of a company, our lives are run like a corporate meeting where any of the employees can randomly jump up on stage to make formal pronouncements in front of the camera whenever they like. So long as there is no company director to moderate affairs, life will remain a bustle of disorder. To live with no clarity of mind, with one's qi scattering as a result, is to have "distorted hsing" and "distorted ming."

Restoring real hsing and real ming is to live "real life," which means being of one body with heaven, earth, and all phenomena. Real life cannot be founded upon the divided and dissipated hsing and ming of later-heaven existence. Real hsing and ming are what create spiritual immortals. Put another way, spiritual immortals are only capable of becoming what they are because they restore real hsing and real ming. Spiritual immortals are not some vague, imaginary thing that exists "up there in heaven." Spiritual immortality is the living of a real life, founded upon real hsing and real ming. If we discover and cultivate real hsing and real ming, then we will become spiritual immortals. If we do not find the real, and remain living lives founded upon distorted hsing and distorted ming, then we will remain as humans.

To be a human is to exist in a realm of possibility. Humans can ascend as well as plummet. When distorted hsing and distorted ming so thoroughly define a person's life that his or her prior-heaven spiritual nature and real ming are totally obscured, then this person will fall. He or she will effectively live as an animal. Totally governed by later-heaven nature, the person will pass his or her life solely in pursuit of temporal, illusory phenomena.

However, if this same person decides to train for self-realization and returns to the state of real hsing and real ming, then he or she will become a spiritual immortal. This is why Taoists teach that humans can rise up and become immortals or descend into animalistic existences.

. . .

Huang Yuanji's core approach to the practice of concentrating shen and aligning the breath is encapsulated in four Chinese characters that translate as, "do not forget, do not assist." This statement comes from Mencius's writings, but it is a key principle common to many cultivation traditions. Regardless of the school, "do not forget, do not assist" lies at the core of Taoist practice.

If our meditation practice is an amalgam of all sorts of specific methods, it is very difficult not to end up with an internal monologue that sounds like an academic roundtable. When discursive thinking arises, the later-heaven mind is in charge. Despite our wish to enter tranquility, if our later-heaven minds "assist" our practice, then in actuality we will do no more than sit on our cushions engaging in delusion.

On the other hand, if, instead of "assisting," we just sit down and space out in unconscious stupor, we are "forgetting." Huang Yuanji's admonition, "do not forget," means to we must maintain the awareness of having been in the Tao all along while we practice. We must recall that we have always been sovereign but that we forgot the supreme within ourselves and mistook ourselves for beggars. Our real hsing and real ming are given to us by the prior-heaven essence of the Tao. They have always been there, but we lose track of them. The "remembering" of our prior-heaven original natures cannot occur if we fail to maintain awareness and fall into torpor when we practice.

"Do not assist, do not forget" is a linchpin instruction because it cautions the student to be neither mentally frenzied nor mentally insensate. If one succeeds at not assisting and not forgetting, one is neither lax nor tense, neither slow nor rushed. If one can maintain "not assisting and not forgetting," then gradually, as with the tuning of a string on an instrument, just as how beautiful notes are produced when the tuning is "just right," one will enter into a truly serene and quiet state. Huang Yuanji calls this state by the name Lao-tzu gave it, "an emptiness supreme, a tranquility deep." When this point is reached, the functions of later-heaven mind are suspended.

In serene quiet, we return to the conditions of our prior-heaven essence. We return to real hsing and ming. We return to the body of the Tao. This state is "ultimate emptiness," because there is nothing done or created, and in it there are no worries, no passions, and no delusions. One cannot create emptiness. If one tries with all one's might to create or perpetuate this empty state, one will have already strayed far away from emptiness. Real emptiness is the condition of self-suchness, non-doing, and naturalness. It is the original state. There is no need for anybody to add anything to it nor remove anything from it. All that is needed is to leave all things to rest in their own places. Let all phenomena be as they are, and liberation will manifest of its own accord.

■ ■ ■

Please pay close attention to something very important that Huang Yuanji says next: "Only when shen is fully empty will the clear and harmonious qi of heaven and earth naturally seek refuge in one another." When one's consciousness is already emptied of the later-heaven mind's worries and distinctions, and one has entered into the serenely quiet condition Lao-tzu called "an emptiness supreme, a tranquility deep," what happens? "The clear and harmonious qi of heaven and earth naturally seek refuge in one another."

When a practitioner reaches this stage, the cultivation of ming and hsing becomes a single thing, and one can no longer speak about hsing and ming practices as separate things. Once one has clarity and tranquility, the universe's limpid, silent, serene, and harmonious energy spontaneously merges with the energies of one's own life. These two energies—those of the universe and the individual—attract one another, such that one's own body and mind resonate in sympathy with the entire universe. One directly experiences the meaning of the Chinese idiom, "heaven and humanity merge as one."

It is important for students of Taoism to keep in mind the principle that our lives are not independent. From the very beginning, we have always been of one body with heaven, earth, and all the things that exist. Of course, this statement often leads directly to the question, "Given that we're already one with the universe, what's the point of Taoist cultivation? Even if I don't cultivate, isn't everything already one?" It is indeed true that we are already one with the Tao, whether or not we choose to cultivate the Tao. However, there is still a distinction between people who have achieved these teachings and the rest of us who have not: we who have not realized the Tao do not *know* that we are one with it, and because we lack this experiential knowledge, we see ourselves as independent individuals, and therefore devote our lives to trying to hold on to things and establish distinctions between this and that. In our thoughts and behaviors, we build selves that seem to be independent of heaven, earth, and the ten thousand things. From there, we create our own suffering due to our illusions and the passions they ignite. We are, as Taoists say, lost.

Even though oneness is indeed real, having a mere intellectual awareness of this principle is of little actual use. If one does not truly know oneness, one will remain lost. It is by cultivating the Tao that one proves to oneself that the individual and the universe are in fact one. When one has clear, direct knowledge of this truth, one's distinction-making mind recedes, and one experiences a life that is vast, endless, and borderless. The oneness of the universe and the individual that cultivation gradually reveals was there all along. But for a Taoist practitioner, that oneness is felt in a way that is degrees of magnitude away from the quality of most people's lived experience. This is the principal reason why one has to actually cultivate.

To reiterate, we humans are fundamentally at one with the heavens, the earth, and the myriad things, but it is only when we align our shen and breath in harmony to enter into the state of emptiness and nonexistence that the empty qi from the universe's own source resonates within our individual lives. Only when that happens can we, as Huang Yuanji says, "change inexhaustibly and be unfathomably marvelous." He refers to this state when he says "within this emptiness, there is substance." This concept corresponds to the Buddhist teaching that "true emptiness is transcendent presence." The Tao's emptiness is positive.

If one talks about "empty nonexistence," most people find it incomprehensible. Some might even be taken aback and protest, "Yikes, emptiness and nonexistence, that sounds terrifying! What's the point of seeking *that*?" However, in Taoist cultivation, the reason one learns to enter emptiness is that its marvelous function is to house "substance." This so-called substance is the source of all genuine ability, genuine energy, and genuine wisdom. When Huang Yuanji says, "within this emptiness, there is substance," he is speaking of what Lao-tzu called "doing nothing and yet having nothing remain undone." At first glance, it may seem as though wu wei, or non-doing, is a very negative teaching. But in Taoism, it is precisely because one does nothing that one leaves nothing undone. Conversely, the more one does, the more things are left undone. It is ultimately due to our doing that we fail to reach the profound workings of the Tao.

■ ■ ■

Huang Yuanji's next statement is, "How is mind illuminated? Only when empty is it numinous. When numinous, it is illuminated."

What this statement means is that, once one's mind is empty, the divine light of one's original nature manifests, as though one cracked open a treasure chest containing all things. Of this state of mind, Huang says, "In a mind illuminated, the multitudinous principles are all complete, and the myriad phenomena are wholly encompassed." Within the divine illumination of emptiness, one returns to the body of the Tao, the state of harmony and completion of all things and all phenomena.

If one should enter into this state, one will encounter two distinct circumstances. The first Huang Yuanji calls "yet to move," which describes one's condition while later-heaven thinking is still yet to stir. This is the original state of the Tao, of which Huang says, "it is vast and mighty, without knowledge and without knowing. This is called 'thoughts not arising within, thoughts not entering from without.'" In this condition, as one is without thoughts, one's mind neither wanders outward, nor lets the endless variety of external stimuli wander in. When this condition manifests, there is just radiant brilliance—the state of essential nature, which we also call hsing.

If emptiness only ever led practitioners into the above condition, they would spend whole days stuck in it, incapable of emerging to handle the affairs of everyday life. However, emptiness also leads to another condition, called "contact," in which the later-heaven mind begins to function as a response to encountering phenomena. Of this state Huang says, "When the illuminated mind comes into contact with things, it moves. Sensing, it thereupon responds. Encountering roundness, it becomes rounded. Yielding to angularity, it becomes angled. Vivacious and uninhibited, its unfathomability is like that of a swimming dragon." A sign that a Taoist cultivator has true attainment is that this person will not merely *dwell* inside his or her original nature. Rather, he or she will be able to *function* from within essential nature.

An achieved person's actions are different from normal people's. Most of the thoughts that stir up in normal people's minds are based in delusions. In a mind that has no master, almost all thinking originates from craving and distinctions. Conversely, after a person realizes hsing, although thoughts will still arise in his or her mind, they will do so without there being any attachment or reified distinction. In a cultivator with deep realization, thoughts simply come in response to whatever circumstances arise, so that whatever needs to be taken care of can be taken care of. When the work is finished, the practitioner lets go right then and there, and the issue is resolved. This sort of thinking is unlike that of normal people—when most of us get stuck in rumination, we struggle to disentangle ourselves and let go. When mental functions are based on an illuminated mind essence, the mind flows with life, and thoughts manifest in spontaneous accord with actual necessity. Any issue, once resolved, leaves no traces of sequela behind it in the mind. Resolution is followed by liberation.

Huang Yuanji summarizes mind's fundamental nature, hsing, by quoting an ancient Taoist maxim: "In tranquility there is primordial shen, in movement there is true intent." In this aphorism, "tranquility" and "movement" refer to how hsing presents itself when an adept is resting in tranquility, and how it functions when the adept springs into action. When hsing manifests in a state of stillness, it is called primordial shen (this synonym for prior-heaven shen will be described in detail in chapter 7). When hsing functions in a person who is engaging in doing it is called "true intent." We normal people, who have not allowed hsing to manifest by illuminating our minds, are exactly the opposite of what the above maxim describes. When our minds are tranquil, they just become dim and torpid; when our minds are active, they bounce around in the chaos of thought.

To finish this section, let us look once more at the relationship between mind and hsing. Hsing is the prior-heaven, transcendent nature of mind. It is one, both with itself and with Tao. If our thoughts and emotions are in constant tumult, our minds will never return to their essence. In the absence of this proverbial master, chaos reigns. However, we cannot aspire to simply bring our lives to a halt and remain in the state of prior-heaven mind nature. We must also act. If prior-heaven mind cannot manifest and perform its function in our lives, revealing hsing is meaningless. Thus, there is a "substance and function" relationship that binds hsing and mind together. To truly illuminate one's mind and reveal its original nature is to obtain "real mind"; to obtain "real mind" means to allow the mind's substratum, hsing, to manifest itself in one's actions.

Hsing's presence in an individual is referred to as "primordial shen." Its activity is referred to as "true intent." Before any of us existed as individuals, what we call hsing was empty, primordial qi. Put another way, it was the empty unity of qi and shen that is the Tao's own essence.

■ ■ ■

Huang Yuanji ends the above discourse with advice on how to practice and descriptions of states that arise in practice. When one single-mindedly applies oneself with the same unbroken focus of a cat stalking a mouse, the scatteredness of mind disappears, and one reaches a state where one's inner being and the outside world become merged together. If one's hsing cultivation reaches this stage, then ming training will naturally become easy, because it will be carried along by the current of one's cultivation of mind nature. Hsing skill is the dominant factor in Taoist practice, because "ming" (this word, which refers to life, the body's energies and essences, as well as destiny, will be explored in depth in chapter 6) cannot be cultivated on its own. Thus, since ming training relies upon the guidance of the mind, it is hsing cultivation that always takes the lead.

Huang mentions "mountain sprites and water spirits" whose ming training is so good that they can perform feats like physical transformation. There are people who, like these "sprites and spirits," have extraordinary abilities, which they obtain without cultivating mind nature. Day after day, they furiously train their skills, but they do not attempt to illuminate their minds and see their natures, nor do they understand what the goals of cultivation are. If one trains like this and develops supernatural abilities—and then uses them to chase after selfish desires—one is far worse than a common thief. To use one's attainments to perform foul, shameless deeds in order satisfy one's greed is tantamount to turning one's back on the Tao and galloping directly away from it. No good ends will come to one who lives like this. Greed and temptation are dangers that linger around those who eschew hsing training.

Not long ago in China we had a period of "qigong fever," when huge numbers of people trained in qigong every day. Certain "grand masters" showed off their supposed supernatural powers, seducing people with claims of having various abilities, while promising to teach methods that would bring about this or that result. Their dangerousness lay in getting people to desire such attainments.

If not supernatural attainments, what exactly does a Taoist practitioner seek to cultivate? The fact is that many of us misunderstand the most fundamental objectives. To cultivate the Tao is to return to the prior-heaven state, which cannot be done while craving and greed are still present. However, there are those whose training is guided by greed itself. If one trains for twelve hours a day simply as a means to satisfy some craving, then even if one becomes exceptionally skillful, one's situation is still extremely precarious. Even if one ends up in radiantly good health, because the seeds of craving remain, great peril never leaves one's side.

Taoists warn against "walking into fire and among demons." When they say this, they do not mean that some sort of demon out there will come to harm a practitioner—what they are speaking of are the mind's own demons. If one does not cultivate one's mind nature and instead just trains this or that skill, one runs the risk of activating energies that are dormant in normal people's bodies and being unable to control them. One also runs the risk of being able to control these energies but being too unwise not to misuse them, and thereby bringing calamity upon oneself and others. In genuine cultivation of the straight and narrow path, there is no "walking into fire and among demons," because what one cultivates is one's mind itself. When one empties the mind, there remain no more such demons, as it is from mind that they are born.

3

玄關一竅

THE PORTAL OF THE
MYSTERIOUS PASS

The two words, "refining mind," are the one and only gateway into Dharma, traversed by thousands of realized ones and myriad sages. Aside from this, all of it is not the Great Tao. One must know that the seeds of endless births and deaths in samsara all stem from not mastering thought, from false discrimination and delusional thinking, and from performing countless types of perverse and dissolute acts.

Thus, when the ancients exerted themselves, they necessarily first firmly tethered the horse of thought, and tightly locked up the monkey of mind. Why? For a thought's motion is the passage of a thought from birth to death; and a thought's cessation is where a thought's nirvana is found. It is in this that the Tao is accomplished—what more could there be? One only need master a single thought to naturally arrive at the undifferentiated and indistinct, the realm without thought and without cogitation.

Even if sometimes thoughts arise and the mind stirs, that is only due to phenomena being sensed, causing movement; it is not causeless, spontaneous movement. If the mind moves only in response to phenomena, it is the mind of no mind, and even as it responds to myriad occurrences, it remains the true mind. Conversely, if the mind is of a mind, then even if one silently sits in shamatha vipassana, *there is only false mind.*

Students, to arrive at such conditions, could it be easy? The key is no more than keeping a grasp on a single thought, all the way up to bhutatathata *naturally occurring, to perfect clarity spontaneously thus, to shen thoroughly interconnected with creation and transformation, to integrity equaling heaven and earth. The only fear is that, when the mysterious pass becomes active, you are absent-minded and indifferent.*

If you can everlastingly hold and perpetually foster, not slacking the slightest, encountering demons without retreating, receiving slander without quitting, being solely of one heart and one mind, taking your empty, intelligent, marvelous essence and conserving and nourishing it always, naturally improving by day and month, then the mysterious pass will appear.

The portal of the mysterious pass is our source for the elixir in the cultivation of the Tao; do not merely seek it in great samadhi and profound stillness. Confucius said: "I wish for benevolence, and here benevolence is." If one needed to wait for great samadhi and great stillness before one could obtain it, Confucius could not have so simply and easily pointed the way.

We see when students are cultivating, suddenly they become still and concentrated, not knowing or sensing anything at all. Then suddenly arises the mind of knowing awareness. Of the future there is not a thought, of the past there is no remembering. Pristine and unblemished, it is heavenly primordial oneness qi's original face.

From the cultivating and upholding of a single thought, gather, obtain, cook, and refine; seal, solidify, warm, and nurture. Slowly but surely, you will naturally become an unfathomable immortal.

Yet, in lesser samadhi and lesser stillness, one can also glimpse the heart of heaven coming to return. If one's personal affairs are hurried and hasty, and one's thoughts and considerations are beyond number, and one's engagements are disturbing and troublesome, then these things will be like arrowroot climbing and creeping up the tree that attracted the vine, sprouting more tendrils the higher it rises, becoming more chaotic as its tendrils multiply, never coming to a stop. In the face of such circumstances, what can be done?

So long as you are able to shed light back on the present thought, your entire mind will be wholly illuminated. You will be like a drunken fellow who is lost and asleep at the roadside, in the instant when a bowl of cold wa-

ter is splashed across his head and face. Abruptly and with a shock you will come to, and you will begin to realize you have been in a muddled stupor in the midst of an empty dream. This is the portal of the mysterious pass.

Once, the Old Immortal of the Southern Pole Star showed Master Skinny Crane that true primordial mind essence is indeed sought through the mysterious pass. The mysterious pass accompanies both movement and stillness. At all times it is present. But if one does not sense its stirring, then it is impossible to know it. The Old Immortal had Skinny Crane try having another person call his name, and of course Master Skinny Crane replied to this person, saying, "I'm here!" Who was it that responded? Although Skinny Crane said it was his mouth, yet the governor of this reply was his true primordial mind essence. He was, within the space of his response, directly taking his true primordial mind essence and, out of the void, holding it out to let others see. The Old Immortal of the Southern Pole Star's example truly and aptly showed the way.

Thus we know that even when knowing and sensing do not arise, and myriad sense objects have disappeared, as soon as there is a call there is a response, and the true primordial is clearly revealed. Also, when knowing and sensing have arisen, and myriad sense objects are active, as soon as there is a call there is a response, and the true primordial is exposed. On this basis contemplate the following: when knowing and sensing have not arisen, the mind is naturally thus; when knowing and sensing arise in profusion, the mind is also naturally thus. This is because it is empty and yet numinous; being empty, then how could it have birth and death?

The only thing to fear is that, when disordered delusions coil and confuse, and when human affections tug and enwrap, you will not see them as empty, and will therefore be incapable of severing them. This is the fundamental reason people are unable to reach the Tao.

In sum, this portal is but the moment of the present breath; it is not before, it is not after. If, when a person is quiet and alone, suddenly somebody calls his or her name, and instantaneously he or she responds, that is the mysterious pass. A moment after this response, yin and yang split into two pieces, and this is the mysterious pass no more.

The mysterious pass is the moment when the taiji is about to split, when the two pieces are about to halve. Movement is not it; stillness is not it, *either. It is in the gap where stillness at its extreme stirs, and where movement at its apex stills! It is said that movement and stillness are endless; the mysterious pass is also endless. You students must skillfully grasp this teaching.*

■ ■ ■

Before we dive into the third discourse, let us take a minute to gather our minds. It is easy for our minds to go running off, so let us return to our breath and feel our bodies, so that our bodies and minds become one.

While in tranquility, try using your primordial shen to read. You do not need to analyze so much. The sentient brightness within you is capable of understanding my words, because what I am speaking is the language of your primordial shen. So just return to your original state. If there are things you cannot clearly understand, just let them pass without pursuing them. Remain stable in the present moment, and then naturally you will understand that which you are meant to understand. This will work because the place within you that is vast and spiritually connected already has sufficient wisdom.

If you return to the original aspect of your mind nature, then you will understand what I am saying upon reading it. "Ah, it's like *this*." However, if you work too hard to try and distinguish and analyze what "*this*" is, then your eyes will have reached the next sentence while your mind is still analyzing the last one, and there will be no way for you to keep up.

Using primordial shen is just like dancing. Dancing always follows the beat, here and now. If you miss the last beat and you step on your partner's foot and you think, "uh-oh, I made the wrong step again," just as you start worrying about the last beat, you will then miss *this* beat, and you will fall even further behind. You have to come back to the beat that is playing right here, right now. You cannot dance to the beat that already passed, and you cannot dance to the beat yet to come.

This is the art of life. Really living means always living in the now. If we wish to really live, we cannot stay fixated on the memories of the past, especially if that means being regretful and remorseful about things that happened long ago. Those events are already following their courses, and there is nothing we can do to change them. The things of the past will never return; the passage of time cuts them away in one fell swoop. If we wish to really live, we cannot stay stuck daydreaming about the future, either. The future has yet to arrive—what we think of it, we ultimately think in vain. So long as our minds are focused on the past and the future, we lose out on living in the present moment.

Because we are prone to living in the future or the past, when it is time to enjoy life, we often miss out. A person who is wealthy enough to eat the finest foods available will not fully experience the beauty of the cuisine he or she has ordered if, upon seeing it, he or she is triggered into thinking, "oh goodness, in the past I was so poor that I could never afford eat like this." Such a thought easily leads to worries about becoming poor again in the future, and soon enough, the food begins to lose its flavor.

If you have a lot of years and experience under your belt, do not let life revolve around reliving your memories. Let what has passed truly pass. If you are in the early stages of life, do not constantly think toward the future, as there is no way to accurately imagine what things might be like, anyway. All sorts of things may one day come to pass, but then again, they might not. If you can really and truly walk each and every step in the present moment, then what is meant to come will come. Be assured that things will work out on their own.

■ ■ ■

Huang Yuanji's third discourse is entitled "The Portal of the Mysterious Pass." The mysterious pass is such an important concept in internal alchemy that it is indeed emblematic of the entire path. The opening line of this discourse points us to a crucial concept in Taoist practice, which is that "refining the mind is the foundation." As we discussed in chapter 2, Taoist cultivation is not a question of pursuing external things, because anything one creates or obtains will eventually disappear. Cultivation is a question of returning to the prior-heaven state of one's mind, and thereby to one's "real" life. The refining of one's mind is the root of cultivation, because without mind, there is no life. Life is the active mind.

Buddhism teaches that the myriad "dharmas" are no other than mind.[1] What this means is that all perceptible phenomena are but manifestations of our own minds. We perceive some things as beautiful because our minds have the experiences and sensations of enjoying beauty. We perceive other things as ugly because our minds display ugliness. But from any standpoint external to our own minds, objects have no objective beauty, nor have they any objective ugliness. Beauty and ugliness are found within our own minds' responses and distinctions.

Our minds can fall into states of confusion and chaos. When this happens, we pursue innumerable external phenomena as the mind is yanked along by endless proliferations of thoughts, unable to rest in its own being. But our minds can also awaken. Awakening the mind is the goal of Taoist cultivation. Awakening is the mind coming back to itself, no longer being swept away by external objects or by thoughts.

Regardless of whether one is undertaking a hsing (mind nature) practice or a ming (life essence) practice, one always practices by refining the mind, because both hsing and ming practices rely upon the activity of the mind. Since internal alchemy emphasizes cultivating hsing and ming in tandem, this tradition includes a category of methods for physical training and transformation. Nevertheless, we must be cautious not to mistakenly conclude that cultivation requires training our bodies day in and day out. There is zero value in deluding ourselves about our bodies, thinking that we need to train for some sort of magical power like being able to fly. All the changes of the body and its energies come about in concert with the transformation of mind. If our minds awaken, if our minds are clear and tranquil, and if we become capable of resonating with the source of energy in the universe, then our bodies will change. In this way, we will indeed see progress in our ming training, but such success always comes from the same foundation: refining the mind.

■ ■ ■

The mysterious pass is a unique part of Taoist inner alchemy's process of refining the mind. All traditions can be said to teach refinement of the mind's nature, but the idea of the portal of the mysterious pass is found only in Taoist alchemy.

Taoist alchemical practices identify numerous "caverns" located in the human body, also called "portals." The three *dantian* are a well-known example. There are also different pathways along which qi and blood travel, including the conception meridian, the governor meridian, the thrusting vessel, and so forth. There are usually convenient methods one can use to get started with practices involving these "portals," but the mysterious pass is quite special, in that it does not refer to a particular location in the body, nor to any of the organs. Anybody who says that there are places in the body that can be given the name "portal of the mysterious pass" is mistaken.

The mysterious pass is called a "portal" only in a metaphorical sense. The key point is that the mysterious pass is a pivot or turning point of inexplicable marvelousness and profound subtlety, which serves as a "gateway" to making manifest our prior-heaven states. It is an energetic turning point found at the threshold of the transformation from later heaven into prior heaven. Because we humans live in a later-heaven state in which the prior heaven is no longer apparent, the later-heaven aspects of our being are dominant. However, the goal of those of us who are walking the cultivator's path is to return to our prior-heaven state. In the process of going back to prior heaven, there are certain crucial points in the functioning of qi when the later heaven becomes inapparent and the prior heaven manifests. In these brief instants, there lies an extremely subtle and marvelous turning point, found between movement and stillness. It lies where movement, having reached its apex, gives rise to stillness; and where stillness, having reached its maximum, gives birth to movement. It is found between existence and nonexistence; it is as though present, and as though absent. It is the moment of transition.

The mysterious pass is referred to as a "portal" because this condition in which the later heaven pivots toward prior heaven is neither something that happens purely in the mind nor something that happens purely in the body. The mysterious pass becomes active in a state that connects the body and mind, just as it connects prior heaven and later heaven. When the mysterious pass appears, it is *as though* some sort of portal opened.

One of Taoist internal alchemy's unique aspects is that it always speaks of the merging of body and mind, as well as the integration of shen and qi. When this integration occurs, body and mind become an indistinguishable oneness. At this moment, a transitional state appears, and it is as if a portal has suddenly opened, even though this "portal" does not exist in any particular location. This is a broad summary of the meaning of "the portal of the mysterious pass."

Speaking more specifically, there are different mysterious passes, which is why Huang Yuanji ends his discourse saying, "the mysterious pass is also endless." For instance, there is a mysterious pass between the arising and disappearing of thoughts—this is the mysterious pass used in the practice of illuminating one's mind in order to glimpse its nature. There is also a mysterious pass in the stirring of qi, found at the moment when our bodies' yang qi arises—this mysterious pass is used specifically to gather medicine in order to refine the elixir. In chapter 4 we will discuss how one uses that mysterious pass to "stoke the fire and gather medicine." This chapter's discussion emphasizes the mysterious pass that pertains to the movements of thoughts and to the practice of illuminating the mind to see its original nature.

■ ■ ■

In the phrase "illuminating the mind to see its original nature," "mind" refers to thought. Our thoughts are numberless. Yet, while countless thoughts arise all throughout the day, no matter how many millions of them there might be, they are never actually any more than the single thought that occupies the present moment. We are capable of mastering thought because our previous thoughts that ceased to exist and our future thoughts yet to come are both actually just the singular thought that exists in the present moment. Our thoughts can rise to the heavens or plunge down into the earth; they can pull us toward confusion or epiphany; they can be ordinary or sagacious. This is why Chan Buddhists say, "awaken to one thought, and you're a buddha; be lost in one thought, and you're an ordinary person." So the question each of us must ask ourselves is, "Is my mind lost or awake in thought right now?" Observing the mind is a practice that we must always apply in any type of Taoist cultivation. When we observe our minds, we do so by observing the present thought. Mastery of this practice or lack thereof determines whether or not we are capable of awakening.

In the Buddhist commentary *Awakening of the Faith in Mahayana*, attributed to Asvaghosa, there is a theoretical framework known as "a single mind opens two gates." It explains that our minds can either reside in "suchness of reality" (*bhutatathata* in Sanskrit), or else in the endless cycle of creation and destruction. To reside in suchness is to have a sage's mind, while to cycle through the arising and extinguishing of thoughts is to have the mind of an ordinary person. The two gates—the later-heaven gate leading to ordinary existence and the prior-heaven gate leading to immortality and buddhahood—are opened by the very same mind. There thus lies a mysterious pass in between later-heaven discursive mental chaos, and a mind that illuminates thought to return to its self-nature.

People who have found their original natures by illuminating their minds function directly from the essence of mind; they respond to whatever comes before them without thinking. Another way of saying this is that their later-heaven thought processes have changed and now function in a sublime way. When such people think, they are not dragged along by thoughts. They are knowingly aware. They think and yet are free of thought.

■ ■ ■

In this chapter, Huang Yuanji describes a simple means anybody can use that directly points to the nature of the mysterious pass. Huang points out that even though our minds may be scattered from morning till night, if a person calls our name while we are in the midst of mental chaos, we will still instantaneously respond, "Yes?" This response comes spontaneously and of its own accord. But who really answered? At that very moment, look within. Your sudden response was a reflection of your prior-heaven mind at work. The true, original essence of mind—the real mind—can manifest and be experienced at any time. This is possible because all of our later-heaven thinking is actually a function of the real mind. The only obstacle is that, amid all the rising and falling of our thoughts, we never realize this is so.

In fact, the only reason our minds are capable of being filled with thoughts is that the essence of our fully clear, awake, and sentient minds is always functioning. To illustrate this point, Chan Buddhism frequently offers stories where somebody asks a Chan master, "What is Buddha?" The Chan master then calls the person's name, and he or she replies, "Yes?" The Chan master says: "This." *Koans* such as these teach us that buddha nature can be experienced right here, right now.

■ ■ ■

Here we will begin discussing this chapter's selection from *The Oral Record of the Hall of Joyous Teaching*. The first sentence of Huang Yuanji's third discourse tells us that refining the mind is the overarching method common to all who become Taoist immortals, sages, and realized humans. While there exists a great variety of ways to practice, when we trace them to their roots, we always find the same two words, "refining mind." If the heart of any method or practice is something other than refinement of the mind, then it is heterodox, profane, and left-handed—it is not of the Great Tao.

That we are able to be born and die over and over again in the infinite wheel of reincarnation is because we have the seeds of a soul. Where do these seeds come from? They are created because false discriminations and illusions arise whenever a person has no mastery over his or her thoughts. Whenever our true minds are not returning to themselves, we birth multifarious thoughts. As our minds stir thoughts into motion, we end up chasing after our ideations in a state of loss and confusion. While we are in such states, we create all manner of karmic seeds.

In our human lives, we have all different kinds of life experiences. If we feel attached to any of these experiences, we will leave behind seeds in the storehouses of our consciousness. Later on, these seeds will slowly exert their strength; this is the force of karma. The dominant aspect of the collective force of our karma decides where we will transmigrate on the wheel of rebirth. If our minds never turn around to become conscious of their own nature, then our minds lose themselves in the infinitude of objects and phenomena, and thereby give birth to innumerable attachments. It is these attachments that leave behind the plenitude of seeds in the storehouses of our consciousness—or our souls. These seeds propel our motion and leave us without freedom.

The implication of karma is being unfree. Seldom if ever able to be our own masters, we are instead dragged along by karmic inertia. This can be seen in the way in which, if we try not to think about certain things, we end up thinking about them anyway—that is the force of karma at work. When suffering arises we declare that we do not want to suffer, and that we will let go of whatever is causing the suffering, but is doing so really up to us? Those who have not walked the cultivator's path, who lack wisdom, and who have not illuminated their minds in order to see their natures do not actually have the power to make the decision to let go of the sources of their suffering. Karma itself propagates new karma. In addition to our own karma particular to our individual lives, there is also the collective karma of the societies we live in, which Buddhism calls "shared karma." Because of it, in much of our behavior we have no freedom. Instead, we are under the control of the force of society's karma.

Nevertheless, if one traces all karmas back to their fountainhead, what one will find is thought. In the span of time it takes for a single thought to come and go, all types of karma can be created. If one can be aware of one's thoughts in the present moment, then one's thinking will be conscious, and for as long as that moment of consciousness lasts, there is freedom. This is how to have self-control and be one's own master. Above we discussed how the force of karma is built out of the long-term aggregation of innumerable thoughts. Be that as it may, the key to enlightenment lies right here, with whatever thought is present in this moment.

If one is awake to and aware of one's thoughts in the present moment, then all delusion is instantaneously extinguished, and one has nirvana right here, right now. "Nirvana" is a Buddhist term referring to the cessation of all passions and delusions and the return to the fundamentally empty state of all phenomena. In Taoist terms, it refers to the return to the original, prior-heaven state. If one is awake and absolutely sincere within the space of the single thought occupying the present moment, then for that moment, one is enlightened—one is an immortal or a buddha.

Of course, the above is not to say that karma that took shape over a vast period of time will be totally resolved by being consciously awake for the duration of a single thought. Soon enough, when the force of one's karma once again rises to dominance, one will be lost to thought once more, and one will then return to a normal person's state of being. Mental activity can alternate between deludedness and awakeness. To fully become a buddha or immortal requires awake awareness that is ever present during each and every thought, allowing no more reversions to confusion.

No matter how far away that goal may be, complete enlightenment still begins with nothing more than being aware of the present thought. The key is always found in the thought that exists right here, right now. We have discussed how we cannot do anything about thoughts that have already come and gone, so there is no need to try to control them. Much less can we control our future thoughts. What will our future thoughts be? None of us have any idea! So the essential point at the center of Taoist cultivation is found within the space of the single thought occupying the present moment. Staying present with and remaining conscious of this thought is extraordinarily important.

There is a mysterious pass that lies between being deluded by the thought occupying the present moment—or being conscious of it. When, in your present thought your passions and delusions are extinguished, in an instant your fundamental, prior-heaven nature of mind becomes manifest. Therein is a mysterious pass—a threshold state where qi becomes active. We need to seize upon this state. Being awake and aware during a single thought is the key to being awake and aware during all of our thoughts, so we must truly apply ourselves to mastery of our present-moment thought. We awaken to the thought that is right here, right now, instead of spinning off in whatever direction it takes us in. Not bounding away with our thoughts is what allows our sentient, illuminating self-nature to resume its central role.

■ ■ ■

If we wish to walk the cultivator's path and achieve the Tao, to become buddhas or immortals, there is actually not a huge variety of methods for us to choose from. A Chan Buddhist saying captures the situation: "There is not much to the Buddhadharma." There is nothing amazing here. The question determining success or failure is simply, can you maintain self-mastery for the duration of a single thought, or not? Starting from mastery of thought, one gradually moves in the direction of undifferentiated, indistinct, amorphous being—the prior-heaven state that is free of thoughts.

Seen from a certain standpoint, cultivation is very difficult, because it impossible to suddenly reverse the powerful forces of karma and habit that took ages to take form within us. But one can also say it is quite easy, because when there is a sudden awakening during a single thought, that thought itself is nirvana, and one has become a Taoist immortal or a buddha during that thought. That this can be true is because, even though karma is resistant to change, like everything else, its fundamental character is empty, and it is therefore not some kind of immutable essence. When all of one's thinking has disappeared into nothingness and the thought occupying the present moment is nowhere to be found, then one need only use real wisdom to observe oneself, and one will be liberated right then and there. Because one can return again and again to the prior-heaven state whenever and wherever one likes, walking the path of cultivation is actually not all that hard.

Is the Tao far away? No—it is right here, right now. The key is whether or not one possesses the lucid wisdom needed to grasp this central point. When one can hold to the mysterious pass that lies between the stirring and cessation of a single thought, then as soon as one's prior-heaven nature reveals itself, one will recognize it. If one can stabilize there, then one will illuminate one's mind and thereby see one's own nature. Returning to my analogy from the second chapter, when this happens, one's inner "protagonist" or "boss" returns to duty. Then, even if one's mind stirs and thoughts arise, although the various "employees" of the mind are back up to their usual business, now one can direct them in unison. No longer do they foment chaos. On the contrary, as though there were an enlightened monarch seated at the throne, all remains peaceful while each "citizen" of the mind goes about its own business in its own place. One's true mind will not waver, even as one continuously deals with myriad stimuli through-out the day. As long as one stays awake, conscious of each and every thought, one possesses "true mind." True mind is not something that can be obstructed by conducting the affairs of daily life.

One the other hand, if one has no skill at being conscious of the thought occupying the present moment, and one has yet to awaken to the essence of the mind (in other words, the "boss" is still off on an endless holiday), then even if one's "employees" buzz about busily day after day, one's efforts at cultivation will be quite fruitless. Even if one sits to meditate or undertakes some other Taoist practice, if one lacks the lucid awareness of prior-heaven original nature, then all of one's strenuous efforts are still nothing more than functions of one's deluded mind, or "false mind." Some people who sit and meditate for half an hour are really just sitting still while their thoughts run wild for thirty minutes. Truly walking the cultivator's path is not just about meditating; it is about returning to the point where one's true mind assumes its central role in every moment of life.

■　■　■

Cultivating to such a level is not easy. And yet, despite being difficult, it still simply starts from the thought occupying the present moment. We must grasp ahold of thought in the present moment, inspect it, and become its master. When our skill has evolved, we will arrive at the realm of self-fulfilling wisdom rooted in absolute reality and perfect, self-aware clarity. This is the stage of being spiritually con-nected to the universe, what Huang calls "integrity equaling heaven and earth."

"Wisdom rooted in absolute reality," called *bhutathata* in Sanskrit, is a Buddhist term. There are ten appellations for buddhas, one of which, *tathagata*, refers to this wisdom. In Chinese, bhutathata is writ-ten as *ru ru*, which literally means "thus-thus." The first "ru" refers to the fundamental reality of all phenomena; the double "ru" implies manifesting in accord with this fundamental reality, without any of the striving and clinging that grow out of an individuated, distinction-making mind. It is from this wisdom that all supernormal, marvelous capabilities can appear of their own spontaneous accord.

Unfortunately, due to the lack of alertness and awakeness that characterizes us as ordinary people, when the mysterious pass stirs and the prior-heaven state reveals itself to us, we invariably miss the opportunity to make use of it. In actuality, even without any cultivation whatsoever, there are many points in a human life when the mysterious pass appears. But since we do not know it for what it is, we do not fully experience it.

For instance, when a flash of inspiration comes to a poet whose writer's block had prevented him or her from finishing a poem, that moment of inspiration represents an opening of the mysterious pass. Similarly, imagine a scientist who has hit a solid brick wall in his or her research that no amount of scouring the mind can overcome. If he or she finally gives up and puts everything down, prior-heaven original nature might suddenly reveal itself with a bright flash of insight, making everything about the conundrum crystal clear. "Ah-ha" moments, too, indicate the activity of the mysterious pass. However, the scientist uses the activity of his or her mysterious pass to make breakthroughs in research, and the poet uses it to write poetry—they do not put the mysterious pass to use to cultivate the Tao. When artists and others use their inspiration to undertake creative efforts, they forgo the opportunity to cultivate the Tao. Their inner light only flashes momentarily, and thus it does not become a source of nourishment for their minds.

It is not only poets, artists, and scientists who have such experiences from time to time—all people do. Imagine one morning you awaken and the weather is perfect, like it is in Hong Kong in January, or springtime in northern China, when the warmth of the season coaxes the flowers into bloom. A gentle wind lightly brushes past you as you get out of bed, and your mind is totally free of any errant thoughts or fantasies. Your mood is already good, and you suddenly feel a sort of deep joy well up from within. At this moment, your later-heaven self temporarily subsides and the prior-heaven state appears to you. Yet, in a flash it is gone without you even realizing what it was. Before you know it, you are already thinking about what you need to do today, and, soon enough, all of the rest of your worldly affairs enter your mind. Just like this, you miss out on the mysterious pass.

Because the mysterious pass is incredibly subtle, we must be always alert to the states of our own minds, constantly observing our thoughts' vacillations between delusion and awakening. We cannot slack off. We have to be persistent, always mindfully nurturing our marvelous, empty-yet-sentient essence. It is this that is the essence of our minds; it is this that is our true nature. If we persevere, we will gradually make progress. With progress, the mysterious pass will appear more and more frequently, and our opportunities to enter it will become more and more numerous.

■ ■ ■

Huang Yuanji goes on to explain that the mysterious pass is the primer for practicing Taoist internal alchemy. As though it were an electric outlet that gives electricity the moment one plugs into it, its appearance presents an extremely crucial opportunity. But Huang stresses that we must not limit ourselves to searching for the mysterious pass within very advanced stages of samadhi and tranquility. Rather, we should try and experience it in our daily lives. Doing so is a bit like the Confucian saying that Huang Yuanji borrows, "I wish for benevolence, and here benevolence is." When Confucius said this, he meant that the state of being a person who acts benevolently is never far away from any of us. Rather, as soon as we contemplate being benevolent, then within the span of time it takes to have that thought, benevolence comes to us.

Confucianism has another saying, "without leaving everyday human relations, I travel directly to the time before even prior heaven came to be." Because the Tao is not distinct from daily life, within mundane living we can directly arrive at the prior-heaven state that is like an untouched canvas. If we conclude that the Tao can only be found by cultivating in a deep state of tranquility or samadhi, then there will be no way for the Tao to be expressed in and merge into oneness with our daily lives. Moreover, even if we can reach highly advanced states when we sit in meditation, so long as we are still susceptible to plunging back into mental chaos during the rest of our daily activities, then our cultivation is unreliable. The time we can spend meditating is, after all, limited. Far more of our time must be spent experiencing life.

After Huang Yuanji quotes Confucius, he describes "heavenly primordial oneness qi's original face." The original face of heavenly primordial oneness qi can be experienced in our daily lives, as well as in states of tranquility and concentration, when we are unknowing and unperceptive, not thinking of what is to come nor what has passed, our minds simply quiescent in the here and now. Although, at such times, our minds are empty of thoughts, within this tranquility there remains an illuminating, intelligent awareness. In tranquility, our minds are not deadened. When words like "unknowing" are used to describe tranquility, they are not meant to imply that we become insensate like pieces of stone. Our pure and unblemished prior-heaven awareness remains present, allowing us to experience our prior-heaven "original face" during practice.

Once one has an experience of "heavenly primordial oneness qi's original face," one continues to cultivate by steadily keeping it in mind. It is through refining the elixir in such a state that one will be able to become a spiritual immortal. When Huang Yuanji says, "gather, obtain, cook, and refine; seal, solidify, warm, and nurture," he is listing specific skills used to refine the elixir. All of the skills spoken of here are applied while one is in the prior-heaven state. The prerequisite for their use is illuminating one's mind to see one's true nature, so that one does the work of cultivation via prior-heaven mind.

Huang Yuanji describes how we can experience our original faces while in profound tranquility or samadhi, but again, we should not limit ourselves to doing so only while actively cultivating such states. What Huang Yuanji refers to when he speaks of "the heart of heaven coming to return" can just as well be experienced in brief moments of light concentration or simple quietude. The "heart of heaven" is synonymous with numerous terms peppered throughout this chapter, including prior-heaven mind, original mind, and true mind; "coming to return" simply refers to its becoming apparent. The idea of the heart of heaven coming to return is a paraphrase of the *Book of Changes'* written description for the hexagram "Return," which represents the first stirring of yang qi. Its description is written, "the first yang line comes to return," and it is drawn as a single line of yang rising up from below: ䷗.

We need to engage with the mysterious pass in different conditions and at different times. Huang Yuanji acknowledges that in daily life we might have multitudes of discursive thoughts that entangle and embroil us like messes of vines. When this happens, we need only, with a single thought, turn inward and observe ourselves. With a single thought, we turn our light around (this "light" refers to the shining of observant consciousness), and observe our own selves. When we return our awareness and do this, we find that our chaotic thoughts actually disappear instantaneously. We become suddenly serene and clear because our discursive thoughts were never things that truly exist within us. Huang compares getting lost in chaotic thought to being passed out drunk—the moment somebody splashes a basin of icy water upon a drunk's head, the drunk will snap awake from his or her reverie, exclaiming, "Oh! Just now that was all a dream!" When our scattered thoughts suddenly vanish under the light of awareness, we can experience the opening of the mysterious pass. This is just one of the many situations in which it is possible for the mysterious pass to appear.

■ ■ ■

Subsequently Huang Yuanji points out the true, primordial essence of the mind. He wants us to know that our true minds fundamentally exist and function at all times and all places. Whenever we think or engage in any sort of activity, external conditions stay in constant flux but our true minds stay the same. Our true minds do not become active in response to the arrival of certain conditions, phenomena, or states. By the same token, when conditions, phenomena, and states disappear, our true minds do not disappear with them. Our true minds are active at all times and places, in any and all circumstances. This is why we can turn inward and make our true minds apparent wherever and whenever we wish.

Huang Yuanji summarizes this discourse by repeating that the portal of the mysterious pass can be experienced during profound tranquility and concentration or in everyday life. One can experience the mysterious pass in the space between movement and stillness, or where one thought has disappeared and the next has yet to arise. In terms of Taoist theory, the mysterious pass is the border between prior heaven and later heaven; it is found in the critical state where taiji divides into yin and yang, and also where yin and yang rejoin and return to taiji. The movement of later heaven is not the mysterious pass, nor is it the pure stillness of prior heaven. Rather, the mysterious pass appears in the gaps where extreme stillness becomes movement, and where extreme movement leads to stillness.

The final sentences of this discourse speak about the movement and tranquility of our own minds. Our minds move or become still in myriad ways. Huang Yuanji alludes to this when he says "movement and stillness are endless." Because that is how our minds are, the mysterious pass manifests differently in different circumstances. When it appears, we need to have the skill that allows us to realize it is present. The true mysterious pass is a crucial turning point—an opportunity when our prior-heaven original face reveals itself. All cultivators must learn how to grasp it, as it is the key to illuminating the mind and glimpsing original nature.

In Taoist alchemy, aside from the mysterious pass found where thoughts arise, there is also the mysterious pass found where qi stirs. This mysterious pass is related to our bodies and to the state where body and mind merge as one. Elsewhere in *The Oral Record of the Hall of Joyous Teaching* and later in this book there will be discussion of the mysterious pass related to qi. This particular discourse emphasizes the mysterious pass of mind nature, which is used to illuminate the mind and reveal its essence.

Our discussion of the third discourse ends here. Starting with this chapter, our discussions will not go through each sentence of Huang Yuanji's original teachings. Rather, they will include a summary and synthesis of each discourse's core ideas, while omitting some of the less central elements, so that the discussions can flow a bit more smoothly. When necessary, readers can compare my explanations with Huang's original text at the beginning of each chapter.

4

進火採藥

STOKING THE FIRE AND
GATHERING THE MEDICINE

*A student inquired about stoking the fire and gathering the medicine. In later
heaven, these are fundamentally two matters, and not a single affair. Today I
will discuss them in detail.*

*Stoking the fire means concentrating shen with indivisible will. Gath-
ering the medicine, then, means employing the qi of external breathing: rising and falling, exiting and entering, allowing it to follow its natural course.*

*If, when yang stirs and medicine is born, one immediately turns the
mind inward, single-mindedly concentrating upon the cauldron of the elixir,
that is stoking the fire. Using the external breath's exiting, entering, rising,
and falling to contain yang is gathering the medicine.*

*Stoking the fire is stoking the fire; gathering the medicine is gathering
the medicine—they must not be muddled up with one another.*

*If one solely uses the external breath's rising, falling, leaving, and re-
turning, but one's shen does not concentrate upon the cauldron of the elixir,
then even though the true mechanism may arise, it will unavoidably diffuse
throughout the entire body, as it lacks an abode to which to return.*

*If one simply notices that yang qi has sprung to life and then focuses men-
tal activity upon it, but does not use later-heaven breathing to contain it, then
the medicinal qi will remain in stasis where it is. This will merely make the lower
reaches of the body robust and cause kidney qi to surge and rise, nothing more.*

In case students do not yet fully understand, I will further analogize: stoking the fire is like adding firewood or charcoal to a metalworker's furnace; gathering the medicine is like pumping a metalworker's bellows. If one merely pumps the bellows, without adding burning coals, then the fire will not be mighty and the metal will not melt.

If one merely adds burning coals, but does not pump the bellows in one's hands, then though there may be firewood or charcoal, it will only warm the interior of the furnace, and no more. How could one hope to successfully refine a useful substance?

Students, contemplate the following: fire is fire, medicine is medicine, stoking is stoking, and gathering is gathering. This is what the tasks of later-heaven methods have always been. But, if one gathers the great medicine in non-doing, and controls timing and firing in inaction, then this means fire and medicine are merged as one, with no distinction between stoking and gathering. Students, you have yet to arrive at this level of practice. Following the moment when yang is born, you still need to be able to ascertain for yourself when the conditions are ripe for real qi to return. Only then can you realistically go from doing to non-doing and from intentionality to non-intentionality.

I teach students to use the method of counting breaths to gather and restrain their minds and wills. Under normal circumstances, when yang has yet to arise, if you practice this method, you can hold your mind steady, so that it will not chaotically wander. Later, at the moment when yang is born and medicine is produced, you must gather it and return it to the furnace to be warmed and nurtured by the fire of shen. In particular, you need to use fire as though there were no fire, and to gather medicine as though there were no medicine. Only thusly will you merge with the primordial mists of heaven and earth's qi, which can regenerate without end and transform without limit.

At the first stirring of yang, use the method of elevating and assimilating. This is the work for you students at this time. It is none other than, internally, ensuring that your mind gathers and does not scatter; and externally, ensuring that your breathing is naturally regulated. That is all.

Students, when sitting to meditate, should you feel the hint of volatile, impulsive, restless qi, this is either because your thoughts are too rigid or because your physical body's yin qi is stagnant and blocked. The appropriate method is to use the ordinary fire of breathing and the primordial fire of real-

ized humans to warm and nurture your tense thinking or stagnant qi, causing them to naturally transmute, after which you will be fine.

What is the so-called primordial fire of realized humans? An ancient one said: "The ears, eyes, and mouth are three treasures; block them fast, don't open them up. Realized humans submerge into the deep profound, floating as they keep watch upon the center of the circle." This is the primordial fire of realized humans. It functions but cannot be used; because one is not using it, it therefore functions. So students, within your own bodies and minds, keenly recognize this fire. Employ this fire, and when it reaches its apex, naturally there will be no more restless qi.

Otherwise, when yang qi is in great plenitude and you are on the cusp of engaging the river chariot,[2] your breathing may become ragged. Should this happen, just let shen and qi be, and think of nothing else. If your mind becomes peaceful and your qi harmonious, then you may employ the river chariot and use the small heavenly circulation method. Students, you may observe and assess what is appropriate on your own.

■ ■ ■

Let's place our attention on our minds for a moment, to observe our thoughts. For a few moments, try to find your thoughts' location. Where are they, where do they come from, and where do they go? As soon as a thought arises, ask, *where is it?*

■ ■ ■

Have you found a location? If you can't, that's nothing to be embarrassed about—it's actually a good thing. I congratulate you on failing to find a place. Thoughts are fundamentally impossible to find, so not finding them is a good thing, as it tells us that there are actually no thoughts to be swept away by.

When you're observing your mind—searching for it but never finding it—then you have no mind, and no mental chaos. That's when your mind can reach peaceful equipoise and cease to be in tumult. That's also when the mysterious pass can appear. In the state without knowledge and without thoughts, there is only your sentient, radiant mind nature. You may still be aware that I'm speaking and may even be able to sense everything in your environment, but you don't make distinctions. It is then that your real mind is manifest.

In chapter 1 we discussed the preciousness of having affinity for Taoist cultivation. In chapter 2 we jumped straight to the primary issue at the heart of cultivation, illuminating mind to see its nature. In chapter 3 we discussed how the mysterious pass gives an opportunity to illuminate the mind and reveal hsing, or mind nature. The ten discourses of Huang Yuanji that I chose to form the basis of this book are interrelated and build upon each other systematically. So, if the mysterious pass has already appeared, and you have a certain level of recognition of the nature of your mind, then what do you do next? That's when you can start to employ techniques, going from hsing to ming as you "stoke the fire" and "gather medicinal ingredients."

What does stoking fire and gathering medicinal ingredients mean? Inner alchemy names three indispensable elements: furnace and cauldron, medicinal ingredients, and temperature and timing. These names were borrowed from so-called external alchemists who attempted to refine minerals and metals into elixirs of immortality, or to turn base metals into silver and gold. The first component of external alchemy was the alchemical furnace, within which elixirs or precious metals were extracted and purified from raw materials, which were also called "medicinal ingredients." From these valueless substances—the crude materials—something of value was created, such as gold or silver. The work of refining was accomplished by paying close attention to temperature and timing. What external alchemists did, in reality, was to elicit chemical reactions and transformations. If you understand anything about chemistry, then you'll know that alchemists had to understand timing and temperature in order to transform the crude materials in their furnaces, because differences in these two factors will lead to entirely different chemical reactions.

An important part of the ancient alchemist's furnace was the bellows, which were used to adjust the temperature at precise times. The bellows also supplied the quantity of oxygen needed for chemical reactions. Adepts had to devote great care to temperature and timing when they tried to create elixirs through "external alchemy." Without a mastery of these factors, results would remain elusive.

Internal alchemists borrowed terms like "refining elixir" and the related vocabulary of external alchemy to use as metaphors. Originally, "elixir" referred to something that was derived from base materials like cinnabar, a crimson-colored mineral also called red sulfide of mercury. Later on, the fruits of this type of alchemy, regardless of whether they were gold or silver, were called "golden elixir." So-called inner alchemy, on the other hand, refers to refining an elixir within one's body, with no need for an actual furnace. Sometimes in this tradition the human body is seen as the alchemical furnace; however, sometimes the scope is even broader, meaning heaven and earth can be seen as a vast alchemical forge. When one takes the entire universe as one's furnace, a more exalted elixir results.

■ ■ ■

The "medicinal ingredients" mentioned above are synonymous with what Taoists identify as the "three treasures" of the human body: jing, qi, and shen. There is an important distinction between the prior-heaven (or primordial) three treasures, and the later-heaven three treasures, which we will discuss in detail in chapter 7. For now, it is sufficient to say that jing, qi, and shen are refined through progressive steps of transformation and sublimation. In a symbolic sense, this transformation is similar to the process of taking base metals and refining them into precious metals and then elixirs of immortality that external alchemy aimed to accomplish. Internal alchemists refine coarse jing into the more subtle qi, and then lead this subtle qi to return into the midst of the primordial shen, making shen and qi merge as one. After that is accomplished, they then embark upon a journey of yet further return, into the body of the Tao. This is how the internal elixir is refined, one step at a time.

In the process of refining the elixir, a practitioner must pay attention to "temperature and timing." In the context of inner alchemy, these words refer to the functioning of the primordial shen—the functioning of our consciousness. The capability of consciousness to observe is called "fire," and it can be modulated and assisted by the breath, which is akin to a furnace's bellows. The three indispensable components of inner alchemy (furnace and cauldron, medicinal ingredients, and temperature and timing) will reappear again and again in later chapters, but in this chapter the focus remains on "stoking the fire" and "gathering the medicinal ingredients."

What does it mean to stoke the fire? If one returns to the prior-heaven state of one's original nature, or if, in meditation, one enters into a state of serene tranquility, then the energy of the body will become aroused and transformations will occur. In the vernacular of Taoist alchemy, this is when "yang is born." When yang qi arises, one must use prior-heaven "true intent" to softly and gently observe it. To pay attention to yang qi in this way is to "process" it, which leads it a step further in its transmutation and sublimation.

What, then, does it mean to gather the medicinal ingredients? To do so is to coordinate one's breathing and subtle pathways in one's body to make use of the energy that has just arisen, sublimating it yet further. The process of stoking the fire and gathering the medicinal ingredients takes one from the use of hsing skills to the use of ming skills; it is a process of using that which is prior heaven by nature to transmute that which is of later heaven.

Herein lies a key step in Taoist practice, that of going from "doing" into "non-doing." In the beginning of our training, we start with a set of concrete techniques that tell us how to use our minds and our thoughts. In the beginning, stoking the fire and gathering the crude medicinal ingredients are discussed separately, and not as a single task. However, when we reach a higher stage in the practice, then we employ the "methods of non-doing," or wu wei. At this stage, the work of stoking the fire is formless and inapparent, and the two tasks of stoking the fire and gathering the medicinal ingredients merge together as one. The aims of inner alchemy practice are naturally and spontaneously accomplished within a state where primordial shen is active. To practice in this way is to follow wu wei.

■ ■ ■

There is a general sequence that must be followed as we refine the internal elixir. Summarized in three sentences, it is: first, return from later heaven to prior heaven; then use prior heaven to transmute later heaven; and finally, merge prior heaven and later heaven into one.

This "merging" takes the practitioner into the Tao, culminating the entire process of inner alchemy.

Anyone who has the desire to practice inner alchemy must start by finding the prior-heaven state. The previous chapters on illuminating the mind to see its nature and the portal of the mysterious pass present the ways in which one can go from later heaven toward recognizing prior heaven. Because most of us normal people live in a purely later-heaven state, we have absolutely no idea what prior heaven is. We have no experience of the prior-heaven state, and very likely do not even know that it exists; thus, we become completely lost in the external world. We chase after delusions and things that lie beyond ourselves, like entertainment, sex, competition, fame, and wealth, eventually going totally astray. When we live like this, it's pointless to try to imagine what the prior-heaven state might be like. If we wish to have the chance to discover that which is prior heaven within later heaven, our first step is to find the "original appearance" of the mind's nature. Once we find the mind's original nature and allow it to take primacy, returning to the empty, nonexistent, clear, and tranquil prior-heaven state becomes a real possibility.

When in the prior-heaven state, we connect and unite with what Taoists call "unified prior-heaven qi," "empty and nonexistent primordial qi," or "the energy of the universe's own essential nature" (these names are interchangeable). This state exerts effects upon both the hsing and ming aspects of our later-heaven existences. With regard to hsing, or mind nature, the prior-heaven state transmutes and eventually eliminates our deluded thinking and our prior-heaven thought patterns. With regard to ming, or life, the prior-heaven state connects one with the universe's unified ocean of qi. This energy is capable of sublimating the turbid later-heaven qi in our physical bodies, causing our bodies' jing, qi, and shen to fully transform.

When the work of using prior heaven to transmute later heaven is done skillfully, then prior heaven and later heaven blend into a single, integrated whole, and one returns to the essence of the Tao. This is how one simultaneously cultivates hsing and ming—by going back to the realm of being merged in the reality of the Tao. The entire process of inner alchemy is summarized by the principle of returning from later heaven to prior heaven; then using prior heaven to transmute later heaven; and finally, merging prior heaven and later heaven into one.

It is here that we can see some of the differences in emphasis between Taoist alchemy and some of the cultivation methods of Buddhism. Chan Buddhism, for instance, does not speak of things like gathering medicinal materials and stoking the fire. Instead Chan talks about "walking through the single door into profundity," "walking directly through the single door," "cutting in with a single swing of the blade," and "leaping directly to the essence." In Chan practice, one illuminates one's mind to see one's nature, and then, having arrived in the prior-heaven realm, one remains there, safeguarding and nurturing this state. One settles down in the prior heaven, and all that is later heaven in one's being directly returns there, too. One no longer employs any specific techniques to use prior heaven to transmute later heaven. In short, the Chan way penetrates right to the very basis. That said, its methods do not necessarily contradict those of Taoist alchemy. In inner alchemy, the methods of Chan Buddhism are seen as a type of alchemy—in fact, they are regarded as the highest-level alchemical method, which is presented in chapter 10. With this method, one directly refines one's shen in order to return to emptiness. One does not employ any other methods, because practicing like this takes one right back to the prior-heaven state. This is the practice of wu wei, or non-doing, and as such it does not make use of any methods that involve intentionality.

The above path certainly exists, but it is lofty and difficult to tread. It is extraordinarily difficult to penetrate straight to the core of reality. If a person can really and truly alight upon the prior-heaven state and stay there, then, in that condition, the fire will spontaneously stoke itself, and the medicine will gather on its own. Chan Buddhists do not speak about the work of stoking the fire and gathering the medicine, but that does not mean later heaven is not transmuted by prior heaven in their practice. Real Chan practice, as taught by truly enlightened masters, leads to physiological changes, transformation of practitioners' qi, and the development of supernormal abilities. Real Chan does not take place in a dull void. All of the above needs to be understood before anybody can try to judge whether Taoism or Buddhism surpass one another, or which cleaves closer to the truth. Simplistic conclusions should be avoided.

I devoted an entire section of my book *Probing the Mysteries of Taoist Inner Alchemy* to discussing the parallels between Taoist alchemy and Chan Buddhism. One should not assume that Chan practice solely involves hsing cultivation at the expense of ming. Just because Chan Buddhists do not speak about ming does not mean that they ignore ming in actual practice. Rather, the essential state sought through Chan cultivation is one in which hsing and ming are merged as one; both aspects are included in its embrace.

When Buddhists criticize Taoism, they sometimes do so without having fully understood Taoism, in which case their views are one-sided, and the object of their criticism does not even really exist—they are only criticizing the misunderstandings they hold in their own minds, whereas the details of the aspects of Taoism they are talking about may be nothing like what they imagine. Some Taoists who criticize Buddhism are just the same. The irony is that when one judges and criticizes something one does not fully comprehend, one is actually criticizing one's own thinking, and nothing more. It is best, then, to refrain from comparing and contrasting things we do not fully understand. We should simply diligently cultivate the practices that we enjoy, "penetrating deeply through the single entryway," instead of casting aspersions at others in a deluded manner.

■ ■ ■

Let's take a look at Huang Yuanji's discourse at the beginning of this chapter. In the first sentence he directly points out that stoking the fire and gathering medicine are two distinct things in later heaven.

"Stoking the fire" means concentrating shen into undivided oneness. To do so, one gathers one's mind, letting shen become a unity that does not make any distinctions, a unity that can only be described as serene awareness. The so-called fire is the capability of consciousness to observe—a capacity that is often likened to rays of light. Once one has stoked the fire by gathering one's awareness, if one places awareness upon the body, one will exert an effect upon it. Concentrating shen upon one's body is akin to applying the heat of an alchemical furnace to it. Doing this leads to transformation.

"Gathering the medicine" means to make use of one's breathing by connecting one's exhalations and inhalations with the rising and falling of the energies of the body. If one does this in a natural way, letting things follow their own course, then the result in one's body will be the accumulation of "medicine." Here, "accumulating medicine" refers to the gradual accrual of transformations in the raw materials of our existence: jing, qi, and shen. By making use of the breath, one promotes these energetic transformations within one's "alchemical furnace."

If one does not stoke the fire and gather medicine, then the energetic changes one brings about in one's body during practice will naturally dissipate. For example, when one is at the stage of refining jing and transforming qi, if one meditates skillfully, then there will definitely be changes in one's jing and qi. But if one does not use the techniques of stoking the fire and gathering medicine, jing and qi will fail to fully sublimate—they will never completely transform into something more rarefied. Instead, partially refined jing and qi will actually fuel an increase in passion and desire; whenever one gives rein to one's desire, jing and qi will be lost as a result. This creates a situation where it is impossible to complete the task of refining jing into qi.

■ ■ ■

Huang Yuanji talks about stoking the fire and gathering the medicine when "medicine is born." Another term he and other alchemists use to describe medicine being "born" is the "birth of yang." To understand this concept, we need to take a close look at what "yang" means in this particular context. There are numerous layers of meaning for the words "yin" and "yang" in Taoist alchemy. According to the well-known philosophical definition of yin and yang, they are two things that should be equal and in balance, because in philosophical terms yin and yang are indivisible—they are inextricably paired, and neither can exist in the absence of the other. Philosophically speaking, it can't be said that yang is good and yin is bad. The two are equals.

However, in the practice of inner alchemy, yin and yang take on special meanings. In this context, yang can refer to the prior-heaven state. Thus, the idea of "yang being born" can mean that one has returned to the prior-heaven state and connected to prior-heaven qi, and that this qi has become active in one's body.

So, in inner alchemy, if "yang is born," what should one do? Refine the elixir! One should stoke the fire and gather medicine, in order to sublimate it. Again, "yang" here is not used in its philosophical sense. It is being used in a context specific to inner alchemy, which requires practitioners to "refine yin until it turns into yang." According to the internal alchemy teachings, once a practitioner has succeeded in becoming "purely yang," he or she will have become a spiritual immortal.

In this context, yin refers to that which is of a post-heaven nature, and yang refers to that which is prior heaven. Thus, reaching the "pure yang" state means that all of a person's post-heaven elements have transformed into the prior-heaven state. The moment when "yang is born" is the moment when the energies of the body carry the potential for energetic change. At this moment, one's mental activity should gather upon the dantian, which is the furnace for creating the elixir, in order to stoke the fire. At the same time, to gather the medicine one should follow along with the rising and falling of the breath, as doing so will envelop the medicine created when yang is born, preventing it from scattering.

The above paragraph describes the early stages of training, when stoking the fire and gathering medicine are two separate things. At this stage they cannot be discussed as a single phenomenon; they have to be discussed separately—but side by side. This is because if one only knows how to harmonize with the rising and falling of the breath when one's body's yang qi becomes active but does not know how to engage the function of primordial shen by gathering one's consciousness, then, unable to find its proper destination, one's true qi will disperse all over one's body until it is gone. True qi needs a place to return to. That destination lies within the prior-heaven state of primordial shen itself.

■ ■ ■

The rising and falling of the breath we speak of here is, in fact, a matter of the small and large heavenly circulations.

The rising and falling of qi along the path of the small heavenly circulation more or less follows along the *du* (governor) meridian on the back, until it reaches the top of the head, from which point it descends along the *ren* (conception) meridian. This orbital circulation, which has the body's dantian at its center, is what allows jing to transform into qi.

Outward manifestations of "the birth of yang" may be different in men and women, but the underlying energy is the same. Some of the possible manifestations include feelings of sexual stimulation or sexual pleasure, as well as arousal of the sexual organs. When that takes place, if the practitioner can maintain clear and tranquil single-mindedness, then the work of moving the small heavenly circulation will refine jing and turn it into qi. However, if the practitioner's mind loses clarity and tranquility, then it will go bounding off with sexual desire, and the energy will scatter until it is lost. When that happens, the meditator is not really training. He or she is just "following the current and becoming a human," not "going against the current to become an immortal" as inner alchemy teaches.

The coordination of breathing with the large heavenly circulation is not limited to the pathway of the du and ren meridians. Rather, it is akin to a form of full-body breathing, or even the breathing of the universe. With each in- and out-breath, the entire body breathes. If one does this, then when one inhales, each cell in one's body takes in qi. When one exhales, each cell releases qi.

Again, at this stage, gathering the medicine and stoking the fire need to be done in coordination. If one only gathers medicine without using fire—meaning one does not gather one's shen in the way described above—then there will be no place for the yang qi to return to once it is active. It is necessary to regulate one's shen so that it concentrates into oneness in order for the work of stoking of the fire and gathering the medicine to truly cause yang qi (which here means that which is of a prior-heaven nature) to transmute yin qi (those parts of one's body and mind that are of a later-heaven nature). Conversely, if one only stokes the fire without gathering the medicine—in other words, one does not coordinate later-heaven breathing with the gathering of one's shen—then the medicinal energy brought about through the arising of yang qi will simply stay where it is. Qi remaining where it is may cause one's lower dantian region or one's sexual centers to be quite aroused and invigorated, which can lead to heightened sexuality and horniness, but it will not allow one to advance to higher stages of internal alchemy.

■ ■ ■

Huang Yuanji later uses the analogy of a metalworker getting a furnace going, which evokes the imagery originally associated with external alchemy. The idea of "gathering medicine" in fact comes from external alchemy, so it is only natural that Taoists use such analogies to describe processes that exist in internal alchemy. In inner alchemy, breathing is akin to the bellows, while stoking the fire is much like adding coal to a furnace to increase the size of the blaze within. It is easy to understand how, when a metalworker is lighting a furnace, he or she needs to work the bellows and add coal in a coordinated manner in order to successfully transform the metals being worked.

Up to now, this chapter's discussion has unfolded from a later-heaven standpoint, so fire, medicine, stoking, and gathering have all been treated as distinct concepts. It is important to keep in mind that there are higher levels of internal alchemy practice, so we should not become attached to the particulars of this stage. There is another stage in which, as Huang Yuanji says, one "gathers the great medicine in non-doing, and controls timing and firing in inaction." What this means is that when one reaches this stage, one has gone from doing to non-doing, and instead of gathering "small medicine" one gathers "great medicine." Great medicine exists in the prior-heaven state that primordial jing, qi, and shen inhabit. As long as a practitioner at this level remains in non-doing, he or she will automatically gather medicine in a state of deep tranquility that includes both firing and timing. At this stage, one no longer stokes the fire and gathers medicine as two separate acts. Regulating the temperature and timing blend as one, and there is no distinction between stoking the fire and gathering medicine.

The stage I am describing here is the same as the practice done by Chan Buddhists that I mentioned before. In this sort of practice, one uses a single teaching to return to the original prior-heaven state, which allows qi to transform naturally, of its own accord. This is also Taoism's loftiest practice—it is the level in which nothing is done, and yet nothing remains undone. However, Huang Yuanji makes it clear to the students he was specifically addressing during the discourse above that they have not yet arrived at this step. He tells them that such a state exists, but explicitly says that those students need to embark on their paths from the standpoint of later heaven. Huang Yuanji's point is that one must know what level of practitioner one is when yang is born—one has to be able to discern whether one is in a state of doing or non-doing.

■ ■ ■

Huang Yuanji next offers practical instructions to the student who asked the question that inspired the discourse above. The method he describes is counting the breath in order to gather the chaotic mind. It is possible to bring serenity to our typically chaotic, orderless churn of mental activity by counting our breaths.

Most of the time, there is no yang being born in our body and therefore no medicine to be gathered. We can use the practice of counting breaths to prevent our minds from running around chaotically and help them to become serene and stable. If they stay serene and stable for a long enough period of time, yang will be born. Then, when yang is born, we can employ the methods described above— gathering "medicine" to return it to the furnace and using the "fire" of shen to warm it and nourish it.

"Warming and nourishing" has a specific definition. It means using one's totally concentrated shen—which is called "fire" in internal alchemy's symbolic language—to continuously "warm" the object of concentration, a bit like one were slowly stewing a meal in a pot. When doing this, it is important to be careful to let the mind's prior-heaven functioning play the primary role. When stoking the fire and gathering medicine, one should not use excessive later-heaven mental activity, which is based upon the mind's tendency to make distinctions. Huang

Yuanji expresses this key point of practice somewhat enigmatically by saying "use fire as though there were no fire," and "gather medicine as though there were no medicine." What he means is that although one has to *use* fire (meaning concentrated awareness), one must do so without engaging the later-heaven mind's tendency to differentiate things. This is because the effectiveness of this practice comes from letting the mind just observe things, without making distinctions. Similarly, while one must gather medicine, one has to do so without any attachment to the so-called medicine. One has to let it transform on its own, as this is the only way for its changes to follow the prior-heaven patterns governing primordial qi's movements. It is also the only way for this process to continuously unfold, without getting interrupted by later-heaven mental activity.

One must know what to do when yang is born in one's own body and starts to cause physiological reactions. One should use the small heavenly circulation method I just mentioned, which will elevate and assimilate the yang qi as one "stokes the flame and gathers the medicine." That is the method that the typical student can use in the early stages of training.

In summary, the practice described above has two main features. The first involves regulating and concentrating shen so that, instead of scattering outward, shen will radiate its awareness upon one's own being. The second feature involves letting harmony come to the gross breath so that it becomes very natural and moves in concert with the observant awareness of one's primordial shen.

■ ■ ■

The next part of Huang Yuanji's discourse centers on concrete practical advice. It starts with the problem of a practitioner sitting to meditate only to find that he or she is beset by restless qi that makes it impossible to be tranquil. This phenomenon almost always arises from one of the following two causes: the first possibility is that the practitioner's attachment to something has caused his or her mind to be so tightly wound that relaxing is difficult; the second involves blockages in the body's yin qi. The mind and qi influence one another. Sometimes, if one's breathing is irregular, yin qi will become stagnant, thereby affecting one's mental state. In other instances, if one's mind lacks clarity and tranquility, worries and discursive thinking will become preponderant, thereby leading the body's qi to become restless or even chaotic. The mind and qi need to have rapport.

The way to resolve this obstacle is by using two different types of "fire." We actually already encountered these two types of "fire" when discussing "stoking the fire and gathering the medicine." One of these "fires," which is of a later-heaven nature, is called "ordinary fire." While practicing internal alchemy, to make use of "ordinary fire" means to let one's breathing become harmonious. The second type of "fire" is the prior-heaven fire of realized humans; in fact, it is another way of saying "primordial shen." A practitioner can use these fires to "warm and nurture" him- or herself. Practically speaking, what "warming and nurturing" implies is safeguarding oneself by causing the turbid, restless qi in one's being to spontaneously transform until it is gone. This is done simply by letting one's breath become harmonious while engaging the non-differentiating awareness of primordial shen. It is important that the turbid and restless qi be allowed to transform naturally and spontaneously. When practicing inner alchemy, we must do so without attachment to the very goals we seek. So in this case one only simply applies the "two fires" to "warm and nurture" one's being. Without being forced, turbid and restless qi will transform of its own accord.

Huang Yuanji borrows a sentence from Wei Boyang's *The Seal of the Unity of the Three* to explain what realized humans' primordial fire is. This line reads: "The ears, eyes, and mouth are three treasures; block them fast, don't open them up. Realized humans submerge into the deep profound, floating as they keep watch upon the center of the circle." To access the primordial "fire" mentioned in the paragraph above, one must first return to the state occupied by realized humans—the state in which the primordial shen is in charge.

From the standpoint of Taoist cultivation, the ears, eyes, and mouth are called the "external three treasures," and they correspond to the "internal three treasures," which are jing, qi, and shen. Most of the time, our jing, qi, and shen are busily scattering outward. Shen dissipates through our eyes, in whatever direction we direct our gazes;

qi dissipates out from our mouths; and jing dissipates via our ears. When our ears hear sounds, we get carried away by them, dissipating our jing in the process. There is an old saying that describes how the act of speaking exhausts qi: "When you move your mouth, your shen and qi disperse."

If we can prevent our internal and external treasures from dispersing outward, then we can restore the state where our true natures play the primary role. A way to express this is having our true natures return to "the gateway at the center of the circle." "The center of the circle" is a term with several different definitions, including the three dantian, but it can also simply mean "within the body." In this latter sense, "the center of the circle" is not a specific bodily location, and rather refers to a condition that can be brought about through practice. When we inhabit our bodies without letting our three treasures scatter away, the "primordial fire of realized humans" becomes active. Operating on the levels of both mind and qi, it naturally guides the processes of "stoking the fire and gathering the medicine," and transforms the restless energy of the body as a result.

■ ■ ■

When Huang Yuanji speaks of the "river chariot" in this discourse, he is still referring to the small heavenly circulation—the pathway we discussed above—which takes a circuitous route as it ascends along the back and then descends down the front of the body. Another term inner alchemists have for qi moving along this route is "turning the river chariot." When one reaches the stage where "true qi" is produced, it will move along this pathway automatically, in a process Taoists call "the river chariot making its circuit." In proper training conducted in the prior-heaven state, qi cycles through the small heavenly circulation of its own accord. As I explained earlier, when one guides qi in the body using intention, one is, by necessity, in a post-heaven state. Thus, letting the body's "true qi" move and transform on its own through the prior-heaven small heavenly circulation is preferable to trying to move qi on purpose.

Regardless of whether one is experiencing restlessness in one's qi or feeling mental peace accompanied by harmonious qi, one can do the heavenly circulation training mentioned here, because this training is capable of pacifying restless qi. When yang qi arises, using small heavenly circulation training will also have the marvelous effect of transmuting jing, qi, and shen, restoring them to their prior-heaven natures.

The general definition of "stoking the fire and gathering medicine" introduced in this chapter bears reexamining. Each day, our human bodies take in large amounts of "raw materials." The food that enters our bodies through our mouths supplements our bodies' later-heaven jing. The air we breathe is also a "raw material," one that is easily forgotten and yet so crucial that going without it for just one minute will cause problems. Life cannot go on without breathing, and the quality of the air we constantly "eat" has an impact on the quality of our lives.

Although the importance of the air we breathe is undeniable, there is yet another type of raw material that is even more important to inner alchemists, namely the "food" we provide to our minds. This is the "diet" upon which shen subsists. While most people are well aware that it is best to eat food with the highest-quality ingredients, few people know anything about regulating and gathering qi. A small number of people who have reached a high level of training may know how to refine qi, but not many of them know how to refine shen. The sustenance of shen is in fact even more important than air. It is possible to live for a minute without air, but for the mind to lose its sustenance for that long will bring life to an end.

What is the mind's "food?" Well, we gather it constantly, through mental impressions. For instance, while reading this book, one obtains "food" that is then processed by the mind. When listening to a class, one also absorbs mental sustenance. One's mind functions endlessly as a receptor for external influences. The way in which keeping different kinds of company will cause one's personality to take on other people's characteristics demonstrates the nature of the mind to absorb "mental food." The mind's "diet" is extraordinarily important. From the perspective of Taoist cultivation, if one has the opportunity to mingle with sages or adepts who have reached the level of spiritual immortality, then the "mental food" one consumes will be of a very high quality.

We need to refine the sustenance of jing, qi, and shen in our bodies, undertaking this task in such a way that we obtain more than we lose. This task starts with refraining from wastefulness and protecting the jing, qi, and shen that we already have. When our minds are engaged in wild, chaotic thinking, or when we're locked in frustration, we exhaust shen. When we use our bodies to hustle and bustle in an endless stream of activity, we exhaust jing and qi. It thus behooves us to learn to be judicious in how we use our three treasures, while also increasing our intake of high-quality sustenance. On the basis of this foundation, we are then able to process and transmute the "materials" of jing, qi, and shen.

■ ■ ■

Inner alchemy is in some ways analogous to heating a furnace by working a bellows—this is "stoking the fire and gathering medicine." Without stoking the fire that is made possible by concentrating shen and letting its awareness turn inward, the energy we accumulate will not transmute. Instead, it will diffuse until it is gone. Teachings on concentrating shen and gathering medicine are specifically intended to make it possible to transmute the energies in our bodies, so that jing transforms into qi, qi transforms into shen, and shen returns to emptiness. Each of those steps refers to distinct stages of energetic transformation in the human body.

As stated above, when beginners stoke the fire and gather the medicine, these are two separate actions. But when one reaches a relatively high level of practice, the two are no longer distinct acts. At higher levels, the methods we practice are formless, and even the concepts of stoking the fire and gathering medicine disappear. Then what one practices is in actuality a method of non-doing. Such practice is empty and nonexistent.

Huang Yuanji's discourse in this chapter introduced the human body's ability to transform and transmute its energies. This discourse represents the transition from hsing practice to ming practice—or going from working with the mind's nature to working with the essences of life. Despite this change in focus, refining the mind remains the foundation of all practice. The crucial question we each need to ask ourselves to determine what level we are at is: "Has my prior-heaven mind taken the fore, or is my mind still engaged in discursive, chaotic mental activity?" The challenge before us is to eventually learn how to stay with our "true minds" at all times and places, no matter what we are doing.

5

虛無之氣

THE QI OF EMPTY NONEXISTENCE

As I teach, I am aware that some students have struggled for many years but still do not fully comprehend this singular qi, so it would be best for me to first offer a thorough, preliminary exposition.

This singular qi of empty nonexistence is also called "the qi of true oneness," "the jing of true oneness," "the innate primordial qi of the cosmos," or "the unified qi of clear emptiness." The names are as many as they are varied, but none of them is satisfactory, as what is essential is none other than that which is without sound or odor—a truth that cannot be thought of or analyzed. It is not within, nor is it without. When concealed within the corporeal body, it is called dharmakaya.

As difficult to contemplate and reckon with as it is, this qi is at once as distant as the farthest reaches of the cosmos, and yet incredibly close by. Confucius's declaration, "I wish for benevolence, and here benevolence is," is enough to show that this primordial qi—the self-such nature of the cosmos— has not been separate from us for even a moment. To separate from this qi is to be unable to obtain life; how could one do so and become a human?

Yet, what must one first do to be able to search for this qi? Although becoming attached to the notion of "searching" is to make a tremendous error that will add layer upon layer of obstructions, it must still be searched for. The only way to do so is to relinquish everything, so that one has not even a thread of attachment and remains uncolored by the myriad circumstances of life. Therein lies this insubstantial, inexistent qi. You have long studied, and your skills are advanced. I believe you already understand this principle and have no doubts.

You must know that this insubstantial, inexistent, singular qi is the same for the heavens, the earth, humans, and all other things. The principle is the same whether one is wealthy or impoverished. Even if you pass through the most extreme sufferings and privations, this qi will not change or move. The qi of breathing can be ample or weak, it can ebb and rise. But this primordial qi is neither ample nor weak, nor does it ebb or rise.

Scholars with shallow and crude understandings do not realize that, in the human body, clearness and turbidity as well as brightness and darkness all come about due to later-heaven qi's functions and movements. Thus, they seek insubstantial, nonexistent, singular qi within that which is clear and bright, and they assume that it is not to be found within that which is dark or turbid. Little do they know, this primordial qi is not present because there is clarity and brightness, nor is it absent if there is darkness and turbidity.

It is especially important to realize that this primordial qi is fundamentally inapparent, without form, and without color. It is, in fact, the root essence of later-heaven jing, qi, and shen, as well as the governor of prior-heaven jing, qi, and shen. Thus, this empty, nonexistent, singular qi births yin and yang in prior heaven, then falls into later heaven to be concealed within yin and yang.

In general, if one is able to cleanly sweep away idle thoughts, complicated ruminations, and all other obstacles arising from the stirrings of mind that give rise to thinking, leaving behind not even a fiber or a speck, then one's ability is sufficient. And yet, for young people whose qi and breathing are robust, it is easy to arrive at the cusp of true qi, while for those who are advanced in years, it may be difficult to harmoniously regulate qi and blood, to conserve and nourish numinous light, and to harvest this modicum of quintessentially yang jing. In such instances, what should be done? I will share with you students the principles for another process of harvesting and refining.

The Book of Changes *states: "Silent and motionless, responding and then connecting." Students, when primordial qi has still yet to appear, you ought to let your shen's light shine downward. Have this shen fire go and impel the metal trapped within the palace of water to stir in response. In due time, fire in water will cause a reaction, as though real gold were released from* ore. This *will sense*, and that *will respond*, even more swiftly than shadows and echoes. The ancients taught latter-day students not to gather while silent and motionless; they taught us the method of having shen's light shine downward. Only at the moment when there is connection does one engage, in order to gather qi which is wholly of prior heaven and utterly real. It is this qi that acts as the basis for the elixir.

This is not to say that the qi that stirs is itself primordial qi. You must know that primordial qi was never not present, even before there was form. Pellucid, empty qi cannot be seen. When it is on the cusp of taking form, that which takes form is not itself the qi of real oneness. That which takes form is no more than that whose splendor derives from the qi of real oneness. When it becomes active within vagueness and indistinction, it is as if something recognizable is present. But recognizing it is like glimpsing an object's shadow and thinking one has glimpsed the object itself. In actuality, nothing has been seen at all. At the moment when it clearly displays itself, "it is released and expands to fill the six directions."[3] Neither the sky nor the earth can contain it. This qi is that which is said to birth the heavens, the earth, humanity, and all things. Yet, although it is immeasurable and boundless, this qi is not distinct from mind. That is what is meant by "it can be rolled up and hidden within the miniscule."

If we use this as the basis of our thinking, then the mists of creation are still yin and yang true qi. But that which governs this true qi has, from the very beginning, always been ultimately real primordial qi. Do you follow? That is why ancient, realized immortals probed its mysteries in order to know its origins and plumbed its spirit in order to understand its transformations. They refined their bodies and returned once more to the unified qi; they refined this qi and reverted once more to empty nothingness. Their key was none other than making use of the false in order to let the real take shape.

We have also heard that an ancient said: "The qi of real oneness—look at that which has no form, listen to that which has no sound." But if one does things this way, how can one concentrate qi into the broomcorn millet pearl?[4] Well, sages have a method to seek and absorb this qi, gathering it within a single two-hour period. The method is returning the shining of the light, in which "I" feel, and "the other" responds.

When the qi of true oneness has already appeared, it remains invisible. Yet, if this is so, how could one ascertain it, and then gather and absorb it in

order to become an immortal of empty nothingness? Well, sages use the man-
ifest to give form to the unmanifest; they use the substantial to give shape to
the substanceless.

That which is substantial and extant is obscure, indistinct true yang;
that which is empty and substanceless is the dragon and tiger double-eight
new moon qi.⁵ The key is nothing more than using that which has form to
refine and extract the formless primordial qi. Only in so doing can it be made
into the elixir.

Students, today you have heard my teaching on the qi of real oneness.
Understand that you must never again mistake later-heaven yin-yang and
prior-heaven yin-yang for the qi of the true oneness, and you will all be close
to the Tao.

■ ■ ■

In chapter 2 we spoke about the "three alignments," which means
letting alignment come to the body, the breath, and the mind. Let
us begin by aligning our postures, so that we sit in the lightest, most
relaxed manner we can. Your whole body should be relaxed, but your
back should still be somewhat straight, so that you are not twisted or
slouching in any way.

Once you have aligned your posture, allow your thoughts and
your awareness to settle onto your breathing. Observe and feel your
breathing for a few moments, allowing it to naturally become longer
and more even.

This leaves one last step, "aligning the mind," which is the basis
for creating mental tranquility. Most people are aware that serenity of
the mind is a fundamental component of authentic meditation practice, but that knowledge does little to resolve a question that can dog
practitioners for months or even years: How exactly does one get one's
mind to become quiet?

■ ■ ■

I once shared a room with an old professor who was quite the ex-
trovert. He said that his mind was simply never quiet, and he wanted
to know how he could cultivate the Tao. I told him that it is normal to have a brain that seems to never stop working. A professor's

brain might be full of complicated ideas that make it unusually difficult to find peace, but all people's brains are active all day long. All we
need to do is observe ourselves for a few moments to realize that our
thoughts are in constant motion. Thus, we should not make it our
aim to suddenly bring our mental activity to a halt and enter into a
state of extraordinary calm. This goal in and of itself is a very potent
thought that will, somewhat ironically, make it even harder for us to
calm our minds. The situation is similar to a person suffering from insomnia whose desperate craving for sleep upsets the very balance of
body and mind that is needed in order to fall asleep. The more an in-
somniac wants sleep, the harder it is to get it.

Of course, I am not saying that when quieting the mind there is
no need to arrive at a state where one has very few thoughts, or perhaps none at all. Such a state is indeed an excellent basis for practicing
internal alchemy, but it cannot be arrived at by repressing or inhibit-
ing one's thinking. In other words, one should not try to think of a
way to quiet down the mind, because thinking about quieting down
thinking is fundamentally unquiet! One can easily end up stuck in a
state of anticipation, thinking, "Ugh, when will I finally be tranquil?
When will I enter the kind of meditative state I'm looking for?" This
is a deluded approach to quieting the mind.

■ ■ ■

The most fundamental point anybody hoping to enter into tranquility
needs to grasp is this: You are not your thoughts.

We normal people have a habit of identifying ourselves with the
act of thinking and with our thoughts. Once this habit is established,
the very next thing we do is go chasing off after our thoughts. When
we do this, there is no distance between us and our thoughts, and
we lose our "real selves"—we lose the "protagonist." The reality is
thoughts come and go constantly, without ever coming to a standstill.
There has never existed a thought that was capable of becoming solid
and staying in place. Therefore, the only thing that is necessary to do
to break this habit is to directly observe thoughts—to shine the light
of awareness upon them. When we observe, we engage that which
we are at our cores: numinously aware consciousness. All of us possess

the same illuminating capacity to observe, and the very thing we use to observe thoughts is our self-nature.

When we observe our thoughts, we temporarily separate our thoughts from our true natures. As we look at our thoughts, we find that they ceaselessly come and go, and that they are utterly devoid of solid form. As soon as thoughts are born, they expire, not remaining for even a moment. When we can see this, there is no need whatsoever to control our thoughts, nor is there any need to quiet them down. Because our thoughts ultimately do not exist—meaning they are not fixed, substantial things—they are no different from the insubstantial objects that we see in our dreams.

We can have any number of dreams while we sleep at night, but the very moment we wake up, we discover that none of the things populating our dreams really exist. Before we woke up, we regarded all of those things as real, as though they were totally solid objects. They may have caused us to cry in our dreams, or to laugh. Our thoughts have a similar effect over us in the daytime, so "waking up" by using awareness to consciously observe our thoughts is imperative. This allows us to recognize that, in essence, our thoughts are empty. They are nothing.

Thoughts arise and dissipate, appear and disappear. As thoughts arise, as long as one quietly pays attention to their intrinsic quality, one will discover that one is not the act of thinking, nor is one the thoughts themselves. If one's self were to be found in the act of thinking, then when thinking ceases, how could one continue to exist? When the act of thinking ceases and no thoughts are present, not only does one still exist, one's existence actually improves, because one comes closer to one's real state of existence!

Thus, we must not identify with the act of thinking, nor with the thoughts that thinking creates. When our minds move—including when they do so chaotically—we have the ability to notice, with immediacy and vigilance, that although we have given rise to a thought, the thought is by no means "me." When we observe our minds this way, slowly but surely the ripples of thought will settle down, and our quietude deepens. Quietude of this sort is uncontrived; it is simply the natural result of engaging the mind's nature.

■ ■ ■

Here is an equally important point: one can neither expectantly await tranquility, nor grasp on to it when it appears. If one succeeds at becoming tranquil, one must not treat it as something that must now be maintained at all costs. The moment one has the idea, "I need to maintain this state," distraction has already begun.

The only thing one needs to do is remain alert and observant, allowing thoughts to rise and fall, letting them come into being and pass away on their own. In time, one's powers of wakeful awareness will become stronger, and eventually one will even be able to apply this practice of observance to daily life. This is the start of living more consciously. From then on, at any time throughout the day, the moment one has a destructive impulse, one will know.

In Chan Buddhism there is a phrase, "if you are aware of it, then it is not wicked." Here, to "be aware" means that when your mind is producing discursive thoughts, you are aware that this is going on. If there is awareness, then having a mind full of discursive thoughts is not a problem. Another way Chan Buddhists say this is, "fear not the arising of thoughts, fear only that awareness comes too slowly." There is nothing to worry about if thoughts arise in your mind—they can only cause trouble if your awake nature lags slowly behind, as though you've forgotten to remain aware.

■ ■ ■

Quieting the mind is an art. One needs to find the knack for it, because one cannot make oneself tranquil by way of brute force. If one is convinced that one needs to struggle with thoughts, one will probably come up empty-handed in the end. In fact, this is a good way to end up facing a crushing defeat, because there is no way to win against thoughts in a fight. The reason for this is that the wish to defeat thoughts is itself a thought—this wish is itself the "enemy." There is no chance of emerging victorious from a battlefield where thoughts wage war against thoughts.

The proper way to practice this art—to attain "victory"—is to see thoughts clearly, recognizing them as nothing but paper tigers that do not necessitate struggle. This means at any and all times being able to accept one's present state, without needing to struggle against it. One simply peacefully coexists with one's physical and mental state at any given moment. Rather than attempting to change or control one's state, one accompanies it, allowing it to continue however it is. Amid this combination of aware and accepting observation, a certain type of transformation will take place, and a new quality of mental serenity will arise.

■ ■ ■

The theme of this discourse is "the qi of empty nonexistence," a concept Huang Yuanji discusses in numerous chapters in the *Oral Record of the Hall of Joyous Teaching*. He refers to it at different times with different names, including "the qi of prior-heaven oneness," "the clear and empty qi of oneness," "the single qi of the heavenly origin," and so on. His discourse at the beginning of this chapter contains a focused examination of this recurring concept.

The first thing we need to be aware of is that, although we are using the word "qi," we must not confuse it with the qi of Taoism's "three treasures": jing, qi, and shen. Both words come from the exact same Chinese character—氣—but the idea of qi that Huang Yuanji presents in this discourse is not defined in contrast with shen, whereas the idea of qi as part of the three treasures is. It is crucial to understand that in books on Taoist alchemy, the word "qi" appears in lots of disparate theoretical contexts, meaning that this word has numerous distinct uses that may not be interchangeable. We must be cautious not to prematurely conclude which kind of meaning is being conveyed when we see this word.

So what, precisely, does "qi" mean when it refers to "the qi of empty nonexistence?" Here, the word "qi" points to the realm of fundamental nature and the roots of our origins—the Tao itself. When we see the word "qi" in "the qi of empty nonexistence," this means that the Tao is being discussed from the standpoint of energy.

Of course, the Tao is primal and fundamental. It is an illimitable entity—no concept or definition suffices to draw borders around it. The Tao is not a thing, either, meaning that there is nothing I can pull out and show people so that they will know what the Tao is. The Tao will never, ever turn into a limited, objectified entity or substance that can appear before us. This is why Taoist cultivation relies upon awakening and firsthand experience.

Nevertheless, while it is impossible for anybody to conjure up the Tao for us to see, it is still possible to use symbols and metaphors to allude to it. Things that are proximal to the Tao can be used to help us attain a certain appreciation of it. Thus, there are two important perspectives from which the Tao is often discussed. The first standpoint relates to the teachings on the mind, in which fundamental nature and primordial shen are used to explain how the Tao is akin to illimitable consciousness. The other major standpoint is energetic. Here, *qi* is used to express the limitless nature of the Tao's energy. We can say that the Tao exists both as unlimited consciousness and unlimited energy. The Tao contains infinite information, encompasses all things, and transcends all things. Yet, while the Tao has a transcendent nature, at the same time it is not outside or separate from all the objects and phenomena in the universe. Quite the opposite, the Tao accompanies all things and all occurrences. All that exists is within the Tao; nothing leaves the Tao.

So, to discuss "the qi of empty nonexistence" is to discuss Tao. Be careful not to see the word "qi" and then conclude that we are talking about something other than the Tao itself, such as particular energies in the body. This discourse also revolves around Tao, but we are speaking from the standpoint of qi instead of the essential nature of the mind. (But even so, remember that in this context qi is not actually distinct from shen, because the Tao encompasses both shen and qi.)

■ ■ ■

The Tao can be said to be the ultimate basis as well as the final goal of all religions and all forms of cultivation. The Chinese character for Tao—道—covers the broadest possible scope, within which fall all religions, all methodologies, and all doors leading to liberation. All methods of cultivation are akin to roads, and "road" is precisely what the character "Tao" means. The place we need to arrive at is upon the road; the places where we begin our journeys are also upon the road. We come from the Tao and we go toward the Tao. In fact, nobody has ever once left it.

Confucians use the character for Tao, as do Buddhists. Different schools of thought use this word in their own characteristic ways that are colored by their systems of explanation and interpretation. This is just like what happens when people take photos of the same scene from different angles. If we were to all go and photograph Victoria Harbour this evening, the angles we took our shots from would yield very different photos, despite the fact that we were all shooting the exact same subject.

The Tao can be discussed from entirely different angles. A discussion from the standpoint of the qi of empty nonexistence reflects a perspective that is unique to Taoist inner alchemy, showing what sets this tradition apart from others. When Confucians use the word "Tao," they tend to be speaking in terms of morality. They hold that humans have an innately moral nature, in the form of a conscience that accords with heavenly principles. They teach that acquired selfish, material desires take one away from the Tao, so in order to return to the principles innate to the universe one must eliminate personal desire. Arriving at sage-hood is a question of merging into oneness with the universe's moral laws.

When Buddhists use the word "Tao," they are mostly concerned with the "middle path" that exists between two of their teachings, the first being that the nature of all objects and phenomena is emptiness, and the second being that all objects and phenomena arise due to dependent origination. Buddhism teaches that the creation of any given object or phenomenon is always dependent on causes and conditions. Because of this, objects and phenomena cannot be said to have absolute, independent existence, and thus their essential nature is emptiness. And yet, this empty nature is not a nihilistic oblivion, because the very nature of emptiness itself is to manifest as dependently originating objects and phenomena. It is through dependent origination that emptiness makes itself apparent. The "middle path" lies between mistaking that which is inherently empty as absolutely real on the one hand, and nihilistically rejecting all things as illusory on the other.

Because of our habitual grasping, humans tend to treat things that are essentially empty as though they absolutely exist, and then we attempt to own and control them. By attaching to objects and phenomena in this manner, we become oblivious to the emptiness that is inherent in all things. Once we lose sight of things' true nature, we then create suffering for ourselves. This is why Buddhism exhorts people to "awaken to emptiness," which means realizing that all things and all occurrences are empty. Realizing this means no longer becoming attached to things and having what the *Diamond Sutra* calls "a mind that functions but does not abide," meaning that one no longer becomes mentally stuck upon any objects or phenomena, because one clearly understands that they all have the same empty nature. Realizing emptiness destroys the obstacle of mental defilement and the barrier of mistaking the seeming for the real. This allows one to obtain liberation and enter nirvana.

The way that Taoists use the word "Tao" does not contradict Buddhist and Confucian usages, nor is it completely unrelated to them. But the Taoist use of this word is unique in that it puts a special emphasis upon "the qi of empty nonexistence," which allows Taoists to interpret the word "Tao" from an energetic standpoint. An emphasis on energy is one of the defining characteristics of inner alchemy theory, which is why it teaches simultaneous cultivation of the mind's nature (hsing) and the essence of life (ming). Whenever inner alchemy discusses shen it also discusses qi, so when it offers teachings such as "illuminating the mind to see its nature," at the same time it broaches the topic of "the qi of empty nonexistence," which is the kind of qi that exists at the level of the Tao.

■ ■ ■

Viewed from the perspective of qi or energy, the Tao is a limitless energy field that is always and everywhere present. We know that at the level of the Tao the entire universe is merged into a single unity. However, this teaching is not meant to imply a sort of merging in which there are absolutely no conditions and distinctions. Rather, the teaching is that, in terms of a certain fundamental essence, all things are connected and united.

At our own relatively coarse level of experience, we are able to perceive all kinds of distinctions. Here is this object, over there is that object; your body and my body are not the same. Yet, if we were to go deeply into things' essential nature, we would see that they are all embodiments of the Tao, part of an interconnected energy field. If we were to try to force this connection into a scientific-sounding term, we might call it "the universal unified field." Ultimate, universal unity is found in a unified energy field. This field is "holographic," in that it contains all of the information in the universe.

In the very beginning, before the ten thousand things emerged in differentiation, they shared a single pure, undifferentiated existence. Later, the yin-yang information contained within this unity emerged and gave form to countless objects and phenomena, including the world that we inhabit. Our world is defined by differentiation, but the Tao remains a part of it, and has never not been connected to the world's myriad objects and phenomena. That is why it can be said that the Tao intrinsically connects and interweaves all things.

We can imagine individual people as like the individual waves atop a vast ocean. At first glance, each wave appears to have an independent existence, but this is not really so. The basis of each wave is the boundless ocean. The ocean is the waves' fundamental nature. It is from the ocean that waves come, and it is to the ocean that they return. In fact, each wave is holographically interconnected with the ocean as a whole, and waves and ocean are all one.

We can borrow the above analogy to represent the "the qi of empty nonexistence" or "the unified prior-heaven qi" of the Tao. Imagine the absurdity of a wave that believes itself to be truly independent and tries to do everything in its power to separate itself from the ocean. *That* is akin to what we do when we assume ourselves to have an existence that is separate from the heavens, the earth, and the ten thousand things. What we do in our minds is no different from being a wave that believes it is independent of the ocean. This is a misapprehension, an unfounded illusion.

Humans' senses of self are just like that wave. At essence, the self is not a real thing. Humans create their selves through clinging, meaning that our sense of independent existence arises due to misperceptions. For this reason, in Taoist alchemy the sense of self that we tend to believe in is called "the false self." I might believe that I am this body, treating the body as "me." I might believe that I am a professor at such and such university, seeing this external identity as "me." In your family you might be a father or a mother or have some other role, and treat this role as "me." You might identify with a career, believing "I am a doctor" or some other title. At a deeper level, we identify with our ways of thinking, particular thoughts, and even our theories, possibly thinking, "this theory is *my* invention." We may also identify with physical sensations or hold that certain emotions are actually our selves. These different "selves" exist at different levels and have different implications, but all of them are arise from misconception.

What, then, is "the real self?" Who am "I," really? The real self can be described using the Buddhist term "no-self." One must apply wisdom when engaging with such a term, because the terminology we are using here—self, false self, real self, no-self—is prone to causing a kind of confusion that can't be resolved through semantics. When the term "no-self" is used, it is definitely not meant to imply that there is nothing at all, that nothing exists, or that there is no real life to speak of. Buddhist teachings are not nihilistic. Rather, no-self is the self that exists absent of all of the external, clung-to "identities" of the sort I just listed. If one identifies with a limitable "small self" because one is clinging to later-heaven objects and phenomena, that is the opposite of no-self. Such a "small self" is only an idea that arises in one's thinking mind. It is not something that really and truly exists.

Humans are interconnected with the Tao and therefore are one with it. The "I" that is interconnected and one with Tao is our fundamental nature, which is also called "the real self." The real self does not make distinctions, nor does it attach to anything. So, on one hand, we can say "humans have selves," referring to that in us which is of the Tao, connected to the Tao, and one with the Tao. At this level, an essential nature exists. Yet, on the other hand, we can also say "humans do not have selves," meaning that there is nothing real in an "I" based upon clinging to extrinsic factors that can represent us and be worn like mental clothing. In a very crucial sense, Taoist cultivation means freeing oneself from the false, illusory self in order to find one's real self. The real self does not hold on to even the thought of "I," because whenever one has an "I," one isolates oneself from the Tao.

In the end, the question of self cannot be resolved using words. Sometimes we speak of "no-self" to describe the inner experience of not having an "I" and its concomitant clinging. However, other times we talk about "self" from an external, objective viewpoint as we discuss existence and the fundamental source of life—Tao.

■ ■ ■

Empty, nonexistent qi is a limitless ocean of energy. It is both interconnected with and one with our essential natures. Typically, we limit ourselves by identifying with our physical, flesh-and-blood bodies. Deluded by that which has form, we never directly perceive that we also exist as an energy field that is formless, inapparent, vast, and boundless. On rare occasion, in the stillness of the very early morning, one might suddenly have a sense of endlessness and borderless-ness with no beginning or end, nor any concept of the passing of time. When this happens, one catches a glimpse of what is meant by "limitless Tao" and "the qi of empty nonexistence."

There are many layers to this qi. It is called empty and nonexistent because it does not appear to have any of the properties that qi is typically thought to have—we cannot see this qi, and it is not the type of qi that might be felt flowing here and there. The types of qi we can feel are later-heaven qi. Even the true qi that becomes active when we sit in meditation is not the qi of empty nonexistence. For this reason, we need to clearly understand the relationship between the qi of empty nonexistence that is all things' original source, and the later-heaven qi that operates during inner alchemy practice.

In inner alchemy practice, there is a harmonious, mutually cooperative relationship between prior-heaven and later-heaven qi. It is important not to confuse the mechanisms of the body's later-heaven qi with prior-heaven qi. For instance, when our minds become tranquil, the functioning of the body's qi will react, causing different sensations to move from one part of the body to another, possibly leading to a sense of flowing energetic currents. Such currents reflect a type of qi, but this is only the body's true qi, not prior-heaven, empty, nonexistent qi.

Speaking more generally, people who do not practice inner alchemy also have qi. In fact, there is no activity that is not related to qi, because qi is the energetic support for everything in the body. Some cultivation systems, as well as Chinese medicine, analyze qi in great detail. They describe which kind of qi supports eating and digestion, which kind of qi supports locomotion, and so forth. Different types of qi allow all of the body's various functions to operate.

However, the focus of this chapter is not the type of qi that Chinese medicine typically describes. Rather, at issue is the relationship between true qi and the qi of empty nonexistence. If one becomes excessively concerned with the reactions and experiences arising from the body's qi functions while cultivating the Tao, it is very easy to end up confining oneself to the fairly rudimentary levels of qi in the human body while forgetting all about the qi of empty nonexistence. Then, when one concludes that one's true qi is abundant and functioning optimally, one may then assume that one has obtained the Tao. But later, if qi isn't working well, one will think one has lost the Tao. This is why it is crucial to remember that the qi we are concerned with is unlimited and illimitable. It is present at any given time and place. If one's body is in great condition, it is there. If one's body is in poor condition, it is still there. In this way qi is just like our minds' essential nature.

■ ■ ■

This "thing" we are discussing from a number of different angles is always there—it is simply up to us to experience it. Paradoxically, despite everything I just said, Taoist alchemy *does* emphasize the cultivation of later-heaven qi's functions. Whether one is "refining the elixir" or "gathering medicine," there are many methods that require *doing*, and this doing always begins with later-heaven qi. The solution to this paradox lies in understanding the entire process of inner alchemy cultivation and all of its methods.

Internal alchemy works by creating a kind of "opportunity" or "turning point" that arises while the body's yin qi and yang qi are in intercourse. This "turning point" is what makes it possible for prior-heaven qi to emerge. This means that in internal alchemy one seeks within that which is later heaven for that which is prior heaven, and after having realized it, one uses prior-heaven qi to transform later-heaven qi. Later-heaven qi can be thought of as the dregs of yin qi; it is these very dregs that are subjected to the alchemical process of sublimation and transmutation. Thus, there is dialectical unity between prior heaven and later heaven in Taoist alchemy.

Discussions of the Tao sometimes begin from the standpoint of qi, and sometimes they begin from the standpoint of mind. In either case, it is important to avoid becoming confused and thinking qi and mind are two separate things. There is a core concept in internal alchemy that can be summed up in the phrase "mind and qi are not two." In this phrase, mind refers to mental energy, consciousness, and psychological activity, while qi refers to the substrate underlying mind. We can better understand what this phrase means by comparing qi to a horse, and mind to its rider. In a certain sense, horse and rider are distinct—the person on the horse's back is definitely not the horse. But the two are intimately linked, mutually influencing and affecting one another. In a very similar way, when the mind moves, qi moves. When a thought arises, the qi in one's body stirs along with it. Conversely, the movements of qi will also have an impact one's mental state. One's psychology influences one's physiology, and vice versa. This is the reason why hsing and ming need to be cultivated together.

As for whether it is mind or qi that plays the decisive role, just as the rider controls the horse, mind takes primacy over qi. That said, qi can counteract the mind, just like a horse that refuses to take directions or even throws off its bridle and bolts away. There are times when we become psychologically distressed, and the chaotic thoughts racing around our minds refuse to settle. This happens as a result of our qi being too frenetic because it is poorly regulated. Qi of this sort carries karmic force that will impact one's state of mind. If one doesn't have quite a bit of inner strength and self-awareness, one can neither redirect nor control such qi. This dynamic also works in the opposite direction. Thus, mental distress, delusions, and scattered thoughts also have an impact on the body's qi.

Many diseases of the body are actually brought about by psychological problems that eventually manifest physiologically. In such cases, if we neglect to find a disease's psychological source and instead attempt to solely heal the body, what we are doing amounts to treating symptoms while ignoring their causes. Taking medicine may bring some relief, but soon enough the problem will be back, because the psychological state that is causing physical malaise remains unchanged. In analytical psychology there are a number of techniques for teasing out the relationship between bodily phenomena and their psychological origins. Sometimes, the search for the roots of a psychological problem can also reveal the cause of a physical illness.

If body and mind are "not two," then this means they are interconnected, but saying "body and mind are linked" is a very general statement. The specific medium body and mind rely upon to maintain their connection is qi. Qi is not air, nor is it breathing. Rather, within our bodies there exists a type of energy far more profound and subtle than anything contained at the flesh-and-blood or even cellular levels. Anybody who trains fairly skillfully and accumulates enough experience will be able to directly perceive this energy's currents in the body.

■ ■ ■

Subtle later-heaven qi may be felt as currents, but how does one experience the prior-heaven, empty, nonexistent, primordial qi that is the focus of this chapter? The principles are actually the same as they were in our earlier discussion of illuminating the mind in order to see its nature. One must arrive at a very quiet and serene state of mind, allowing one's essential nature to become apparent. This works because essential nature and the qi of empty nonexistence are inseparable, like two sides of the same coin.

A person who has just embarked upon the Taoist path is incapable of fathoming his or her essential nature, and therefore is also incapable of experiencing the qi of empty nonexistence. What he or she must do is begin by working with that which has form in order to refine that which is formless. This avenue to attainment, which is unique to Taoism, amounts to finding a road in a land without roads, or finding a method to apply oneself to when one is at a loss as for what to do. We begin our cultivation of that which has neither form nor appearance by using our human bodies. This means slowly accumulating experience through training that starts with the workings of the human body's later-heaven qi.

One example of such practice is turning one's mind inward to observe a "portal" in the body, such as the dantian, in a process called "concentrating shen and entering a gateway." Doing so allows for a connection and interchange between body and mind, and in time the body will respond to the mind's observant gaze, leading further to a state of harmonious accord. This will then produce energetic transformations such as "the creation of medicine" and "gathering medicine." From this basis of searching for prior heaven within later heaven, one will slowly come to realize prior-heaven qi.

■ ■ ■

Above, I expanded upon the general themes of Huang Yuanji's discourse at the beginning of this chapter. Before we closely examine the specifics of his discourse, I must point out that I will gloss over some sections of his teaching, or else discuss them only briefly, but I will examine other sections in detail.

Huang Yuanji begins his discourse by acknowledging that although many of his students have practiced painstakingly for years, they still have not clearly comprehended the prior-heaven qi of empty nonexistence; much less have they directly experienced this qi, which is of the Tao. This qi is actually not supposed to be discussed, because describing too many things that pertain to later stages of cultivation can cause practitioners to develop conceptualizations that get in the way of progress, especially if they are treated as goals that have to be strived for. Some things are not meant to be revealed in words; other things should only be described to a student who has reached a certain level, in order to give instructions when the specific need arises.

However, sometimes students remain confused about what cultivation entails for such a long time that it is necessary to offer a clearer explanation. When a teacher offers such an explanation, it is like sketching a simple map of Hong Kong and roughly tracing a route through the city. Having such a map might aid a student in his or her travels, but the danger is that the student believes the map to be "reality," thus becoming a person who spends all day wandering through the map of Hong Kong in his or her mind, instead of actually exploring the city. Naturally, this kind of mistake will derail one's cultivation.

Clear verbal explanations can be beneficial, but they can also be deleterious. Huang Yuanji offers this explanation as a preliminary for those students who have yet to experience unified, prior-heaven qi, otherwise known as the qi of empty nonexistence.

■ ■ ■

In the second paragraph of his lecture, Huang broaches various alternative names for the qi of empty nonexistence, including "the qi of true oneness" and "the jing of true oneness." One must be cautious here, because the word "jing" in this term is not the jing of the three treasures, which are jing, qi, and shen, even though the character (精) and pronunciation are the same. Here, the word "jing" is used almost as an adjective, connoting something marvelously fine, sublime, and quintessential. Whenever the names of the three treasures appear in discussions of the qi of empty nonexistence, they are not meant to imply the jing, qi, and shen of the human body. Rather, they appear in terms like "the innate primordial qi of the cosmos" or "the unified qi of clear emptiness" to describe the Tao itself. When reading books on internal alchemy, always seek to know precisely what their vocabulary alludes to.

Its names might be "as many as they are varied," but just what is this so-called qi of empty nonexistence? At the heart of the matter, it is nothing other than a featureless, incognizable "reality." This "reality" is the unadulterated truth that has existed all along, never becoming embroiled in the illusory nature of later-heaven existence. Huang Yuanji starts by talking about qi, but then moves to talking about the state it occupies, because it is only by ourselves occupying this state that we can directly experience the qi of empty nonexistence. With the lines "without sound or odor—a truth that cannot be thought or analyzed," Huang Yuanji is alluding to the type of mindset that practitioners need to develop.

Earlier I stated that, if one wishes to truly enter into a state without thinking, one cannot treat it as a goal and strive after it. Nevertheless, it is only when one has genuinely stopped thinking and analyzing—when later-heaven scattered thoughts have disappeared—that one will be able to directly experience the limitless, vastness of existence.

To paraphrase Huang Yuanji, this sort of experience is neither internal nor external. It is not limited to being inside the body, because, not being a thing, it cannot be tied to any particular location. At the same time, it is not external to one's body, because it is not a thing one can seek beyond one's body. It is hidden within form and mind, and another name for it is *dharmakaya*.

This realm or state is impossible to describe in words, as well as impossible to arrive at through rational thought. No matter how one turns it over in one's mind, one will never be able to hold it in the grasp of reason. However, that does not mean that the qi of empty nonexistence is far away. Were someone to declare that it is in the far-flung reaches of the universe, this would require giving it a concrete definition. The reality is that this qi transcends both remoteness and proximity. Having no edges and no borders, it is neither close at hand nor far away. The only way it can be said to be far off is in the sense that it is quite removed from the way we everyday people experience the world. In other words, because we can't perceive the Tao's qi, it seems as though it is in some faraway celestial realm. But really, this qi is so close to us that even the word "close" is inappropriate. The qi of empty nonexistence is actually what we really are. Even saying "close" misleadingly implies that there is separation.

. . .

There is no distance between the actual Tao—the actual qi of empty nonexistence—and any of our lives. Our lives and Tao are one. Huang Yuanji uses a quote we have already seen from Confucius to illustrate this relationship: "I wish for benevolence, and here benevolence is." What Confucius meant is that, if one wishes to act benevolently, just the thought, *I wish to live as a person with a benevolent heart,* is already benevolent in and of itself. Because the desire to become benevolent *is* benevolent, this means anyone can realize benevolence anytime, anywhere.

Huang Yuanji borrows Confucius's teaching in order to explain that primordial qi exists self-suchly, innate to everything in the universe. Not for one moment has it left us; not even for the span of a single breath has it been separate from us. Were it to leave us, we would have no way of surviving. Just as fish cannot live outside of water, we can't help but pass our entire lives within the Tao.

The Tao is a formless, featureless, boundless ocean that fills everything. We exist within it; none of us will leave it. To truly leave it would be to not be, as all beings are functions of the Tao, meaning it is a background that is impossible to separate from. There is no distance between us and the Tao, and yet, precisely because it not removed from us, we don't notice it. This is precisely the reason why the Tao is so difficult to experience.

■ ■ ■

When we use the word "seek" to describe our efforts to find the Tao's primordial qi of empty nonexistence, this creates a problem. The more we try to search for it, the further away it seems to be. This is because the act of seeking presupposes a distance, meaning that as we go off in our journeys of seeking, we actually add to our obstacles.

Classic Taoist writings can seem to be full of contradictory messages. Sometimes they tell the reader to seek the Tao, but later they say that it cannot be sought after. This can be a source of confusion, but it is really a matter of the same words taking on different meanings in different contexts. When Taoists say one must "seek the Tao," they do not mean there is some particular method that allows one to go and find it. Rather, they are describing the path of cultivation *as though* it involved something external to us. Taoists indeed frequently say that we left the Tao, and so they remind us to return to our roots and our origins, and to cultivate the Tao. When they do so, they are addressing our present, relative circumstances, which can be *described* as being separated from the Tao.

On the other hand, when a Taoist says that the Tao cannot be sought, he or she is acknowledging intrinsic reality. In reality, there is no method or practice that will allow us to find the Tao by acting as though it were external to us. But if it is true that the Tao cannot be searched for, what should one do? The answer lies where Huang Yuanji says: "The only way is to relinquish everything, so that one has not even a thread of attachment, remaining uncolored by the myriad circumstances of life." This means restoring an unadulterated, here-and-now state of mind in which one is looking for nothing, pursuing nothing, and free of the thoughts of gaining or losing anything. In this state of mind, one allows all objects and phenomena to be as they are. One does not try to make additions to the entirety of all things, nor does one attempt to eliminate anything. One does not get caught up in anything, nor does one become colored by anything. One returns to placidity, to non-doing, to being what one is.

When abiding in this state, it is possible to experience the limitless energy field that is the qi of empty nothingness. This state comes from such complete relinquishment that not even a tiny thread of attachment remains. But this state cannot be desperately striven after. As I said earlier in this chapter, one cannot struggle against one's present state of being. Rather, one needs to use wisdom while shining one's observant gaze upon one's present state. That is what will enable one's being to transform, uncompelled, by virtue of its own nature.

■ ■ ■

The qi of empty nonexistence is also called "the one, empty, nonexistent qi." It is the original source of all things and phenomena, and from its own standpoint there are no differences between the cosmos, the earth, humanity, and all other beings and objects. Even less do wealth and poverty mean anything to this qi. All things are of the same Tao and follow the same principles. In terms of this qi, you will not get more of it because you are wealthy, nor could you be lacking in it because you are poor. That is why it is said that the Tao operates selflessly between heaven and earth. All people, without exception, can come into resonance with it.

The Tao is innately with us, and it cannot be lessened or increased. It is itself a limitless being. In no way will it change because we are born or we die, because we are suffering, or because of any other circumstances our lives. It also will not change on account of how our bodies' qi functions or the way we breathe. Plenitude or paucity of this or that do not affect the Tao. The true Tao is neither gained nor lost; we cannot have more of it or less of it. It is as it has always been. It has always been just as it is now.

Qi can function in different ways in people's bodies, yielding different states. Sometimes our qi is very clear, sometimes it is quite turbid; sometimes our spirits are very bright, other times they feel dim. People whose insights are not deep fail to grasp that these disparities are only reactions to changes in the movement and functioning of qi in the body. The Tao—the qi of empty nonexistence—is unaffected by any of these changes. Do not think that because your qi feels muddy or polluted that you are "without Tao," and that you must do some special thing or other in order to get the Tao. That which is truly of the Tao cannot leave you for even a millisecond. Given that it is always present, the only thing you need to do is discover and recognize it.

■ ■ ■

Huang Yuanji devotes part of his discourse to pointing out that changes in the functioning of qi in the body have no impact on the primordial qi of empty nonexistence. After that he elucidates the true nature of the relationship between primordial qi and later-heaven jing, qi, and shen. The primordial qi of empty nonexistence—meaning the Tao itself—never becomes manifestly apparent in any concrete way. It is formless and trait-less. Nothing can be found that so much as indicates its presence. It is called "empty and nonexistent" because it does not appear as any object in the later-heaven realm, nor is it subject to the distinctions intrinsic to later-heaven existence.

Elusive though it may be, the qi of the Tao is still the root of our later-heaven jing, qi, and shen. These three treasures not only come from the Tao, they are governed by it. There are both prior-heaven and later-heaven aspects to jing, qi, and shen, which we will expand upon in detail chapter 7. For now, it suffices to repeat Huang Yuanji's pithy summary of this relationship: "Empty, nonexistent, singular qi births yin and yang in prior heaven, then falls into later heaven to be concealed within yin and yang."

When Huang Yuanji says "cleanly sweep away idle thoughts, complicated ruminations, and all other obstacles arising from the stirrings of mind that give rise to thinking, leaving behind not even a fiber or a speck," he means that the secret to realizing the qi of empty nonexistence lies in doing away with the chaotic tendency of the mind to fill itself with idle, random thinking. As this tendency fades away, instead of constantly birthing new thoughts, the mind becomes spotlessly clear. This principle is the same as that implied by the phrase I mentioned above, "mind and qi are not two." The key point is that the path leading to realizing the qi of empty nonexistence is actually a process of refining the mind. What is required of the cultivator is to restore the mind's prior-heaven essential nature.

■ ■ ■

In the next part of his discourse, Huang Yuanji offers an expedient method that allows people to begin cultivation from within the milieu of later-heaven existence.

Young people with plentiful jing, qi, and shen may be able to experience the vastness and mightiness of the qi of empty nonexistence quite quickly. However, this is harder to achieve for older people whose physical bodies are no longer in great health and whose qi and blood are harder to regulate. The question thus arises, what can people whose three treasures have been depleted do to coax forth a direct experience of the qi of empty nonexistence, and thereupon gather it as purely yang jing? ("Purely yang jing" is yet another synonym for the qi of empty nonexistence. Here, the word "jing" does not relate to the triad of jing, qi, and shen and instead simply means "quintessential." The term "purely yang jing" treats the qi of empty nonexistence as though it were a quintessential energy. Practitioners must "gather" this energy, so that prior-heaven qi can transmute the dense, turbid later-heaven qi of the body).

Addressing those of his students who were advanced in their years or had compromised health, Huang Yuanji offers a method for gathering and refining the constituents of inner alchemy. It starts with a simple instruction: if one has yet to experience the emergence of prior-heaven qi, then it is suitable to turn the "light" of one's shen inward, so that it radiates upon one's lower dantian.

The word "shen" encompasses our later-heaven psyches as well as prior-heaven primordial consciousness. Shen shines like a light on whatever object we place our awareness on. This "light of shen" is usually expressed in our eyes—specifically, it inhabits our gazes. Whenever we gaze upon anything in the external world, the light of our shen diffuses outward. This means that if we peer at an object, it takes the "light" of our awareness with it, away from us. For this reason, it behooves Taoist cultivators to "return the light," which is a term that refers to shining the light of shen found in the eyes' gaze inward upon one's own being.

It is incredibly easy for our minds to flit away and diffuse outward, so we need to recall the light of shen and let the radiance of observance shine inwardly upon our own bodies. In this practice, one does so by observing the dantian. Taoists use the *li* trigram (☲, a symbol for fire) to represent shen, while using the *kan* trigram (☵, a symbol for water) as well as the term "water mansion" to represent the dantian. Shen is symbolized by fire because awareness is likened to light; the dantian is symbolized by water because it stores jing. In inner alchemy the two need to meet and merge. However, in typical people, the factors represented by the kan and li trigrams tend to remain separate, because the mind habitually wanders off, while the energy in the "water" of jing tends to drain down and out of the body. This condition is called "kan and li failing to conjoin."

If the light of one's shen turns inward and radiates upon one's body so that it converges with the "water mansion," shen and qi will then blend with one another, creating a state which Taoists call "water and fire nourishing one another." This phenomenon, which is comparable to lighting a stove so that a pot of water on top of it comes to a boil, will cause jing and qi to undergo transformation. When fire and water "nourish" each other—meaning that one has entered a state in which body, mind, shen, and qi are all indistinguishable—certain reactions will occur in the body.

Continuing the analogy of boiling a pot of water, if we do not use this practice, then the light of our shen—"fire"—may remain as though above the pot of "water" remaining below it. As the heat of this proverbial "fire" scatters up and away, the "water" beneath it will remain unboiled; without boiling, the water will be unable to turn into steam. In this analogy, "steam" represents the sublimation of jing into qi and the subsequent rising of qi in the body as it leaves the "water mansion." If it does not sublimate and rise, the energy in the "water" of jing will remain destined to eventually flow down and out from the body.

■ ■ ■

The above practice reflects a very important principle in Taoist internal alchemy. This principle is present whether we are speaking about the mating of yin and yang or the mating of shen and qi. After one causes shen and qi to conjoin by shining the light of shen downward into one's dantian, there will arise a harmonious state of body and mind that indicates intercourse between true yin qi and true yang qi (true yin and true yang are described in detail in chapter 8).

The yin and yang of our beings originally derived from the Tao before separating into yin and yang. Thus, when true yin qi and true yang qi return to one another, it is very easy for prior-heaven qi of true oneness—the qi of the Tao itself—to appear. In other words, the joining of true yin qi and true yang qi presents a moment when it is relatively easy for a cultivator to experience the primordial qi of empty nonexistence.

When the one qi of prior heaven emerges, Taoists call it "medicine." It is the "basis for the elixir," and it is used in all of the subsequent steps of internal alchemy practice to dissolve and transform the later-heaven, physical body. The principle of this practice is called "going from later heaven to prior heaven, and then using prior heaven to transmute later heaven." It is analogous with the overarching process of cultivation that was outlined in chapter 3.

■ ■ ■

Huang Yuanji concludes his discourse by reiterating that primordial qi is always present, and that it is not synonymous with the types of qi with specific forms and functions that move around inside our bodies. But he also makes the caveat that it is sometimes necessary to initiate cultivation from within that which has form, as a way to search for the pivotal point at which prior-heaven qi becomes apparent. So, while prior-heaven and later-heaven qi need to be clearly distinguished when discussing theory, at the same time, they should not be seen as diametrically opposed to or severed from one another.

The above statement is especially applicable to the practical starting points for Taoist cultivation. A teacher cannot expect students to be able to begin practicing if the starting point is fixed at the furthest limits of abstruseness and nebulousness. Beginners have to start within that which has form and appearance, even if the real goal is to reach that which has neither of those things. So, while we cannot remain attached to the formed and apparent, we also cannot treat form and formlessness as irreconcilable opposites.

The final segment of Huang Yuanji's lecture returns to the nature and role of the qi of empty nonexistence, which we have already discussed in detail. Primordial qi is immeasurable and boundless, but it is nowhere other than the mind, and thus, "when it is released it expands to fill the six directions, but it can be rolled up and hidden within the miniscule." The Tao is just like the mind, which can expand to encompass and merge with the entire multiverse, and which can also contract into a single point of numinosity.

In sum, one cannot find the Tao in any particular place, so Taoists often say that it is "so enormous that it has no exterior, and so tiny that it has no interior." As for the different types of qi functioning within the human body, they all derive from the movements and intercourse of true yin qi and yang qi. What governs this true qi is the ultimately real, primordial qi of prior heaven.

6

性命雙修

THE COUPLED CULTIVATION OF
HSING AND MING

The study of coupled cultivation of hsing and ming is not unique to my path. No sage of any of the three teachings of Taoism, Buddhism, and Confucianism could have taken any other path. One starts by using hsing to establish ming. Afterward, one uses ming to fully realize hsing. Finally, hsing and ming merge as one, in order to return to the essence of empty nothingness, which is completion.

The mind's fundamental nature is empty and nonexistent. It is indistinct, absent of objects and phenomena. However, it must be an insubstantiality so absolute that it contains the utterly substantial; a nonexistence so ultimate that it contains the utterly extant. Knowing this from the start, a student will not fall into the sidetrack of insensate oblivion.

When students begin to practice, they must relinquish all concerns, until there is not a speck or a thread of stain. At the moment when emptiness is absolute and tranquility is profound, there is light without object, there is something without form; one is in limitless depths, where nothing can be perceived. But a numinous light shines upon entire vast world systems, meaning that the mind is limpid and silent—what Buddhism calls great bodhi and tathata, *and what Taoism calls numinous knowing and real knowing.*

As soon as a person has a physical body, the single spark of his or her truly numinous aspect is mired in dust and grime. Great cultivators must thus eliminate thinking and rid themselves of worldly concerns, instead nurturing the traces of this spark—this is the practice of illuminating the heart in order to see its essential nature. If you all probe deeply into what I am telling you, you will begin to realize that the basis of essential mind nature is never not present in your life. It does not exist only when you are tranquil. Yet, it is through tranquility that we nurture it.

When the heart becomes serene, much as ice and snow melt without the knowledge or sensation that they are melting, a ray of numinous light will suddenly appear. Not only do others not know when this happens, one has no sense of it oneself. At this moment, all things become utterly pellucid, no thoughts are born, and it seems as though there is nothing—from the heavens to the earth to the ten thousand things—that is not in one's own embrace. And there is no time—from antiquity to the present to ten thousand years hence—that does not flow through one's own being.

This is what Mencius called "nurturing vast qi." It is the zenith of enormity and righteousness, filling all between the cosmos and the earth. Only by seeing the mind's nature in this way does one truly see it. Only by nurturing the mind's nature in this way does one begin to directly nurture it.

When this is accomplished, one's shen skims over the surface of profundity, and one's qi penetrates the heavens of great harmony. One is quiescent, limpid, pure, and coalesced. The Tao will be attained if one does not then enter into trance states, which turns this sacred teaching into a font of bizarre occurrences; and one does not latch on to some object or phenomenon, which causes this sacred teaching to trickle away into confusion.

Although, in daily life, you will still have countless affairs and interactions, you will act by allowing things to take their natural course, letting your behaviors be governed by your fundamental nature. This is like Yu the Great who tamed the floods, working as though he was not working, such that when he was finished, his accomplishments benefited all beneath heaven, but he did not recognize his merits. Likewise, his name was heard everywhere under the sky, but he paid his fame no mind, as unaffected as a baby's knowing to love and look up to others. This comes entirely from innocence. Though there may be nothing that is not known, and nothing that cannot be done, you will not actually be aware of knowing, nor will you have a sense of capability. Existence, and all the things in it, will all transform in unison.

Students, if you realize this Way, because you penetrate the myriad, and the myriad are interwoven with the one, then by virtue of what things are, when you refine jing, you will obtain primordial jing; when you refine qi, you will obtain primordial qi; and when you refine shen, you will obtain primordial shen. Thus, longevity can be had, and spiritual immortality can be approached. Regardless of whether you are in the pristineness of youth or you have a worn-out body, regardless of whether you are old or young, talented or simple, rich or poor, so long as your actions are meritorious and you possess integrity, you will naturally become a highly realized sage.

Although this is called the "Marvelous Way That Is Empty and Non-existent," it is actually the great freedom of tathata, complete and eternally enlightening. People of the past said one must be able to "do a somersault atop the point of a needle and come to a stop in a flash of lightning" in order to be substantial within emptiness and extant within nonexistence, and to avoid digressing into unclear, ill-defined side-path teachings.

Students, this is where cultivation comes from: the first step is a mind that neither comes into being nor is extinguished. This allows your mind's nature to be always present. The next step is a breath that neither enters nor exits. This allows your life's essence to be endlessly preserved.

An ancient said: "When the mind is upon the dantian, the body has a sovereign; when qi returns to the primordial ocean, longevity has no end." Is this not indeed true? Alas, the cultivators of today do not realize that clear purity is our basis and authenticity is our ancestor. Some solely apply themselves to emptiness and tranquility, not understanding that that which must be studied and that which comes through epiphany are one, for as above, so below. Others engage only in striving, not understanding that the de of the universe and the ways of governing the world are one and the same.

Some succeed in realizing the source of the mind's nature and see the marvelousness of creation but fail to realize that the mind's nature is qi's essence—and that it is through qi that original nature functions. They cannot see that without the mind's nature (hsing), life's essence (ming) could not be born, and that without life's essence, the mind's nature has no way to exist. They vainly proclaim that perfecting the mind's nature can affect life's essence, not knowing that by establishing life's essence one can perfect the mind's nature. For those who vainly hold to the mind's nature without being able to establish life's essence, whenever qi moves, shen goes with it. Till their very ends, they remain unable to cut off passion and desire or stop their qi from scattering as their shen wanders. Far less can they escape from birth and death.

In light of the above, cultivating hsing is of vast importance, and refining ming is of urgent concern. Even though this is true, nowadays, those who wish to refine ming just close their eyes and sit in stillness, dimming their minds in silent illumination, vainly keeping watch on the yin shen in the trigram li, never gathering the yang qi in the trigram kan.[6] If their thoughts stir and their shen is distracted, longevity will elude them—how, then, could they hope to exit the wheel of transmigration? Moreover, as for those who vainly work toward void-like silence, unyieldingly keeping watch on their yin shen, such that they haven't even a single spark of yang qi and vitality is gone from their view—how can they hope to be spiritual immortals after they die?

Even if one has the five numinous capabilities of being able to appear anywhere in the manifest universe, knowing past lives, reading others' minds, or seeing or hearing anything in the realm of form, in the end these all come from yin shen. If shen has not entered qi, if qi has not returned to shen, if yin and yang have not merged, if shen and qi have not mated, if the breath goes in and out, and if shen still stirs and moves, then even when the mind enders samadhi, that is only because the yin shen has been forced there. In the end, if one has still yet to successfully refine imperturbable yang shen, then life and death remain beyond one's grasp, and the seeds of transmigration remain.

If that is the way you cultivate, how are you different from any ordinary person?

■ ■ ■

From a certain standpoint, one of the important qualities of quieting the mind is "here and now-ness." Here and now is not a special place or point in time. In fact, here and now is not a place or time at all. Here and now are your existence in every moment. You take them with you wherever you go.

Wherever you are, that is "here." Walking down the road, the road is "here." Returning home, home is "here." Going to bed, your bed is "here." "Here" can never be tied to any particular place, just as "now" is not a set time.

One of the biggest problems we everyday people have is that we live inside the thoughts that fill our heads—seldom do we come back to right here, right now. This means we do not actually live where we're living. We live as though elsewhere.

If, right now, you were listening to me present this chapter in a lecture, how much of the time would you really and truly be listening? A lot of the time you might not really be listening at all, and instead your mind might take you elsewhere, as you think about what is going on at home, what happened yesterday, or something from the more distant past. Or you might look into the future, thinking about tomorrow, or all the things you need to do before the Chinese New Year holiday. When this happens, your mind is not letting you inhabit the present place and time. Instead, you inhabit your imagination.

Of course, no matter how far away your mind wanders, you cannot not be right where you are right now, because what you really exist as is what is right here, right now. Your fundamental, original being is the here and now. Your true being is here. Another way of saying this is that your essential nature is this place at this moment; the Tao is this place at this moment. Given that this is true, the feeling of "not being in the here and now" is in fact a chimeric perception. We cannot *really* leave the here and now, but what our minds do do is take us into all sorts of dream states. While we are dreaming, our consciousness can *seemingly* visit the past or the future, but the reality is that we never truly leave wherever it is we actually are.

So, in terms of actual practice, making our minds tranquil in order to cultivate the Tao simply means having our minds return to the place where our fundamental beings already are: the here and now.

■ ■ ■

Our true beings are the here and now; our real lives are also the here and now. The only problem is that our minds do not stay in the here and now, so we fail to be consciously aware of the present. This causes us to be missing a certain quality. And yet, at any time we can become completely present in the here and now. If we do so, then our minds will quiet, and we will come into resonance with the Tao.

There is no method that can be used to be right here, right now. If you tried to use a method to do so, the method itself would take you away from the here and now. The fact is that you are here, now.

You have never left the present—you only dream that you are else-where. So the only question that needs to be answered is, how do you wake up from dreaming? Waking up is all that needs to be done.

Ceasing to think about the past and the future and fully experiencing the moment at hand is the highest art of life. Mastery of this art means that when you stroll down the street, you do so completely. Your consciousness, your character, and the whole of your body and mind are all walking down the street. Mastering this art means that, whatever you are doing, you are completely merged with it as it is happening. This is the way to live fully and abundantly, to your heart's content. This the way to truly feel the rhythms and melodies of life.

The fact is, though, that most of us live in a scatterbrained way, doing everything as though we were of two minds about it, instead of engaging fully. Whenever we do anything, a good portion of our attention and thoughts run off in other directions, leaving us present enough to complete our tasks, but too absent to achieve a sense of fulfillment. Instead of fulfillment, we are left with a feeling of emptiness—one that we end up trying to fill, again and again, long into the future. The only way to truly find the flavor of whatever we do in life is to experience things fully, thoroughly, and heartily as they are happening. That is why I say that being right here, right now, is the highest art of life.

■ ■ ■

We are always either missing the last beat, or skipping ahead to the next one. Rarely do we really live in step with the rhythms of life. When we are young, instead of fully experiencing our youthfulness, we try and model our lives after grown-ups, or try to live like somebody we admire. When we get old, we feel like we did not really live out our youths, so we envy the way young people live, and try to re-enter that stage of our lives. But this means that instead of deeply enjoying what it is like to live as an old person, we miss that too.

If a person misses out on most of his or her life, this person will be filled with feelings of remorse and regret instead of the fulfillment that comes from immersing oneself in the flavors of life. Truly living is not a question of possessing some kind of advantageous status. Truly living means that, regardless of what one's conditions are and regardless of what one's status is, one lives one's life fully engaged. If one can truly live in the present moment, one is rich, because from this a sense of good fortune and happiness will come. However, if one misses out on really living because one is constantly lost in remembrance of the past and hopes for the future, then one's life will be little different from a dream.

The meaning of "to cultivate the Tao" is to wake up from this dream and live an awake life. Wherever one is, one's mind and body must be fully present with whoever else is there and whatever events are unfolding. This is the only way to really be alive. If, whenever one goes out, one spends one's time missing one's home, spouse, and kids, then one misses out on life in the world. And if whenever one returns home to one's spouse and children, one spend one's time pining to go back out—perhaps thinking, "life away from my family is so simple and peaceful, my lover and my kids are incredibly frustrating"—then one misses out on life in the home. This is no way to live, and I would not wish it upon anybody. So, whatever one is doing, one must do it fully, with one's body and mind fully present, forgetting about the past and forgetting about the future.

Some people might worry, "If I actually live in the present like you say, then will I be able to make plans? Won't major problems arise in my life if I don't concern myself with what will happen tomorrow?" There is really no reason to worry. There is nothing we can do to manipulate the past; it is gone, and it is unchangeable. We also cannot manipulate the future, as that which needs to be done tomorrow can only be done when tomorrow arrives. If one truly attends to the tasks at hand at any given moment, then what is meant to happen will happen, and what is fit to succeed will naturally be a success. This is because the cumulative result of dealing with the things before us in the present moment is that they will all come to completion.

Of course, when I say not to live in the past or the future, what I mean is that one should not let oneself cling to the past or get lost in thoughts about what is to come. One needs to be conscious of whatever is unfolding in the here and now, but that does not mean one can never contemplate the past and future. The key is that, when life requires one to think about the future and create a blueprint for dealing with what is yet to come, one is wholly present while using the present moment to make plans. What one is thinking about might belong to the future, but the thinking itself still belongs to the here and now.

It is important not to misunderstand this teaching. For example, if one needed to return home after a trip, but one had not allowed oneself to do any thinking about the future, then of course one would have no idea which day to start the journey home. When the time finally came to leave, one would be stuck, frantically trying to get a ticket at the last minute. So, the teaching is not that one must never think about the future—one absolutely may think about and plan for it. But, when making plans, one must be wholly alive within the act of planning. Then, once one's plans are ironed out and one's tickets are bought, one lets these things leave the mind, and returns to the here and now.

■ ■ ■

When we talk about the present moment, this has nothing to do with some objective span of time that can be measured with a timepiece. The present moment is a phenomenological sense of time, felt in one's own internal consciousness. That is why it is possible to think about the future while still remaining fully present in this moment. Living in the here and now is simply a quality of awareness—it is unrelated to the concept of time as it might be defined by a physicist or anybody else.

"Now" is a moment that is overflowing with life, not a dead concept. Being in the now does not mean forgetting all about yesterday, refusing to think about tomorrow, and suspending all of one's plans. One will still clearly remember yesterday, precisely because living fully in the moment means that the things that happened will have left a deep impression. At the same time, if one lives wholly in the here and now, yesterday's memories will not be a source of trouble, and one will not drag around the burden of the past as one goes through life.

If one is in the present, each moment of one's life is a source of fulfillment and enrichment. Using the analogy from chapter 3, one will feel like one is dancing in step with the beat. One's life will turn into a dance, timed harmoniously with the exquisite rhythms of being.

On the other hand, if one never manages to catch the rhythm, instead trying to catch up with the last beat or wondering how to get ready for the next one, one will constantly be out of step with the here and now. One will not live like a person who is dancing, but like a person who is jerking about on the dance floor, oblivious to the music of life.

■ ■ ■

Regardless of whether one is cultivating hsing (the nature of mind) or ming (the essence of life), living in the present is a crucial skill. This chapter's theme, the "coupled cultivation of hsing and ming," is an extremely important topic. Taoist internal alchemy is sometimes simply called "the study of hsing and ming." This term is used in some classic Taoist alchemy writings to encompass everything that this path of learning includes. In *Awakening to Reality*, Zhang Boduan wrote, "Lao-tzu and Shakyamuni opened an expedient door with the study of *hsing* and *ming*, teaching people to cultivate so that they can escape the cycle of transmigration." In the afterword for *The Oral Record of the Hall of Joyous Teaching*, Huang Yuanji declares that the book "is a full exposition of the study of hsing and ming that leaves nothing out." Hsing and ming are core matters in Taoist philosophy, and they are constantly discussed.

Naturally, the first question students always ask is, "What exactly are hsing and ming?" There are many things in Taoism that resist definition, because as soon as we try to define them, we limit them. Nevertheless, in a broad sense, hsing and ming are the two basic aspects of our being. Hsing pertains to the aspect of our lives that includes our will, awareness, and mind. Ming pertains to the physical aspect of our lives, including qi and the various constituents of our bodies. Ming starts as a general description of our gross physical bodies, but moves on to more subtle understandings of jing and eventually qi.

The relationship between hsing and ming is similar to what is implied in the phrase "mind and qi are not two," which arose in chapter 5. Hsing and ming are not exactly the same thing, so they can be discussed separately. But, at the same time, they are not two wholly separate or distinct things. In actual reality, these two aspects of our beings are inseparably linked to one another.

This simple phrase, "coupled cultivation of hsing and ming," covers a large swath of what Taoist cultivation is meant to achieve. In some early texts on internal alchemy, this expression was used in critiques of Buddhist cultivation; some early Taoists believed Buddhist practice only develops hsing, while ignoring ming. They also felt that qigong and other similar arts of inner development only addressed ming, without cultivating hsing. In other words, these ming-focused arts included numerous methods for training skills related to the body and qi, but because they did not teach people how to illuminate the mind to see its nature, they did not lead to liberation. Thus, the early inner alchemists determined that the Great Way lies in the paired cultivation of hsing and ming.

If one's practice only affects ming while leaving hsing untouched, one will experience all manner of sensations and reactions in the body, but one will not find one's "protagonist," and as a result the real goal of cultivation will remain elusive. People whose practice does not address hsing pour time into their bodies, and in return they create reactions in their qi meridians as well as certain physical changes. But because they do a poor job of cultivating their minds' natures, their thought patterns follow their base desires instead of becoming more refined. Because they have not developed their hsing, a great many qigong "masters" end up boasting of having supernormal abilities (which they may well have), advertising themselves, and seeking to profit from their abilities. Once they establish themselves in their roles as "masters," many of these practitioners end up exploiting others for influence, money, and sex. This is how they ultimately end up as cult leaders.

Just as it warns of the risks of cultivating ming without cultivating hsing, internal alchemy also teaches that if one only develops hsing without transforming one's body and qi, then one will end up with highly refined mental energy that has no physical basis. When a person cultivates in this way, because the body's qi has not been transmuted it can still influence the mind, and at the end of the practitioner's life his or her mind will go wherever qi takes it instead of reaching true liberation.

■ ■ ■

Texts from Taoist alchemy's nascent period treat the coupled cultivation of hsing and ming as the trademark that sets them apart from other traditions. However, as time went on later teachings became more nuanced, and instead of making the overgeneralized statement that nobody but Taoists cultivates both hsing and ming, they began to divide their discussions into more detailed analyses of various methods and levels of practice.

In his discourses, Huang Yuanji teaches that Confucianism, Buddhism, and Taoism are all authentic paths, and that they all cultivate both the mind's nature and life's essence in combination. Huang's stance may lead some to wonder whether or not Buddhist or Confucian teachings mention the phrase "coupled cultivation of hsing and ming." This term, and indeed this thread of discourse, is never explicitly brought to the fore in their classical writings. However, this does not mean that the type of cultivation they teach is at odds with the coupled cultivation of mind nature and life essence.

It is important to keep in mind that although hsing and ming can be discussed as two separate things, they can also be discussed from a higher standpoint—from the level of the original source—in which case they are indistinguishable and cannot be discussed as two distinct aspects of being. Within the body of the great Tao, hsing and ming are fully united.

Given that hsing, ming, and the relationship between them can be discussed at different levels, we cannot simplistically declare that Buddhists cultivate mind nature but do not cultivate life's essence. Thus, the "mind nature" that Chan Buddhists awaken to should be understood as that which exists at the level of the source of all things, and not at the level where mind nature and life essence can be viewed as two distinct concepts. If a Chan Buddhist illuminates his or her mind nature, or hsing, what he or she awakens to includes ming, and in fact can be said to represent the highest form of alchemy. In the same way, in Taoist alchemy, the highest methods do not focus on hsing and ming. Instead, they directly teach the refining of shen to return to emptiness. These teachings aim to bring one straight back to the Tao, where the nature of mind and the essence of life function as one.

Ming is not mentioned in Buddhist teachings on cultivating dhyana through seated meditation. However, in Buddhist cultivation of the "four dhyanas and the eight concentrations," body and mind merge as one, meaning that hsing and ming merge as one. In true samadhi, there is no distinction between hsing and ming. Moreover, when a Buddhist practitioner enters samadhi, transformations will occur in his or her physical body and the qi meridians, instead of solely at the level of mind.

■ ■ ■

With its declarations that "all things are only mind" or "all things are only consciousness," Buddhism may seem to only pay attention to mind and mind's essential nature, while glossing over the material realm as well as the physical body. However, the "consciousness" pointed to in Buddhism's teaching that "all things are only consciousness" is a comprehensive, total concept. Buddhism holds that the most fundamental, deepest-level of consciousness is called *alaya-vijnana*. Alaya-vijnana is akin to a vast storehouse containing an infinitude of seeds. Among these "seeds" are included our bodies and our qi, which Buddhism conceptualizes as being stored in the form of "seeds of consciousness." Because all things are stored in alaya-vijnana, to truly transform all of the deepest seeds stored at the basis of one's mind is to transform *everything*, mind and qi included.

Buddhism's mind-only teachings are not the same as the philosophical theory of "idealism." This is because in Buddhism the essential nature of mind can be described from a standpoint where mind and phenomena are "not two." At this level, the mind as well as all objects and phenomena are a single entity.

If we take the above into account, we can see that Buddhism discusses the same issues Taoism does, but it uses a different explanatory system and presents things in different contexts. If we allow ourselves to understand Buddhist cultivation in a penetrating, open-minded way, it becomes impossible to simplistically declare that Buddhists only cultivate hsing, but not ming. That is why later Taoist alchemists began to speak about the three teachings joined as one instead of standing in opposition to Chan Buddhism. In fact, not only did they shed their opposition to Chan, they actually absorbed it into their framework, positing that Chan equates to the highest level of inner alchemy practice.

The Southern School of internal alchemy, which is strongly associated with Zhang Boduan, teaches a set of methods for cultivating ming. These practices make it possible for a student to begin with ming and then arrive at hsing. In the end, a student on this path returns to the highest realm of Chan Buddhist teachings—"sudden enlightenment." Complete Reality Taoism, known as the Northern School in internal alchemy circles, was founded by Wang Chongyang. Hong Kong's Green Pine Temple belongs to this school. Hsing methods take primacy in the alchemical teachings of this tradition, to the degree that cultivating hsing precedes cultivating ming. Complete Reality Taoism's relationship to Chan Buddhism is even closer than the Southern School's.

■ ■ ■

It is important to keep in mind that Taoists eventually abandoned their oppositional stance vis-à-vis Buddhism, instead concluding that unity between the two schools is possible. Please do not make the mistake of thinking that Buddhism and Taoism are in constant conflict with one another. In fact, when conflict does arise, it usually stems from quite specific misunderstandings.

Most Buddhists do not know an awful lot about Taoism. Some of them, on the basis of preconceived ideas and dogmas that can be found in Buddhism, are prone to casting aspersions: "You Taoists are busy 'refining' your qi all day long, just trying to attain eternal life. You do all sorts of things with your bodies, but you don't illuminate your minds and glimpse your original nature. You don't transform your afflictive karmic impressions, so you will die, unable to preserve your physical bodies. All that cultivating you do is meaningless. You've wasted a lifetime, living blindly and training ignorantly."

There are also plenty of people in Taoism who do not know much about Buddhism. They often make the following criticism: "You Buddhists who sit and meditate all day long just produce a yin spirit. A yin spirit doesn't have any energy or any real wisdom. It's a vacuous, illusory thing. That's what you get when you just cultivate hsing and don't cultivate ming."

However, there have been highly accomplished Taoists and Buddhists who have taken the time to deeply understand and experience each other's paths, which has led them to discover that there is no irreconcilable difference that separates them. Rather, the two ways are compatible. Of course, the word "compatible" does not mean "the same." Compatibility means that both paths can lead to the same place, and that they do not contradict each other. But that definitely does not mean that Buddhism and Taoism are exactly the same thing. They still have their own unique traits that distinguish them as separate schools.

This situation is a bit like meeting in the same room after entering through two different doorways, or arriving at the same mountain peak via different paths. The person who hiked up the northern route would have seen different scenery from the person who hiked up the southern route, especially while still close to the foot of the mountain, where the paths would have provided totally unique views. However, after trekking up these two entirely distinct routes, the two hikers would arrive at the same exact peak and look at one another with broad smiles on their faces.

The differences between Taoism and Buddhism tend to be found in their *you wei* methods, because you wei practices have determinate formats and specific ways of proceeding. One school's set of practices may be quite unlike another's. On the other hand, Taoist and Buddhist wu wei practices are compatible, to the degree that it is fair to say that all genuine wu wei practice is the same. This is because wu wei methods are methodless methods. They are empty. They contain nothing that is created, nothing that is held on to, and nothing that is distinguished. Given that this is the case, what sameness or difference is there to speak of? When two practitioners who are both at the stage of wu wei practice meet, there are no differences between what they do, so they do not get caught up in distinction-making. However, early on in their cultivation paths, the you wei practices they started with may have been very different.

Thus, Taoism and Buddhism are compatible because they both lead into the practice of wu wei, and they both lead into what Taoists call "the Tao." There is no differentiation within the Tao, but dissimilarities do arise in the interpretation and expression of what the word "Tao" implies, as well as in the pathways and methods that lead in its direction. This means that there are indeed areas of similarity and difference in various schools' ways of cultivating hsing and ming that call for discussion.

■ ■ ■

Within Taoist inner alchemy, or "the study of hsing and ming," there are important questions regarding hsing and ming's interrelationship and the order in which these two things are cultivated that require discussion.

It is generally said that, in the Southern School that was influenced by Zhang Boduan, ming is cultivated before hsing. In the Northern School that Wang Chongyang established, hsing cultivation comes before ming cultivation. The above is the traditional explanation. However, we need to be keenly aware that there are no contradictions between these two ways, and that they are not opposites. Even within the contexts of Northern and Southern disciplines for training hsing and ming, when these two things are spoken about, the implications will differ depending on what level of training is being discussed.

If we envision existence as an endless chain, then every link on the chain represents a distinct phase of hsing and ming. This is like the relationship between accumulating knowledge and taking action. Do we first gather knowledge and then take action, or do take action first and then learn from it? Well, with some links on this chain, knowledge comes before action, while on other links action precedes knowledge. Sometimes we have an experience first, derive knowledge from this experience, and then arrive at a theoretical understanding. Other times we begin with theory, before going into practice and obtaining firsthand experience of what the theory describes. This is a dialectical process in which progress unfolds cyclically.

The question of in what order hsing and ming should be cultivated can be addressed from more than one perspective. In terms of relative import, hsing is more important. If we compare hsing and ming to one another, hsing, which refers to our original nature, is clearly more fundamental. Hsing is our dynamism and self-awareness. Whatever Taoist methods we may practice, we rely upon our mind—our hsing—to practice them. One cannot rely upon one's body to cultivate. After all, there are few tasks that the body can accomplish all by itself. Thus, even when we cultivate ming, the basis of our work lies with the mind's nature. We first rectify our minds, and then we use our minds to restore ming. Observing our breathing, regulating our physical states, or adjusting our postures are all accomplished due to the mind's initiative. Ming, which is associated with the body, listens to directives that come from hsing. Hsing is the leading factor, and so it is unquestionably of greater importance.

That said, we can also consider this issue from the standpoint of urgency, asking the question, "which must be more urgently cultivated, hsing or ming?" The answer to this question is that the cultivation of ming is almost always the more pressing task. This is because the word "hsing" refers to prior-heaven original nature, which, because it is without form or aspect, is therefore ungraspable, and very difficult to begin cultivating with. Regardless of how important hsing may be, if a student does not know how to find its proverbial entry point, the question inevitably arises, exactly how could one begin to cultivate? The answer is that one usually begins with ming. This is because one of ming's roles is to serve as the vehicle or medium that carries hsing. Hsing makes its home in ming.

In a certain sense, our bodies are not especially important. After all, bodies have their limits, and we all eventually die. There is no way to make a physical body last forever, so what is truly important is to locate our prior-heaven hsing and ming, which I sometimes refer to as our true "protagonist." However, one cannot make the above statement without acknowledging the fact that the body is still extremely important. This is because all of our mental activity—up to and including the cultivation of our minds' nature—is inextricably tethered to the point of support that is the body. Our bodies are our foundations.

This point can be illustrated by thinking about what it is like to suffer through a grievous illness. When one is deathly ill, and one's jing and qi are depleted to the point that one is sapped of strength, it becomes impossible to apply oneself to the work of spiritual cultivation. Similarly, when one's body and one's qi are in a highly chaotic state, one's mind is simply incapable of becoming quiet and tranquil.

It is thus imperative that we maintain, regulate, and look after our bodies, in order to achieve a state of relative harmony and abundant energy. That state is the platform atop which our cultivation takes place. Taoists like to say that the alchemical "furnace" we use to refine our "elixir" has to be in good shape. There is no way for an alchemist to refine base metals using a furnace that is on the verge of falling apart. So, not only should we take good care of our bodies as a matter of general principle, we need to pay special attention to them if we embark upon the cultivation path.

Again, the relationship between our bodies and minds is deeply intimate. There is no real separation between our minds and our qi; they are interconnected. Very often, cultivation begins with the physical body—through ming practices. But beginning with hsing and beginning with ming are both viable approaches. Moreover, on each of these paths there are multiple stages at which the practitioner moves from hsing toward ming, or from ming to hsing.

■ ■ ■

To paint a picture in very broad strokes, the process of coupled cultivation of hsing and ming includes the following stages:

First, there is "using hsing to establish ming," which is an approach in which hsing is cultivated prior to ming. This stage involves experiencing and recognizing one's fundamental nature. Nurturing and cultivating the mind's nature is necessary, because only when one has identified one's true "protagonist" is one able to establish life. Ming on its own cannot cultivate itself; the cultivation of hsing and ming both depend on the mind, so one must begin by working on the cultivation of mind nature. A clear, tranquil mind in a state of wu wei is the foundation that allows the body to move toward health and balance. Thus, "hsing is used to establish ming."

Next, there is "using ming to complete hsing." Hsing and ming act upon and influence one another. Original nature, hsing, can only manifest itself when the body and qi are so regulated that they enter into an optimal, harmonious state. In this condition, hsing and qi merge, which lends energy and power to hsing. As both mind nature and qi are purified, they merge, returning to the Tao.

In the final stage, hsing and ming become one. Indistinguishable, completely harmonized, and united, they return to their root source, which is the body of the Tao. The coupled cultivation of hsing and ming is a totalizing process. One can speak about first cultivating ming and then hsing, or vice versa, but in the end the two join into oneness.

■ ■ ■

Approaches where hsing comes before ming emphasize illuminating the mind in order to glimpse essential nature. However, that is because having an experience of original nature, or hsing, is the ideal foundation for engaging in the cultivation of life essence, or ming. This idea finds a similar expression in Chan Buddhism, where there is the saying, "If you have not seen your original nature, then it is pointless to cultivate the Dharma." What this means is that, if you have not witnessed the nature of your mind, and you do not clearly understand what it is, then even though you may be devotedly training for hours every day, you are proceeding blindly.

Such blindness can be seen in qigong practitioners who do not apply themselves to cultivating mind nature. Wisdom and essential nature remain utterly out of reach to them, even though they work with their qi day after day. They run endless circuits of qi through the microcosmic orbit, first achieving one kind of sensation, then another. But it is these very qi meridian sensations that take them further away from understanding their minds. Their lives lack a center point, and they do not awaken.

It is a tenet of Taoist cultivation that hsing and ming must be developed together. Neither can be pursued at the expense of the other, as neglecting either hsing or ming will lead to maladies. If one only applies oneself to ming practices, even if one develops substantial supernormal abilities, one will still lack wisdom, and one's cultivation path will be a precarious one. Supernormal abilities are, in the final analysis, fairly mundane. Modern technology has already given us many things that far surpass the special abilities a practitioner can develop.

I once heard a rumor about a person who trained for three decades in order to develop the ability to breathe flames out of his mouth. When he finally pulled it off he was beside himself with glee, "At last, I did it! A real achievement! I can spit fire out of my mouth!" After some time, he bumped into an accomplished monk and shared an account of his efforts, saying, "I had to train bitterly for thirty whole years, but in the end I finally mastered a real skill." The monk asked him to demonstrate the fruits of his efforts, and the fellow exhaled a plume of flame. Unimpressed, the monk said, "Hopeless. You wasted three whole decades for something totally meaningless." He then produced a lighter and created a flame with a flick of his thumb. "I've got fire, too. Is there any difference between the fire you've got, and this one? I suppose you can use your fire to cook rice. What else is it good for?"

Some people spend their days trying to bring forth supernormal abilities without really knowing what the purpose of Taoist cultivation is. Taoism holds that it is silly to pursue this kind of training, because special abilities have no real value. To Taoists, real value lies in the wisdom that comes from cultivating and nurturing the mind's nature, and which will elevate one's state of being. Wisdom leads our lives back to their true homes.

In spite of the above statement, it is still problematic to solely cultivate hsing. Those who exclusively cultivate mind nature are ignorant of the mysteries of the body, meaning that they are unaware of the principle that mind and qi are indivisible. Even if one practices devotedly in this manner, one's results will not be proportional to one's efforts, because the burdens of the body will drag against progress, limiting how far one can go. Ultimately, the highest realms of cultivation of mind nature will not truly reveal themselves. For people who practice like this, illuminating the mind and glimpsing its nature will be chimerical and unfounded.

■ ■ ■

The above is an exploration of the themes of Huang Yuanji's discourse at the beginning of this chapter. The rest of this chapter discusses specific aspects of Huang's teaching, but instead of unpacking his discourse word by word, I will focus on a few statements of particular importance.

We have already touched upon the meaning of Huang Yuanji's first sentence. When he says that sages from the three teachings—Taoism, Buddhism, and Confucianism—all cultivate hsing as well as ming, he is speaking in terms of the essence of what they practice, even though Buddhist and Confucian sages do not, on the surface, speak about hsing and ming.

Huang's next lines are, "One starts by using hsing to establish ming. Afterward, one uses ming to fully realize hsing. Finally, hsing and ming merge as one, in order to return to the essence of empty nothingness, which is completion." With those statements he summarizes the tenets of dually cultivating original nature and the essence of life. In the beginning, the two factors are discussed separately, so hsing is used to establish ming, and ming is used to complete hsing. But later, the two merge into union and become indistinguishable. Their unity takes hsing and ming into empty nonexistence, where the Tao is cultivated through wu wei methods, or "non-doing."

■ ■ ■

Hsing is empty and nonexistent. It is in communion with the Tao; it originates in the Tao. It is the embodiment of the Tao's prior-heaven nature within our own beings. I say hsing is empty and nonexistent because, within it, there is nothing defined or subjective. However, the sense in which I say "empty and nonexistent" is not meant to negate anything or to sound nihilistic. Rather, this empty nonexistence brims with life force. This emptiness is totally full, and within it is something of "ultimate substantiality," meaning a functional energy that is completely real. Thus, hsing is both ultimate nonexistence and ultimate existence—it is what Buddhists call "that which is truly void and yet contains subtle, profound being." It is not an insensate oblivion.

In Taoist cultivation, one must not go in the direction of insensate oblivion. The goal is not to negate all things and end up in a nihilistic state where one has nothing, knows nothing, and thinks about nothing. In fact, if a cultivator really and truly becomes empty and nonexistent, then he or she will access the unlimited well of "incomprehensible existence," in which lies real energy and real experience.

In sum, hsing is empty and nonexistent. It cannot be grabbed on to, because it is not a thing. And yet, it is that which is empty even of emptiness.

■ ■ ■

How do people who have just begun to study the Tao obtain an experience of their prior-heaven nature? The answer lies in cultivating the mind. One must start with mental tranquility. Typically, our minds are far too polluted with the swirling dusts of the world. The things we worry about and ruminate over from morning till night are excessive, and they cause our minds to scatter. Therefore, we require practices that lead us back to quietude, tranquility, and emptiness. As we discussed in previous chapters, we cannot fight our way back to such a state. Instead, we need to employ expedient methods that help us get there.

Huang Yuanji states that when we are truly tranquil, our essential natures reveal themselves like "a numinous light shining upon entire vast world systems." One should be careful not to take this description overly literally, as though Huang was describing things in the phenomenal world. What this statement means is that the light of original nature shines upon everything without there being any limits or distinctions. Yet, while the experience of tranquility can be likened to blazing light, it is also an empty, silent state that is devoid of thoughts and concerns. Furthermore, while tranquility is often compared to emptiness, at the same time it is a state of fullness that merges with the qi of empty nonexistence. Buddhists call this state "supreme bodhi" and "tathata," while Taoists call it "numinous knowing" and "real knowing."

"Numinous knowing" and "real knowing" describe fundamental nature—hsing—from two different angles. Fundamental nature is empty and yet imbued with life; emptiness and life are its substance and its function. When fundamental nature is not actively functioning, it is in a quiescent state, and it is called "real knowing." But when fundamental nature is actively functioning, it is called "numinous knowing," because in action it reveals its spiritual luminosity and its penetrating, continuous awareness. "Numinous knowing" is the state in which fundamental nature can respond to anything that arises. Of course, while these terms tell us more or less what the word "hsing" means, solely relying upon descriptions will not lead us into these states, so it is necessary to slowly gain direct experience through practice.

Huang Yuanji's discourse begins with an explanation of what prior-heaven hsing is. However, as soon as humans are born into later-heaven existence, our truly spiritual prior-heaven aspects—"numinous knowing" and "real knowing"—begin to be occluded by the dust and grime of the world and its ways. This is like a precious mirror being covered in layer upon layer of dust, until its brightness is so totally obscured that no evidence of it remains. It's also like thick layers of clouds blocking the sunshine, until not a single ray of sunlight can be seen. Thus, we must begin by restoring clarity to our minds before we can directly experience prior-heaven hsing. Cultivation begins with the challenge of getting the spiritual brightness of our minds' fundamental natures to shine forth from amid the tens of thousands of thoughts and worries that constantly fill us.

At a certain stage in our cultivation careers, it is necessary to make provisions to spend periods of time practicing in quietude, away from the "dusty world." This is because we tend to get yanked in all directions by our concerns and commitments in the world, and it is difficult to quickly return to clarity while this is happening. Only later, when we have already reached quite a high level of development, can we practice in the midst of everyday life. When we are at such a stage, our minds function so marvelously that nothing that occurs in the world will steal our presence of mind. One can then be "in the world, but not of the world."

To borrow Buddhist terminology to describe this transition, it is like going from "Hinayana" to "Mahayana," or from the "lesser vehicle" to the "greater vehicle." To practice in the "lesser vehicle" manner, one must cut off external affairs and train in serene seclusion to be able to realize oneself. But then, once one has self-realization, one begins to offer service and returns to the world. This is the stage of "greater vehicle" practice. One who is ready for it lives in the world like a lotus that thrives in the mud without ever being stained.

■ ■ ■

In the beginning, a practitioner has to learn how to enter into stillness—how to enter into a mental state that can be described as empty and nonexistent. Above, we have seen descriptions of this state, and now we are using the word "enter" to speak about achieving this state, but how does one actually *enter* it? We have to deftly apply the reasoning we discussed earlier in order to resolve this question. One cannot force one's way into stillness. Instead, one needs to rely upon wisdom as well as an appropriate method in order to make one's way forward. As a beginner, when one is unable to become tranquil, it is necessary to regulate the mind as though tuning the strings on an instrument. Eventually, after a long period of searching, one will finally find the knack for quieting the mind, and suddenly understand what it takes to get one's own mind to peaceably return to the here and now. One will return to the present, and no longer be beset by excessive and chaotic mental activity.

When one finally reaches quietude and profound emptiness, one will see that one's true nature has always and everywhere been present. This is because one's true nature is something one has possessed all along. It is the most fundamental and real aspect of each person's existence. In the later-heaven world, the gaze of one's awareness is constantly chasing things outside of oneself, and because of this one may never have turned awareness inward in order to observe, recognize, and realize self-nature.

We most definitely cannot create basic nature—hsing—nor can we ever lose it. It is not there only when one is sitting serenely in meditation. Nevertheless, occupying a state of tranquility can, in a sense, both nourish and protect original nature. This is so because fundamental nature can only reveal itself when one is already tranquil, meaning this is the only time one has the opportunity to experience and observe what has been there all along. This is also so because it is only when one is tranquil that one is directly connected to the Tao, as well as the heavens, the earth, and all the myriad things. This connection provides a sort of energetic support that must be present to strengthen original nature. When one is truly tranquil, the numinous light of hsing flashes, "much as ice and snow melt without the knowledge or sensation that they are melting." Still, we might fail to recognize this when it happens, thereby missing out on a glimpse of reality.

When Huang Yuanji says, "much as ice and snow melt without the knowledge or sensation that they are melting," the lack of knowledge or sensation he alludes to is not something negative. What he means is that, when one is truly tranquil, even thoughts like "wow, I'm so serene" do not arise. One who is truly serene does not distinguish his or her serenity. There is no knowledge added on top of tranquility. Thoughts are absent, and all things are limpid and quiescent. This state is like a cloudless midday sky: vast, endless, clear, and brilliant. In it, one merges with the Tao's prior-heaven, empty, nonexistent qi. One experiences existence without bounds.

While merged as one with the Tao, it is as though heaven, earth, and all things fall within one's embrace, along with endless eons of time. Within the Tao, neither time nor space appear, and because of this, all of eternity as well as endless, unlimited space fall within it. The sense of space that one experiences when still is expressed by Buddhist as "all lands and all seas being no further away from oneself than the breadth of the tip of a rabbit's hair." Buddhists refer to the sense of time one experiences in stillness as "the ten times, from the past to the present, from start to finish, being nowhere other than the thought currently in mind." The Tao is beginningless, endless, borderless, and limitless. It transcends space and time. To enter into this state is to have one's original nature—one's hsing—become apparent. It is also to "get" the Tao.

■ ■ ■

Huang Yuanji once again borrows a phrase from Mencius to illustrate his point. Some of us might find this strange and wonder, "aren't Confucians just concerned with cultivating ethics and morals?" However, it was Mencius who first mentioned the nurturing of "vast qi," which is analogous to Taoism's empty, nonexistent qi. When a person's moral development reaches a very high level, he or she connects to the heavens and the earth, thereby obtaining access to an extraordinarily abundant form of energy. A person who reaches this state of moral cultivation will also glimpse his or her true nature—hsing.

When Huang Yuanji describes what it is like to "nurture vast qi," he also warns about two deviations one must be cautious of when in this state. The first is "falling into trance states," which he describes in a negative sense by using a word that means "distant and dim." This term can imply sinking into an insensate state and getting mired in oblivion, but it can also imply a state where confusion and bizarre occurrences come to the fore. If we deviate into what Huang Yuanji refers to as "distance and dimness," we turn the noble pursuit of transcendence and sage-hood into a chase for the novelty or strangeness of altered mental states.

The second deviation is "latching onto some object or phenomenon, which causes this sacred teaching to trickle away into confusion." This statement not only describes a risk that can arise in meditation but also the overall human condition. It refers to a person letting his or her consciousness go running away after this or that external stimulus, instead of letting consciousness return to its source.

There is nothing bizarre or peculiar about the Tao. It is utterly normal. Thus, if one does not fall into either of the above two deviations, one's essence and one's actions will unite harmoniously. Should one recognize one's original nature and then harmonize with it, then even when one is busy with the tasks and interpersonal interactions of daily life one's original nature will still continue to function spontaneously. Rather than present an obstacle to daily living, it will function marvelously within the milieu of one's everyday life. A person who has truly awakened to his or her essential nature applies it in the midst of living life.

Huang Yuanji goes on to say, "Though there may be nothing that is not known, and nothing that cannot be done, you will not actually be aware of knowing, nor will you have a sense of capability. Existence, and all the things in it, will all transform in unison." Here, "not being aware of knowing" and "not having any sense" are used in a positive sense. What Huang means is that when one's hsing is active, one will not think "my oh my, now I've got some special new form of 'knowing' and some new abilities." One's hsing will simply dissolve into unity with the sky above, the earth below, and all between.

Of course, self-awareness is a good thing, so why does Huang Yuanji talk about "not being aware of knowing?" Here it is important to keep in mind that the same word or phrase can be used in a number of different ways, so we need to avoid reflexively interpreting a term the same way each time we see it. Everything that is included in Taoist cultivation revolves around "awareness," meaning that if one is not self-aware, then one's cultivation has gone awry. Thus, when Huang says one is "not aware of knowing," all he means is that when one enters into a state of real tranquility, one's mind does not stir and give birth to new thoughts like, "ooh, now I'm tranquil!"

In a positive sense, the term "self-awareness" means being subtly but lucidly conscious of whatever happens to and within one's own body. There is no confusion in this state. The mind of one who is self-aware does not get distracted and drift off after thoughts about what is occurring, nor does a self-aware person's mind sink into torpor. When Taoism uses the word "awareness" in a positive sense, it refers to one's intrinsically awake nature. This awareness is unmarked by the tendency of the later-heaven mind to make distinctions. It exists at the prior-heaven level.

The ideal state when we sit to meditate is one of "not-knowing," where the later-heaven, distinction-making mind is at rest. But "not-knowing" is nothing like a stupor or fugue. It is not like being a piece of stone. Within not-knowing there is awareness that knows, in a subtle, lucid manner. This awareness remains crystal clear even if one's mind begins to generate thoughts, and even when things are happening in the environment around oneself. With the clarity of this awareness, one knows that thoughts are arising or the environment is changing, but one does not make distinctions.

One's mind will become expansive and open precisely because one is not focused on any particular object. When this expansion occurs, one can hear whatever sounds are made and see whatever objects pass by, without drifting toward or differentiating any of them. On the other hand, if one focuses on a specific sound—for instance, thinking, "ah, that was the sound of a car passing by just now"—one's mind will chase after that sound and fail to register the next one. Once this starts to happen, the mind becomes subject to limitations, as though it were tuned into a specific channel.

Always remember that the "not knowing" extolled by Taoists refers to a state in which the later-heaven, distinction-based awareness that pursues objects external to itself has receded. However, recall that Taoists also instruct students to "be knowing and aware." When they say this, they are referring to allowing prior heaven fundamental nature to perform its duty, which is to be subtly yet radiantly conscious. In the ideal meditative state, there is no distress, no chaos, and no discursive thinking. This is nothing like spacing out or falling asleep. In meditation, one's mind is perfectly clear, but it does not make distinctions. Everybody who wishes to cultivate the Tao needs to personally experience this state.

■ ■ ■

If one truly understands how to access the state in which original nature is manifest, one can then move from cultivating hsing to cultivating ming. This transition—which Taoists call "using hsing to establish ming"—becomes possible because access to true tranquility opens the door to refining primordial jing. If the later-heaven distinction-making mind is used to refine jing, one will end up working with later-heaven turbid jing, and not primordial jing. It is only by engaging one's prior-heaven mind that one becomes able to refine primordial jing. The next chapter is devoted to exploring what it means to refine jing into qi and explaining the nature of primordial jing, qi, and shen, so I won't discuss them in detail here. But in short, when one has entered the clear, unblemished prior-heaven state, the qi one works with is primordial qi, and the shen one works with is primordial shen. When one is capable of cultivating the primordial, the achievement of both longevity as well as transcendence becomes possible.

Huang Yuanji's next sentence describes subtle, radiant consciousness as "the great freedom of absolute wisdom, complete and eternally enlightening." These terms imply that, when one reveals one's nature by illuminating the mind, the experience is nothing like deep sleep or an insensate stupor. It is a state of conscious knowing, where hsing is like a lamp with an eternal flame. Though it may be described as "knowing," this type of consciousness is different from distinction-making mental activity that chases after external objects. Huang borrows an ancient phrase—"do a somersault atop the point of a needle and come to a stop in a flash of lightning"—to explain that accomplishing the complete and eternally enlightening state requires extraordinarily advanced and delicate skill.

"A somersault on the point of needle" is a metaphor for abilities so difficult for the typical human being to achieve that they effectively seem supernatural. In Huang Yuanji's eyes, this is the level of skill a person needs to develop in order to successfully cultivate the Tao. Such skill is as hard to develop as the level of athleticism required for a person to be able to go from running at full speed to standing stock still the moment lightning flashes. When one's skill in cultivation reaches such a high level of freedom and fluency, one touches the substantial within emptiness, and nonexistence gives birth to existence. Emptiness and substantiality merge as one, as do existence and nonexistence. These are the ideal conditions for cultivating hsing and ming together. Achieving them means no longer dabbling in the vague, wishy-washy, close-but-no-cigar states achieved by those who follow side-door teachings and deviant paths.

■ ■ ■

One might ask, in Taoism, what state must a person arrive at when cultivating hsing and ming in order to count as truly established in the practice? Huang Yuanji provides a signpost in the following paragraph.

In terms of training in hsing, one must reach the stage where one's mind "neither comes into being nor is extinguished." When one is there, one's fundamental nature is constantly present. It is stable and capable of continuity. Specifically, having a mind that "neither comes into being nor is extinguished" means that one's mind no longer tends to stir into thought, and if and when it does, it does so as a reflection of the subtle functioning of one's original nature. Having "a mind that neither comes into being nor is extinguished" means one's mind no longer has the later-heaven tendencies to constantly differentiate, to swing between awakeness and torpor, or to be distracted by hindrances and attachments.

From a certain standpoint, it can be said that our minds have never "come into being or been extinguished." This statement is based upon the observation that as soon as thoughts arise, they immediately disappear of their own accord. It can also be said that the mind does not really exist, because it is impossible to actually locate whatever it is that we conventionally call "mind." These observations allow for the argument to be made that the rising and falling of mental activity does not, in fact, hinder a person's innate awareness in any way. This line of logic is reflected in comments I made earlier in this chapter, when I said that thoughts and the even the mind itself are empty, even as their activity comes and goes. However, there is a difference between accepting these ideas on an intellectual or philosophical level and actually experiencing the reality that they point toward. To actually realize the unhindered nature of mind, which neither comes into being nor is extinguished, one must be so unattached to later-heaven thinking that when thoughts arise, it is just as though there were no thoughts at all. When one directly experiences the mind in this way, one's original nature is a constant presence, as though it were a lamp constantly radiating light. When one reaches such a plane, all things are the same, and one's hsing training has been successful.

In terms of training in ming, the point at which one counts as established in practice is alluded to by Huang Yuanji when he mentions "a breath that neither enters nor exits." The idea of a breath that does not go in and out of the body naturally gives rise to a lot of questions. Suffice it to say, if a person's breathing truly stops entering and exiting the body, he or she cannot go on living. Breathing is always necessary, and air is one of the most important "foods" required by our bodies. Thus, "a breath that neither enters nor exits" does not refer to an absolute absence of breathing. Rather, it refers to how, in a state of deep tranquility, one will breathe in an unusual manner that is not characterized by the shallow in-and-out movements of later-heaven breathing.

At this stage, one's breathing will become so subtle that one will not feel the entry and exit of one's breath. One may enter a state called "fetal breathing," wherein the breath is so soft, slow, and deep that it affects every cell in the body. One's mind and one's breathing will merge as one, which means that hsing and ming merge as one. One's ming, or life essence, will be established, unlocking tremendous power to transform and regulate the body. One can, via fetal breathing, enter into samadhi, an enhanced life state that substantially alters one's physical body and one's qi pathways.

■ ■ ■

The final section of Huang Yuanji's teaching in this chapter contains the warning that many cultivators go astray because they fail to grasp that "clear purity is our basis, and authenticity is our ancestor." Others go astray because they "solely apply themselves to emptiness and tranquility, not understanding that that which must be studied and that which comes through epiphany are one, for as above, so below"—this means that they fail to learn how to blend the empty, tranquil state into everyday life. Still others fail to make progress because they "engage only in striving, not understanding that the de of the universe and the ways of fixing the world are one and the same." Such people spend their days in a whirl of busyness, devoted to things that lie beyond themselves, ignorant of the fact that de—which is a facet of one's true, divine nature—has to be embodied in the way one lives in the world.

Some people understand the teachings on hsing, but they have no knowledge of the teachings on ming and qi. The teaching they have missed out on is that hsing is simply qi's original form, while qi is nothing other than hsing in action. Hsing and qi are correlative. If one's hsing was not present to act as the leading factor, one's ming would never have the chance to come into being. And yet, if one's ming was not there to serve as an undergirding support, one's hsing would have nowhere to establish itself. Hsing deprived of a place to settle is isolated and skewed to one extreme.

Huang Yuanji speaks of people who "vainly proclaim that one who perfects the mind's nature can establish life's essence." These are people who are solely interested in the teachings on hsing, or mind nature. Huang counters that without establishing life essence through the transformative effects of ming practices, it is extremely difficult for anybody to perfect the mind's nature. This is because people are invariably influenced by qi. As soon as qi moves, people's mind natures move with it. If one's hsing has not merged into oneness with ming's transformations, there will come a time when the fruits of one's efforts at perfecting mind nature will prove unreliable. Sooner or later, one will find oneself incapable of exercising the self-mastery required to remain detached from one's emotions, and one will instead be swept along by one's temperament. Finally, at the end of life, as one's qi dissipates, one's spirit will scatter with it, and one will be unable to leap free from the cycle of birth and death. Thus, although cultivating hsing is very important, refining ming is also a very pressing matter. These two factors always correspond to one another.

Those who only attach importance to refining ming tend to train with all their might, spending the whole day with their eyes closed in meditation. But with this sort of practice, hsing and ming (or, put in other terms, shen and qi or yin and yang) cannot join together. Even though those who only train in ming may develop extraordinary powers, since they lack shen's guidance, their shen and qi will not return together to oneness. If shen does not enter qi, qi will not return to shen. If yin and yang—here meaning shen and qi—do not merge, then a person's cultivation has missed the point. Thus, even if extraordinary powers arise due to a person's ming training, his or her state will ultimately be undependable.

It behooves students of Taoist alchemical practice to obtain a deep understanding of what it means for there to be communion between hsing and ming. The two must be cultivated in tandem. A practitioner must establish ming from within hsing, and then use ming to perfect hsing. At last, the two must be cultivated as one unto the arrival at the original source, which is the realm of being merged into the reality of the Tao itself.

7

元精元神

PRIMORDIAL JING AND
PRIMORDIAL SHEN

Jing refers not to the fluids of sexual communion, but rather to prior-heaven primordial jing. What is that which we call primordial jing? This jing comes from the beginning, when one's life is conceived. It is the qi of yin and the qi of yang, concentrated into a single coalescence, akin to a dewdrop or a pearl, stored in the heart as yin jing. It is the heavenly one that births water.[7] When it has not stirred reactively, it is just a single qi. When it is affected by stimuli, then in the liver it transforms into tears, in the spleen it transforms into saliva, in the lungs it transforms into mucus, in the heart it transforms into the pulse, and in the kidneys it transforms into sexual fluids. In the cold it becomes a runny nose, in the heat it becomes sweat; when delicious fragrances are smelled it causes the mouth to water, and when flavors are tasted saliva flows. Hence the phrase, "mucus, spittle, sexual fluids, saliva, blood, sweat, and tears—these seven efficacious materials are all yin."

Only when not even a single thought arises as you single-mindedly observe within will the seven orifices all be sealed and primordial jing have nowhere to leak. After continuously concentrating and refining for a long time, one day jing will be born. It will be like waking after a deep sleep into the warmth of spring weather, as a hot coalescence of gentle qi emerges from within the corporeal kidneys. At this time, you must hastily use true intent to gather it back to the earth cauldron[8] that is the dantian, to forge and refine it, to warm and nourish it. Thereupon, primordial jing will constantly be present, and primordial qi will be able to be produced.

However, the medicinal herb can be withered or tender, the fire can be scholarly or martial, and movements can rise or fall. Returning to the stove, warming, and nourishing—all of these things have their methods and degrees, so students must humbly entreat teachers to clearly point out the true mechanism. Otherwise, if there is any ignorance, this will lead to deluded gathering and rash refining, from which few can avoid harm. The dangers herein must not be overlooked.

Thus, in the refining of jing, one must concentrate shen in the center. Externally, one must harmonize the breath, until jing and shen collect and coalesce, and the breath is regulated and peaceful. Then jing will spontaneously arise, and qi will spontaneously transform.

So-called qi is formed of the forging and smelting of primordial jing. But it is concealed within the corporeal kidneys, vague and indistinct, concentrated in one place, becoming qi when in stillness, becoming jing when in movement. If qi remains, then an individual lives; if qi is exhausted, then an individual dies. Qi's role is no trivial matter. Qi's depletion or abundance are the causes of a person's age or youthfulness, as well as strength or weakness. Success or failure in one's work, accomplishment or lack thereof in one's deeds—seldom are these things not dependent on qi.

When it is still, it has neither form nor aspect. There is only the sense of a warm, gentle coalescence whose vapors warm the limbs and flow throughout the entire body. When response to stimuli causes movement, it becomes the virtue of filial or fraternal or sororal devotion, and it connects to the divine; or it becomes actions that are loyal and just, and it plays its part in heaven and earth. Vast and abundant, enormous and adamantine, it has magnanimity that encompasses the universe.

Mencius said, "Accumulate righteous deeds to give rise to qi. Accumulate qi to accomplish valor, which can penetrate metal and stones, and even influence animals." These are the effects of correct qi. Will is qi's commander; qi allows righteous deeds to be accomplished. Without this qi, one becomes timid and listless. In this world, one can possess ordinary gold and jade by buying them. Yet this qi—which accompanies life and death and is common to both original nature (hsing) and life essence (ming)—cannot reach abundance except through the accumulation of profound merit.

Students must know that, before qi has stirred, one must remain tranquil in order to nurture qi. When, by chance, qi reveals itself, one must become active to refine it. An ancient said: "Suddenly at midnight there is the sound of thunder; tens of thousands of windows and doors fly open one after another." This is the sign of the first yang's return. When golden light is seen by the eyes and sweet dew fills the mouth, this is evidence of the appearance of the greater medicinal herb.

Make haste to gather the medicinal herb and have it traverse the passes. Consume it, warmly nurture it. At this time, completely contract the genitals, firmly shut the gate of yang, cut off the external breath, and use the internal shen breath. Do not allow even a drop of leakage; you must have each and every breath completely return to the real, and at each moment your shen must entirely follow these commands. Have this qi enter into the midst of shen, and have shen envelop qi's exterior. In time, the coming and going of the breath will suddenly cease. You will merely feel that there is a spark of numinous light existing vaguely atop the spiritual platform, as primordial qi will already have transformed into primordial shen.

From this point, let qi merge with oblivion and let shen concentrate in emptiness—as though existing and yet not, neither inside nor outside—in order to refine the ultimately empty and numinous shen.

Then do the work of rising, moving shen to the upper dantian. Using the wu wei fire of shen, do the seven-days' refining work of traversing the passes and consuming. Then the skill of the jade fluid will be complete. Henceforth, one will feel neither hunger nor cold, and the four seasons will all be as though springtime; there will be another heaven and earth over which one presides, and one will possess the real self.

Continue training with the step of refining shen to return to emptiness. Replace the zither and the sword, reset the stove and the cauldron. When shen appears, numinous light will shine in all directions. When gathering shen, blend it entirely into primordial qi. If shen should at any time become active, hastily attend to it and take it back to the central palace. It must be made to stay there firmly and continuously, yet with thusness and freedom, until immature yang becomes mature yang.

Then, should stimuli prompt one into action, as soon as a thought arises, one will be able to sit bestride a crane and climb the clouds, ascend to the heavens or enter the earth, and perform any deed to eliminate evil, restore order, save people, or benefit the world. Moreover, one will be able to transform into any number of embodiments, appearing anywhere to offer salvation. Yet one will not find harm in so doing, for one will be silent, tranquil, and traceless. Nor will one find any benefits, for one will remain composed within that which has not even sound or scent.

Indeed, such activity of shen occurs in response to things; it is not that shen will become active of its own accord for no cause. When shen is quiescent, it will be because there was nothing to respond to, and therefore it subsided. It will also not be that shen detests action and therefore became eternally tranquil. Shen's sensations and its responses arise entirely due to things, not due to itself. What is called "eternally responsive and eternally tranquil, eternally tranquil and eternally responsive" or "silent and yet awake, awake and yet silent" both refer to the true meaning of "returning to emptiness."

Conversely, if shen has not been nurtured unto maturity, and it is brought out too early, then it will unavoidably bound away after what it sees, falling onto the demonic path and ultimately dissipating. If it has been nurtured until reaching its prime, but thinking has not stopped, then one's will will still be rooted in desire, and one's thoughts will still be based in intentionality. Thus, even if one's actions are appropriate, one's consciousness will have been impelled to act by that which is you wei, and not by the fundamental essence of that which is empty and nonexistent.

What does this mean? When actions are you wei, it is the cognitive shen that is acting. When actions are wu wei, it is the primordial shen that is acting. When the cognitive shen is in charge, the primordial shen steps back and passively takes orders. When the primordial shen is sovereign, the cognitive shen transforms in its entirety into primordial shen. This is the critical juncture separating the Tao's principles and personal desires; the two cannot coexist. If the cognitive shen has not been transformed, it is next to impossible to sever worldly desires. Should one be incautious with just a single thought, one will slip into the cycle of birth and death, unawares. Hence the saying, "the karmic seed leading to death and rebirth for endless kalpas is precisely what a fool mistakenly refers to as his or her original self."

It is especially important to know that the primordial shen is traceless. The place of greatest numinousness within primordial qi: that is the primordial shen. But it must be that which is like a valley echoing a sound or a shadow following a form. It is aware as a matter of course, and it knows be-

cause it is its nature to know, without relying on even a hair of intentionality, or containing even a thread of contrivance. When Mencius said that any person who sees a child fall into a well will catch a fright and burst with compassion, he was alluding to the primordial shen.

From the above we can deduce that there is nothing—from seeing, hearing, speech, and movement, on through to all other daily activity—where the primordial shen is not playing a role. It is merely that that which is intentional is attributable to the cognitive shen, while that which is done without intent is attributable to the primordial shen. That is really all there is to the debate over what counts as primordial shen and what counts as cognitive shen. Students, you must self-investigate.

If you are able to give your primordial shen sovereignty, then you will return to the realm of emptiness and nonexistence. If you wish to coalesce into oneness, you will. If you wish to multiply, then you will become myriad. Nothing will be beyond your spiritual powers—this is far greater than simply being able to submerge in water without drowning and pass through fire without burning!

■ ■ ■

If one wishes to cultivate the Way, regardless of what tradition one belongs to, it is necessary to enter into a certain state, often described as a state of tranquility, or a condition of conscious awareness. This condition cannot be arrived at through force. One cannot get there through suppression or an internal struggle where self is pitted against self.

In the beginning, we should not directly seek after the goal of quieting the mind or achieving any other particular state. At the same time, we cannot exert no effort whatsoever, like a typical person who does not have a self-cultivation practice. If we do not apply ourselves, our states will remain those of everyday people. The condition a cultivator should occupy is different from that of a person in the world, but it is not a state of urgent pursuit based on an ardent desire to achieve this or that goal.

There is an expression that captures the cultivators' ideal state of mind quite nicely: "choiceless awareness." To start with, this sort of awareness is distinct from our typical mode of consciousness, because in our normal states we tend to be quite unconscious and unaware. When our minds stir and thoughts arise, this happens in a mechanical manner dominated by habit. In our typical states, one thought comes right after another, but we are incapable of recognizing that this is happening, much less playing a decisive role in the process. Rather, under the sway of enormous karmic force, we let our thoughts run hither and tither. When in such a state, what we lack is the type of awareness that allows a person to "observe" or "sense" his or her own thoughts, and thereby be conscious of everything that is occurring in the mind. This type of awareness does not involve the addition of any judgment or distinction. When aware in this way, we do not declare one type of mental state to be "good" and another to be "bad," nor do we affirm some types of thinking and reject others. Rather, this is a state in which we regard all phenomena in the present moment in exactly the same way. We simply maintain this state, not interfering with what arises, yet consciously perceiving it.

Again, in this state of mind, we do not make judgments—we do not label some things as good and others as bad, nor do we strive to arrive at certain meditative states or eschew others. Rather, we simply merge with the condition of our body and mind in the present moment. We thoroughly accompany our own being. Even if our state is unpleasant—for instance, if there is discomfort or even pain somewhere in the body—we do not decide that this sensation needs to be eliminated or rejected. Similarly, if we are experiencing pain or suffering of a psychological nature, we do not oppose our thoughts or emotions. Having certitude that a certain state of mind is negative just leads to further psychological burden. So, we just perceive and observe what arises, so that we can experience things as they really are, and thus understand them.

When practicing like this, we do not operate under the sway of our various long-held ideas, and we refrain from making assessments. We just penetratingly "watch" the things that arise. Maintaining our perceptiveness keeps our minds from becoming foggy and drowsy, while maintaining choiceless-ness keeps our minds from becoming scattered and chaotic. Not foggy, not drowsy, not scattered, not chaotic— it is precisely such a state that allows for cultivation practice.

If we do not observe our own states at all times, then our minds become unfocused and unruly. Practically speaking, this means that we cannot be cognizant of the wild churn of thoughts in our minds. The situation is a bit like leaving our houses unlocked and unattended. Any thief, from a petty miscreant to a hardened criminal, can waltz right in the door and engage in mischief, and there is no way to supervise what is going on. Perceptiveness is akin to being the master of the house; when the master is at home, one is "awake," and the so-called thieves naturally disappear. Choiceless awareness allows our minds to gradually learn how to stay put in one place, and to no longer tend to become scattered and chaotic.

The "perceptiveness" we are discussing here is no different from the principle of "illuminating the mind to glimpse its nature" that we discussed earlier. Our minds are intrinsically perceptive. We possess awareness that is present by virtue of its own nature, and which is cognizant of all things that arise. However, when our later-heaven thoughts become so prolific that they are like thick layers of heavy clouds, they blot out this natural awareness, and our minds become totally lost. Nevertheless, the "awakeness" of our original nature does not actually disappear in this process. It can never disappear. But it is up to us to allow it to become apparent—to "wake it up," as it were.

When we are reading, we also need to maintain a state that is not foggy, not drowsy, not scattered, and not chaotic. Some people read for a little while, and then their minds drift off into sleepiness and they are barely aware of what they are doing. Others read for a while, and then they start to daydream, their minds bounding off to faraway places, leaving no room to live presently in the here and now. In either case, it is impossible to really grasp whatever it is an author is trying to explain. However, if one can maintain choiceless awareness while reading, calling upon innate perceptiveness while carefully reading the words on the page, one will be very clear about what is being conveyed.

■ ■ ■

Huang Yuanji's above discourse revolves around "jing, qi, and shen." We have previously used different terminology to describe the principles of alchemical practice and the sequence in which they unfold.

For example, we have spoken about the process of "returning from later heaven to early heaven" and "using early heaven to transmute later heaven"; we have also spoken about the process of "using hsing to establish ming," "using ming to develop hsing," and "merging hsing and ming as one." To further expand upon the above requires addressing questions related to jing, qi, and shen, as they are fundamental to both the cultivation of hsing and ming as well as the transformation of later heaven into prior heaven. Thus, this discourse examines the progression of alchemical cultivation in a way that is both more granular and more concrete than previous discourses. Its contents are central to the study of inner alchemy.

Sometimes hsing and ming are simply said to be shen and qi, with shen representing hsing (original nature) and qi representing ming (life essence). This is done because qi is ming's quintessence, while shen is hsing's embodiment. If ming is further broken down, then it includes both jing as well as qi, with jing representing the more gross aspects of ming, and qi representing the subtler aspects. Even though jing and qi can be distinguished from one another in terms of coarseness and subtleness, they always belong to the category of ming, while shen is always in the category of hsing.

Great care needs to be taken with these terms, because the words "jing" and "qi" can be used in quite disparate ways in different teachings on inner alchemy and in books on other types of Taoist cultivation. For example, in very early Taoist writings, the character for "jing" is sometimes used in a way that implies "Qi," which is in fact "qi's most rarefied essence."[9] This point can be extremely confusing, because when it is used this way, "jing" actually refers to something even more refined and of a higher grade than "qi!" When "qi and jing" are discussed from this angle, the two characters point to different levels than they do when they are used as they are in this book. It is qi's nature to exist at many different levels, and thus it is imperative to be clear about which of its aspects is being described. A general rule of thumb is that if "qi" is being used to describe the coarsest, most external type of qi, it likely refers to something that is of a lower grade than jing. Huang Yuanji's discourses did not follow that pattern, however. In these pages we use these characters to refer to a progression that starts with "refining jing, transforming qi," proceeds to "refining qi, transforming shen," continues with "refining shen, returning to emptiness," and concludes with "returning to emptiness, merging with the Tao." In this alchemical process, the concept of "qi" represents something of a higher level than "jing."

Regardless of whether one is discussing jing, qi, or shen, all of these things further subdivide into two primary aspects: prior heaven and later heaven. Prior heaven jing, qi, and shen can also be called "primordial" jing, qi, and shen. Later-heaven jing refers to the human body's sexual essences, but it does not *only* refer to those fluids. Rather, the sexual essences are *representative* of later-heaven jing. Later-heaven qi is the qi that our bodies breathe in and out, while later-heaven shen, also known as "cognitive shen," is the aspect of shen that engages in thought. Cognitive shen is a term that represents the tendency of the mind to make distinctions, and therefore refers to discursive mental activity. The endless supply of scattered thoughts that follows us through our later-heaven lives comes from cognitive shen, not primordial shen. Similarly, the gross later-heaven qi we actively breathe is not the same as primordial qi, and the reproductive fluids that can be referred to as the human body's jing essences are not the same as primordial jing.

In internal alchemy, the "three treasures" of jing, qi, and shen are sometimes called "three great medicinal substances." Refining the "elixir" refers to the refining of jing, qi, and shen, but as practitioners, the most important thing to remember is that what we ultimately seek to refine are primordial jing, primordial qi, and primordial shen. In other words, it is the prior-heaven aspects of jing, qi, and shen that have to be used as the "medicinal substances." Later-heaven jing, qi, and shen are incapable of serving as the raw materials for inner alchemy. Trying to refine later-heaven jing, qi, and shen is to abandon the rarefied materials that Taoist alchemy is based upon, and instead to train with the stuff of ordinary mortals. Put another way, if one eschews the prior-heaven "three treasures," one ends up using the exact same basic materials that typical, later-heaven qigong does.

Although the key to internal alchemy lies with primordial jing, qi, and shen, this does not mean that adepts simply ignore the later-heaven three treasures. The relationship between prior heaven and later heaven is dialectic and integrated—the two influence one another. So, while inner alchemy does not refine later-heaven jing, qi, and shen, because prior-heaven and later-heaven jing, qi, and shen are intimately linked, the three later-heaven treasures still have to be trained with, in order to cause the three prior-heaven "medicinal ingredients" to reveal themselves.

■ ■ ■

Inner alchemy cultivation is often compared to building a building, with each step in the process taking a person from establishing a base toward constructing the highest floors.

"Building a foundation," a term used in inner alchemy, is the same as the term for constructing a building's base. However, even before "building a foundation," there is also a process of "refining the self" that must be undertaken before formal alchemical practice can begin. "Refining the self" is mental cultivation that develops one's ability to reside in a state of clarity and tranquility.

One's mind needs to have undergone a certain amount of basic preparation before one can hope to establish a foundation. This is why, in chapter 6, I spoke about how "cultivating hsing before ming" and "cultivating ming before hsing" are actually parts of the same sequential process. The preparatory stage of "refining the self," which involves cultivating the mentality needed for inner alchemy, can be described as a form of hsing practice. But we must recall that the specific subject matter of hsing cultivation varies depending on what stage a person has reached. The psychological preparation that takes place before a foundation can even be built is very different from the cultivation of the mind that takes place later, at quite high levels, such as when one is refining shen in order to return to emptiness. These two stages of hsing cultivation are very distinct.

This book begins with the chapter "Unsurpassed Destiny" because, before one starts inner alchemy practice, one needs to understand the worldview and life outlook that underpins Taoist cultivation. These two things count as components of "refining the self," because they prepare the mind in a way that helps one enter the path of cultivation. If one's mind remains wholly mired in the "dusty world," one will not have the slightest inclination to cultivate the Way, and instead one will invariably veer toward honor, fame, wealth, rank, and the rest of the teeming human world's attractions. "Refining the self" provides a psychological basis for inner alchemy practice, without which it is pointless to talk about the rest of the training process.

"Building a foundation," on the other hand, pertains to our corporeal bodies and training in ming. If we wish to practice inner alchemy, then our "furnace" needs to contain medicinal ingredients, or else there will be nothing to refine. With an empty furnace, regardless of how well one stokes the fire and works the bellows, one's training will be pointless if not downright delusional, and the furnace itself will be damaged in the heat. "Building a foundation" means ensuring that one's proverbial furnace actually contains the fundamental materials of alchemy. This means accumulating the amount of jing, qi, and shen that is necessary to make further practice possible.

Since building a foundation revolves around preparing our bodies' jing, qi, and shen, the matter of protecting and nourishing the later-heaven three treasures is inevitably one that requires attention. I have already said that inner alchemy is not based upon refining later-heaven jing, qi, and shen, but we still have to begin our journeys with later heaven. In practical terms, this starts with learning how to let our breathing become harmonious, which facilitates entry into a state in which the thinking of the "cognitive shen" is naturally regulated. The pacification of the thinking mind allows us to enter into stillness, and thereby preserve our later-heaven life energies. This is what allows jing and qi to accumulate within us. Once jing and qi have accumulated up to a certain level, one possesses a foundation that enables progress to the next steps in cultivation.

■ ■ ■

The process of refining the elixir is a sort of "alchemizing of the human body," by which the energies of the body constantly transform and sublimate, going from gross to subtle. Everything that exists in the universe has a different quality of energy, ranging from the coarse to the subtle. It is impossible to scientifically classify anything on the basis of the quality of its energy, but we can still roughly distinguish between which things have a quality of energy that is relatively coarse and which are relatively refined. These general categories are actually quite obvious.

We can use food to illustrate this idea. Humans cannot subsist on a diet of dirt, despite the fact that soil is full of all kinds of nutrients. Why can we not go straight to dirt for our nutritional needs? The reason is that our gastrointestinal tract's capabilities for receiving, digesting, and extracting nutrients is not suited to soil—from the human body's standpoint, earth is a very coarse substance, and therefore impossible to directly absorb. However, plants *are* capable of extracting water and nutrients straight from soil, and with the aid of sunlight, they perform chemical reactions that gradually turn the organic matter in dirt into the fruits and vegetables that we are able to consume. In terms of this discussion, we can say that fruits and vegetables are more refined than dirt is. Similarly, humans can eat some plants, but there are others that are only edible to herbivorous animals. Again, those plants we *can* eat might be said to have a more sublime level of energy. Cows, sheep, and other herbivores with very strong digestive systems can eat grasses that are inaccessible to us, and their bodies transform these plants' energy into meat, which we are able to consume. Because meat, which comes from animals that eat vegetation, has gone through another level of transformation, it can be said to be of a higher level than plants. My point is not to say that eating meat is necessarily any better for us than eating vegetables—there are other factors to consider—but in terms of degrees of subtlety as well as the organization of life energy, animal flesh is indeed of a higher grade than vegetation.

The point of the above illustration is to remind us that different substances have different levels of refinement. According to Taoist alchemy's understanding, the human body's energies can be divided into several different layers. The coarsest and most external of these layers is the flesh-and-blood body itself. In Taoist terminology, the physical body's most highly refined and subtle aspects—in other words, the essences of the substances that comprise the body—are represented by the character 精, or "jing."

What does jing mean in Taoism? In the very beginning, it is unified energy—it is the primordial jing that originates in prior heaven.

As it evolves along with later-heaven existence, primordial jing can transform into the myriad forces that allow the human body's various functions to operate. Jing's transformations can take it in any number of directions. For example, jing ultimately turns into the different materials secreted by the human body, all of which operate in very distinct ways. One of the important ways in which jing manifests is as our reproductive essences, including semen and vaginal secretions. The importance of these substances to the continuation of life is the reason that they are seen as "essences," and described with the character *jing*. However, as crucial to the miracle of life as they may be, they still only represent later-heaven jing.

■ ■ ■

We need to examine the principles that underlie "refining jing, transforming qi," in order to be sure about what "jing" means in the context of this work. Many people misunderstand this concept, and as a result they confuse the later-heaven jing related to reproduction with primordial jing. Because later-heaven jing has already turned into a substance with a physical form, it is no longer possible to directly transform it into qi. It is already "old," and therefore cannot be used in inner alchemy. If anybody states that this unclear form of jing can be transformed into some kind of qi, he or she is pointing to a side door leading to a crooked path. Even a worldly scientist with no knowledge of Taoism can tell that this is impossible, as the principles behind such a practice are illogical.

So we have to distinguish ordinary jing and primordial jing, but there is a somewhat tricky point we need to be clear about in order to do so. The jing that is refined in inner alchemy is primordial jing. Primordial jing is a relatively subtle form of energy or sustenance found in the human body, and it needs be made to transform into qi, which is an even more subtle and rarefied form of energy. This process is in some ways akin to cooking—when we put ingredients into a pot and add heat, the ingredients will start to steam, meaning that the substances that had been in a liquid state are turning into gases. The tricky point where this analogy breaks down lies in the fact that that primordial jing is formless; it is only akin to a fluid, but it is not actually something in the liquid state of matter. Similarly, qi is merely analogous to something in the gaseous state, because it is something that flows throughout the body, but it is not actually a gas. Nevertheless, we use this analogy because when "fire" (which represents the effects created by consciousness) and "wind" (which represents the effects created by the breath) are regulated in tandem, jing can transform into qi, which means that jing transmutes into a more sublime form of energy. That is the meaning of "refining jing, transforming qi."

Even though primordial jing is distinct from later-heaven, corporeal jing, the two are nevertheless closely related. For this reason, if we are to practice internal alchemy, it is necessary to moderate our desires, to reduce the exhaustion of our sexual energies as much as possible. What principle underlies this statement? Primordial jing is the basic energy of life. If it is called to do so, it will fulfill its function by turning into the body's sexual fluids and energies. Turning into reproductive jing is the route that primordial jing commonly takes, and as this happens it gets used up. Thus, if we constantly consume our reproductive essences, at the same time our primordial jing will constantly transform into corporeal jing, which means that we will lack the basic ingredient for the alchemical work of "transforming jing to turn it into qi."

Conversely, if we sublimate and refine primordial jing before it has undergone the process of turning into post-heaven, physical jing, it will become a higher-level energy. Simultaneously, that change will reduce the strength of the impetus that pushes primordial jing to go in the direction of becoming bodily jing. The natural result of this process is to transform sexual energies as well as to reduce the rate at which they are consumed; both outcomes are closely intertwined.

■ ■ ■

Once primordial jing has transformed into a higher level of energy, it is more accurate to describe it as a type of primordial qi, but it is still of a different level from the primordial qi that we have previously seen described as "the qi of empty nonexistence," "the qi of prior-heaven oneness," or "the unified qi of complete yang." The type of primordial qi that primordial jing can turn into is better described as "that which is prior heaven within later heaven." This means it is a type of primordial qi that is present within later-heaven existence, but it is not the same as what is sometimes called "the prior heaven within prior heaven," which refers to the fundamental source of all that is prior heaven in nature. The most fundamental and original of all prior-heaven qi belongs to the same level as the Tao itself, and it is indistinguishable from primordial shen. The primordial qi we are concerned with at this stage is not of that level.

The unified qi of prior heaven is a limitless ocean of energy. It is not something we need to go and create, because it has existed all along in this universe, and it is in fact the original source of our own life energy. This is different from the trio of primordial jing, primordial qi, and primordial shen. All three of those things are indeed called "prior heaven," but, in this context, that is a designation that is relative to later-heaven life; in other words, it can only be said that there exist primordial jing, qi, and shen after later-heaven life has already begun. The trinity of jing, qi, and shen is the way in which the unified qi of empty nonexistence manifests within the human body. The qi of empty nonexistence (prior heaven within prior heaven) is the ultimate essence; it functions through the three primordial treasures (prior heaven within later heaven).

In terms of their original source, primordial jing, primordial qi, and primordial shen are all simply the one qi of empty nonexistence. All three of them are therefore manifestations of the Tao, and yet they are of different degrees of subtlety and profundity. Jing, qi, and shen operate on three distinct levels within the human body, and each of these levels has some similarity to what are called the "three realms" in Buddhism. Jing corresponds to the relatively gross realm, known as the "realm of desire." Qi is related to the "realm of form," while shen correlates to the "formless realm." Buddhism teaches that one must transcend the three realms, meaning that one can have no attachments to any of them. What lies beyond the three realms? Not primordial jing, not primordial qi, and not primordial shen, but the original source. The source transcends the three realms, and yet it is from this source that the three realms derive, so they cannot be separate from it. In Taoist terms, to "transcend the three realms" is to arrive at Tao, or the primordial qi of empty nonexistence. But here, the word "qi" does not refer to qi alone—it is qi and shen, merged as one, in a state that precedes separation.

In summary, if one wishes to refine jing to transform qi, one must begin with a certain amount of raw ingredients, which in this case means primordial jing. Then one must use specific methods so that it refines and sublimates.

■ ■ ■

"Refining qi, transforming shen" refers to primordial qi transforming primordial shen. One must be careful to note that this phrase does not describe taking primordial qi and transforming it *into* primordial shen. Primordial qi is not something that needs to be created; because primordial shen is of a prior-heaven nature, it is something that has been there all along.

So what, then, does "refining qi, transforming shen" really mean? When primordial shen is functioning and active, its functioning includes qi, because shen and qi are inseparable. However, although shen always involves qi when it operates, because our later-heaven shen is usually playing the primary role in our lives, our primordial shen is therefore typically unable to obtain sufficient support from primordial qi, and as a result it is as though there is a separation between shen and qi. Thus, to "refine qi and transform shen" really means entering into the state that is required to practice inner alchemy—where primordial shen's observant awareness (called "true intent") is active—and allowing vitalizing primordial qi to draw closer to primordial shen, so that the two merge and unify. When that happens, primordial shen receives far more abundant and vigorous energetic support; another way of putting it is that it has a more stable "material" foundation. At the same time, because primordial qi will have found its home by merging with shen, it will no longer be so easy for primordial qi to be scattered by various later-heaven energies and stimuli. At this stage, a practitioner's life enters into a new, heightened state of being, in which primordial qi and shen are one. The functioning of the practitioner's mind and body will reflect this heightened state.

Qi is the basic energy of life. It is relevant to everything that we do in the world, and it determines whether or not we succeed in our undertakings and whether or not we possess a certain force of will. There is a common phrase, "the mind is willing but the body is weak." To be weak means to have insufficient support from primordial qi, and therefore to lack the means to execute tasks.

There are people we encounter in the world who do not seem to need to do any kind of cultivation practice, and yet they are full of charisma and highly capable. Many outstanding individuals in different fields possess charm, the natural ability to lead, and the type of appeal that allows them to rally people behind them. On top of those factors, they also have an imposing force of will that they use to bring their ideas to fruition. Even though these people tend not to know anything about Taoist cultivation, it can still be said that it is the functioning of qi that supports them in their endeavors.

Why is it that some people behave justly and rightly, and others do not? This is also a question of the qi that supports them. When primordial qi splits apart as it becomes a part of later-heaven existence, it can go in any direction and take on any type of character. Thus, even violent tendencies come from qi. A person with a terrible temper is propelled along by qi of a violent nature, which he or she sometimes loses control over. There also exists auspicious, peaceful qi, which is present in people with placid minds and kind dispositions. Qi manifests differently in different types of people, giving them distinctive characteristics. Primordial qi is therefore extremely important to us, as its activity will not only affect the conditions of our biology, but also the types of forces that are active in our lives.

When a person possesses very abundant primordial qi but has not learned to transform it so that it merges with primordial shen, then he or she will be missing the so-called protagonist or master of the house, and as such will generally be unable to guide and control the energy at his or her disposal. The person will likely find ways to disperse this surplus energy, perhaps even engaging in bad deeds as a way of draining down the abundance of qi. At the opposite end of the spectrum, there are also people whose primordial shen is already active in their lives, but because they do not have enough primordial qi to support prior-heaven shen, their wisdom has little force behind it, and is effectively weakened.

The above principles can be expressed using the Buddhist terms "samadhi" and "prajna." Taoists' refining of shen is comparable to Buddhists' "cultivation of prajna"; the refining of qi is somewhat similar to "cultivating samadhi"; and the refining of jing also has some things in common with the "cultivation of ethical conduct." Thus, Buddhism's ethical conduct, samadhi, and prajna have corollaries in Taoism's jing, qi, and shen.

Practically speaking, if one's skill in samadhi is highly developed, one's qi will also be quite abundant. If one's shen has been successfully cultivated, one's prajna, or wisdom, will be quite advanced. Buddhism calls for samadhi and prajna to be cultivated together, warning that if a person merely possesses powers of samadhi without the wisdom of prajna, while such a person will have abilities and energy, he or she will not know how to use them properly and will end up using them in deviant ways or losing control over them. On the other hand, possessing the wisdom of prajna without having any skill in samadhi will mean that there is no power underlying one's wisdom, and thus it will be ineffectual and incapable of affecting anything. These considerations have much in common with what takes place in the process of refining primordial qi and primordial shen.

■ ■ ■

The next question is, what does it mean to refine shen and return to emptiness? Above, we discussed how internal alchemy eventually causes primordial qi and primordial shen to merge together. When that occurs, the result is described with the term "yang shen." In essence, yang shen and primordial shen are the same thing, but primordial shen refers to that which is innate—meaning that all people have prior-heaven shen—whereas yang shen is, in a sense, acquired. What this means is that yang shen describes primordial shen after it fully merges with primordial qi in a person who has reached a high level of inner alchemy training.

Although all people possess primordial shen, we must recall that, for most of us, it is cognitive shen that is active, whereas primordial shen long ago ceded primacy, and its functions have ceased to be manifest. "Cognitive shen" refers to later-heaven, distinction-making consciousness; the constant streams of thought and differentiation coursing through our minds reflect its activity.

To refine shen and return to emptiness means causing fully merged primordial shen and qi (also called "yang shen," as mentioned above) to progress another step by returning to emptiness and going into the Tao. Throughout this process of return, an adept must constantly transform cognitive shen, because it acts like a warehouse within consciousness that contains countless seeds that, if allowed to sprout, will trigger reactions from what Buddhism calls "the qi of habit." These "seeds" function through a person's post-heaven tendencies of thought and distinction-making. They grow into the endless varieties of greed, anger, and ignorance, ultimately leading a person into all kinds of suffering. Therefore, it is necessary to allow these seeds to be "digested."

In Taoist cultivation, it is not sufficient to just sit to meditate or practice techniques of moving qi around the body. Rather, the entirety of the mind's "warehouse of consciousness" must be purified. This work takes place at the stage of refining shen to return to emptiness. Within emptiness, one utterly transforms cognitive shen, and in this process causes yang shen to reach full maturity. In the view of Taoist alchemy, if one's cognitive shen is not sufficiently transformed, then even though one's yang shen might be capable of leaving the body and traveling around the world, one will invariably experience desirous or wrathful thoughts in response to stimuli in the external environment. This is inevitable for as long as there still remain karmic seeds stored within one's consciousness. A vexed mind is a source of real danger for the practitioner.

Yang shen needs to be nurtured through a period of higher-level training that is lengthier, subtler, and more difficult than what came before it. At the end of this training, when yang shen is fully mature, cognitive shen will have been completely transmuted, such that even though it still possesses the facility to think and make distinctions, those things will serve only as shen's subtle, profound functions, and will no longer lead to obstacles.

When an adept has reached this stage, his or her shen will still respond to objects and phenomena as they arise due to the ripening of karma. However, the thoughts that stir and arise in his or her mind will no longer have the ego as their basis, and mental activity will no longer be a product of the mind's desires and attachments. Rather, shen will naturally make its presence known in accord with external conditions, responding to whatever is sensed, and moving as situations unfold. If a cultivator at this level is asked a question, he or she will naturally answer, but the answer will not emerge from his or her attachments. Instead, it will come from a mind that has stirred only in response to external conditions. Once the cultivator's mind has finished responding, thoughts will subside. This is called being "always responsive, always tranquil." What that term means is that even though the cultivator's mind can still stir into thought, it takes only a moment for the mind's activity to dissolve back into nothingness, leaving no traces whatsoever. There is thus no more suffering and attachment, and one's cultivation of the Tao has been successful. This stage is one of real achievement.

■ ■ ■

There are both prior-heaven and later-heaven jing, qi, and shen. The entire process of refining the elixir in internal alchemy lies in their mutual transformations. This process is one of starting with the coarse and transforming it into the subtle. The process includes the step-by-step sublimation of the human body's energies, which is the work of ming practices. It also includes the cultivation of the mind, which focuses upon eliminating clinging and suffering as well as purifying the "seeds" within cognitive shen, so that the mind transforms and occupies the non-distinguishing, limpid state of primordial shen. The entire process of Taoist alchemy's dual cultivation of hsing and ming is found within these tasks.

Ultimately, inner alchemy aims to take one back into emptiness. One returns into and merges with the Tao. One should be cautious not to envision inner alchemy as nothing more than a physical transformation or a biochemical transformation. Its most important factor still lies in the state of one's mind. Inner alchemy's purification of the psyche takes one from the surficial, coarse state of consciousness to one that is both deeper and more primal.

Now we will take a look at some of Huang Yuanji's teachings found at the beginning of this chapter.

Huang's first paragraph discusses how jing is understood in internal alchemy. He says, "Jing refers not to the fluids of sexual communion, and rather to prior-heaven primordial jing." We already discussed this point above: the jing used in inner alchemy is prior-heaven, primordial jing, and not later-heaven reproductive essences. To explain what jing actually is, Huang states, "This jing comes from the beginning, when one's life is conceived. It is the qi of yin and the qi of yang concentrated into a single coalescence, akin to a dewdrop or a pearl, stored in the heart as yin jing. It is the heavenly one that births water." This means that primordial jing is life. It is created from the mating of the two energies of yin and yang, and it comes from a single point of prior-heaven primal life energy that is analogous to a drop of dew or a jewel. It exists within the heart, and, in this state, it can be referred to as yin jing.

In the above paragraph, there appears the phrase "the heavenly one that births water." This expression comes from symbolic numerology. The term "heavenly" here refers to "heavenly numbers," which is the description given to odd numbers in the "River Diagram" and the "Luo Chart" (even numbers are called "earthly"). The "heavenly one" represents the start of the heavenly numbers. The "water" in this term comes from the five phases, and because it is associated with the north it is sometimes called "the water of the north." The ancients linked the digits zero through nine with the five phases to create a system of symbolic numerology that models the universe's genesis and transformation. To make a long story short, within the language of yin and yang and the five phases, the phrase "the heavenly one that births water" represents the formation of the primordial jing of prior heaven.

Of primordial jing, Huang says, "When it has not stirred reactively, it is just a single qi." This means that when primordial jing has yet to connect with and respond to any object or phenomena beyond itself, it is a singular energy. The word "qi" in Huang's sentence is not used the same way it is in the phrase "refining jing, transforming qi." Rather, it refers to the "state of qi" that primordial jing occupies prior to being used in any way. Because this state is one not of coarseness but of clarity and brightness, the word "qi" is used here to describe it.

When Huang says, "when it is affected by stimuli," he is speaking about jing encountering the later-heaven world and responding to it. When this happens, jing turns into the different types of energy functioning in the human body, and in turn it can give rise to the body's different fluids. Huang states, "in the liver it transforms into tears," meaning that when the liver makes use of jing, it turns into the secretions of the tear glands.

Continuing this train of thought, Huang states that "in the spleen it transforms into saliva, in the lungs it transforms into mucus, in the heart it transforms into the pulse, and in the kidneys it transforms into sexual fluids, in the cold it becomes a runny nose, in the heat it becomes sweat; when delicious fragrances are smelled is causes the mouth to water, and when flavors are tasted saliva flows. Hence the phrase, 'mucus, spittle, sexual fluids, saliva, blood, sweat, and tears—these seven efficacious materials are all yin.'" What he means here is that when the primordial jing of prior heaven becomes active in the later-heaven world, it manifests in the form of physical secretions. Later-heaven reproductive secretions are only one of the possible ways for prior-heaven jing to manifest. All seven types of secretions mentioned here are ways in which jing appears when it has already entered later-heaven existence. None of these things can be seen as raw materials for inner alchemy cultivation, and yet the depletion of jing in any of its later-heaven forms will still affect our primordial jing. Thus, one must nurture that which is of a later-heaven nature in one's body in order to avoid depleting that which comes from prior heaven. At the same time, by avoiding depleting that which is of a prior-heaven nature, one ensures that there is always enough of it in reserve, so that it can transform into its later-heaven form when needed and keep the human body healthy. These two factors are intimately related.

■ ■ ■

Primordial jing will only issue forth when there are no thoughts arising. This is not a state that can be reached by repressing thoughts. Rather, it comes when one is absorbed in tranquility, and then, without losing one's serenity, wholeheartedly looks within. In this intro-spective mental state, one's attention ceases scattering outward, and the gateways of the "seven orifices" Huang Yuanji mentioned close, so that energy no longer leaks out through them. At this time, be-cause there are no avenues through which it can seep out, primordial jing will stop ceaselessly pouring into the later-heaven realm. Instead, it will begin to concentrate.

Wholehearted inner observation is the method we use to cause primordial jing to concentrate and become refined. With regular practice, it will become more and more abundant, and at the right moment it will make itself apparent. Huang Yuanji describes this mo-ment when he says, "one day jing will be born." From that moment forward, prior-heaven jing will continue to issue forth and accumu-late day by day.

Huang goes on to describe primordial jing's arrival, saying, "It will be like waking after a deep sleep into the warmth of spring weather, as a hot coalescence of gentle qi emerges from within the corporeal kidneys." This sentence speaks to the subjective experience of having ample primordial jing, which Huang Yuanji compares to awakening from a delicious nap in warm springtime weather, when flowers are in bloom. This sort of warm, fully energized feeling indi-cates that the body's primordial qi is beginning to become apparent, thereby triggering a reaction. When this sensation arises, one can start to practice. If one does not practice at this time, it is easy for primor-dial qi to turn into later-heaven qi.

Because this moment is so crucial, Huang Yuanji continues, "At this time, you must hastily use true intent to gather it back to the earth cauldron that is the dantian, to forge and refine it, to warm and nourish it. Thereupon, primordial jing will constantly be present, and primordial qi will be able to be produced." What this passage means is that, once primordial jing has emerged and grown into abundance, one should refine it so that it transforms into qi. This is accomplished through "true intent."

Most of the time, our cognitive shen is active, making distinctions and engaging in thought. "True intent" is different—it comes from pri-mordial shen's function, which is to observe. To use "true intent" is to bring primordial shen into play by having the gentlest and subtlest of intentions to be observant. True intent is used to lead primordial qi to return to the dantian, so that the dantian will act as a furnace that cooks and nurtures it, thereby gradually purifying it.

. . .

In the passage quoted above, Huang Yuanji mentions "forging and refining" and "warming and nourishing." These are two distinct levels of "temperature and timing" in internal alchemy. When doing so-called forging and refining, one uses a bigger "fire," which equates to increasing the intensity of the blaze heating a furnace. When in the stage called warming and nourishing, the "fire" is turned way down, so that the primordial jing within the proverbial furnace is simmering at low heat. These are the techniques that are used so that primordial jing will transmute into a higher-grade substance, becoming primordial qi. Primordial qi is created via the transformation that occurs when primordial jing is refined.

Huang Yuanji continues, "However, the medicinal herb can be withered or tender, the fire can be scholarly or martial, and movements can rise or fall. Returning to the stove, warming, and nourishing—all of these things have their methods and degrees, so students must humbly entreat teachers to clearly point out the true mechanism." Huang's point is that the process of refining jing and transforming qi is an especially subtle undertaking. Just as with fine cuisine, it is an art in which exacting attention must be paid to the amount of time and temperature at which things "cook." For this reason, in Taoist alchemy one hears the phrase, "one can comprehend the mind's nature (hsing) all by oneself, but the teachings on life-essence (ming) must be transmitted by a teacher." Working alone, one can have epiphanies that fall under the category of hsing, because what one realizes in these epiphanies was already in one's own possession, all along. However, because training in ming involves a wide variety of experiences and specific methods, guidance from an insightful teacher who has already walked the path is always necessary. The role of the teacher is to explain the specifics of the methods, so that one does not engage in cultivation blindly. Never believe people who tell you that inner alchemy cultivation is no more than circulating qi around the inside of your abdomen. Doing that will very easily lead to trouble.

One has to humbly visit a teacher who can clarify the concrete realities involved in putting internal alchemy teachings into practice. Questions that need to be addressed include: When should one be using "scholarly fire," and when should one be using "martial fire"? How should rising and sinking be accomplished in the heavenly circulation, and how should they correspond to breathing? In what manner should one place attention upon the "medicine"—meaning primordial jing—and what constitutes "withered" or "tender" jing? These questions have to be answered, because jing that is too "withered" or too "tender" are both unacceptable. Similarly, just as is the case with preparing a meal, the "fire" of internal alchemy can neither be too ferocious nor too weak. An excessively strong fire will burn the ingredients, while a weak fire will fail to cook them thoroughly. It is in these questions where inner alchemy practice can be seen as something of an art. The only way to get jing to transmute effectively is by learning how to get the "timing and temperature" just right.

Huang therefore warns us, "If there is any ignorance, this will lead to deluded gathering and rash refining, from which few can avoid harm. The dangers herein must not be overlooked." In internal alchemy, if one has not obtained instruction in authentic methods and clearly grasped their underlying principles, and instead trains all by oneself, this is called "blindly cultivating." Doing so can lead to side effects or even endanger one's health.

Of course, these warnings will lead readers to wonder, what can one do if one has yet to meet a qualified teacher? The answer is that one can select a relatively safe method to train with. A method may be considered relatively safe if it does not rely heavily upon later-heaven techniques meant for gathering and refining jing, as they often prove to be chaotic. Methods one can use alone should be very basic and fairly wu wei in nature. There should be a minimum of "doing" at the later-heaven level. Intent should only be applied via observant awareness, so that one can enter into a state of extremely deep tranquility that allows jing to transform qi and qi to transform shen of their own accord. There should be no attempt to intentionally bring about these results. In training this way, not only is there minimal risk, there is also an additional benefit: namely, even if one fails to succeed at realizing the transformation of jing to qi, because one is following a wu wei approach that involves concentrating shen and being observant, one will still be cultivating one's mind nature, or hsing.

. . .

Because students may not understand the potential pitfalls inherent to internal alchemy, Huang Yuanji adds more clarification: "In the refining of jing, one must concentrate shen in the center. Externally, one must harmonize the breath, until jing and shen collect and coalesce, and the breath is regulated and peaceful. Then jing will spontaneously arise, and qi will spontaneously transform." The key point here is found in the term "concentrating shen." If one's shen—here referring to awareness—is not concentrated, then it will scatter. If it scatters, one will effectively be without "fire." Without fire, it is impossible to refine jing.

Thus, shen must be gathered inward, so that one can observe the "center." Here, the word "center" describes a certain state. It is one of centeredness, free of any kind of skewedness, where one resides in total "balance and harmony."

When Huang says "externally, one must harmonize the breath," he means that one should allow the physical breathing that takes place through the nose to become regular, so that the breath will allow jing and shen to "collect and coalesce." Jing and shen will merge together as one's breathing becomes peaceful. This will bring body and mind into a state of balance, where the two are in harmony with each other. Within this placid harmony, primordial jing is able to be generated, and it is also capable of spontaneously transforming. In the above passage, when Huang Yuanji says "qi will spontaneously transform," this does not mean that qi will transform shen. Rather, he means that primordial jing will naturally turn into primordial qi. In this context, primordial qi is the product of primordial jing's refinement.

Primordial qi is stored within the kidneys in an obscure state, where it is concentrated and coalesced. When primordial qi is tranquil—meaning it has not become active—it remains in the form of qi. However, if it becomes active and moves in the direction of later heaven, then it turns into jing. Just as jing can transform into qi, the opposite can happen, and qi can transform into jing. When qi turns into jing, it is following the "concurrent" path of moving into later-heaven existence. This is the direction primordial qi takes in everyday people—qi becomes jing so that it can perform its functions in the body. When jing is refined into qi, its transformation is going "against the current." This is the direction that Taoist adepts move in.

■ ■ ■

The next portion of Huang Yuanji's teaching focuses on the importance of qi. Qi is related to a person's level of health, ability to pursue goals in the world, and chances of achieving success—it is the substratum underlying all human accomplishments.

Primordial qi, like primordial jing, can exist in two states. In its state before it becomes active, it is formless and inapparent. It can be sensed, but it is still not a thing that has any form or appearance, nor can one directly see it. Rather, it is a warm, harmonious sense of something that seems to infuse and flow throughout one's whole body. One can feel it as a subtle energy that fills the whole body with pleasant warmth and a sensation of vigor. Its other state is as the functional later-heaven jing it transforms into when it becomes active in response to stimuli external to itself.

The actions of people who are known for their extraordinary kindness, filiality, loyalty, or righteousness are inseparable from primordial qi—their deeds are its manifestations. Speaking in lofty terms, those who have plentiful primordial qi can take part directly in the workings of heaven and earth. They can connect directly with heaven and earth, act upon them, and possibly even alter their courses of change.

Huang Yuanji borrows from Mencius to describe what primordial qi is capable of, saying: "Vast and abundant, enormous and adamantine, it has magnanimity that encompasses the universe." In the following lines he paraphrases the great sage, stating: "Mencius said, 'Accumulate righteous deeds to give rise to qi. Accumulate qi to accomplish valor, which can penetrate metal and stones, and even influence animals.' These are the effects of correct qi."

It must be said that the "vast qi" Mencius spoke of came to him via strict moral cultivation. This is implied when Huang Yuanji says "will is qi's commander." What he means is that when a person's moral cultivation is very advanced, he or she will naturally possess abundant qi, and it will follow the mind's governance. The methods broached by Mencius are Confucian. Confucian ways of cultivating the mind and temperament are also capable of nourishing and refining primordial qi. In fact, there are numerous pathways of transformation linking jing, qi, and shen. A person can begin at the bottom and work up or begin at the top and work downward. But in the end, it is always the mind that is primary. The mind is qi's master, so no matter what, the state of one's qi is determined by one's state of mind. The elevation of one's mental state will naturally improve the quality of one's qi.

Huang is in fact still citing Confucian theory when he states, "Will is qi's commander; qi allows righteous deeds to be accomplished. Without this qi, one becomes timid and listless." This theory, however, has been fully integrated into the theories of Taoist inner alchemy. "Will" here refers to consciousness's dynamic aspect—it is the quality of one's willpower. Will is capable of acting as qi's master and commander; when qi is regulated, preserved, and nourished, it can serve as the basis that allows a person to perform great deeds of benevolence or righteousness, up to and including sacrificing his or her own life for a just cause. Without the support of qi, a person will lack the inner strength needed to fulfill the heart's wishes and instead be "timid and listless."

Primordial qi is extremely precious. There are all kinds of precious objects that can be bought with money in the human world, but primordial qi cannot be bought, nor can it even be given to you. To obtain it, one needs to perform meritorious deeds, build integrity, and cultivate. Qi is the root of one's life, so it is imperative that one restores and nurtures it. The entire path of Taoist alchemy revolves around cultivating the mind's nature and life's essence, which is nothing other than the work of cultivating shen and qi. Primordial shen and qi serve as each other's supports. The two cannot be separated.

■ ■ ■

Knowing how to preserve and nourish primordial qi is crucial. Huang Yuanji teaches that before qi has stirred, one should remain tranquil in order to nourish it. This means that while primordial qi is in a dormant state, entering into tranquility and eliminating wild movements will conserve and nurture it. Later, once primordial qi has already made its presence felt, Huang says, "one must become active to refine it." This means that one must then use a specified method in order to refine and transform primordial qi, as well as to prevent it from moving in a chaotic way or dissipating.

When primordial qi is quite plentiful, it will lead to reactions described as "the birth of yang," which indicate that true yang has been born (true yang is discussed in detail in the next chapter). When Huang Yuanji quotes the ancient who said, "suddenly at midnight there is the sound of thunder; tens of thousands of windows and doors fly open one after another," he is alluding to a sign that primordial qi has become abundant and true yang is arising. Huang mentions the sound of a thunderclap because one might hear a sound like an explosion at this time. But one must not become attached to this particular sign, as the phenomena that appear are not always the same.

Huang Yuanji continues, "This is the sign of the first yang's return. When golden light is seen by the eyes and sweet dew fills the mouth, this is evidence of the appearance of the greater medicinal herb." With these sentences, Huang is describing more of the occurrences that can accompany the birth of yang. In practitioners of a certain level, when the body's prior-heaven yang energy appears there are definite signs, including visible golden light and a flow of sweet dew in the mouth. These phenomena verify that the "greater medicinal herb" or "great medicine" has come into being. This so-called herb is what is used in the refining of qi into shen. Its appearance also signifies that the time for "gathering the medicine" has arrived.

Saying that golden light appears before the eyes does not mean that one's eyes will actually emit light. Rather, it refers to the light of shen. When jing and shen are abundant, a sort of brightness will seem to illuminate one's field of vision. At a certain point, the mouth will also ceaselessly fill with an unusual type of saliva that only appears after one has been training for some time. In the language of internal alchemy, when there is a "fire" steadily warming the "furnace" that is the body, a sort of fluid will "evaporate" and float upward like steam; when it reaches the mouth it is like a sweet dew. Also known in Taoist literature as "the spirit water of the flowery pond," this fluid is very valuable. When it appears, it should be slowly swallowed and returned to the dantian. This saliva will seem to issue forth in the mouth continuously, as though no matter how many times one swallows it one can never exhaust it. When it is swallowed like this, it will help to regulate gastrointestinal function as well as overall health. Everything, including one's skin, will change as this "sweet dew" nourishes and moistens the body.

■ ■ ■

The next part of Huang Yuanji's discussion focuses on refining qi so that it transforms shen. This is a very high-level practice, so we will not discuss it in great detail here. Huang opens this part of the discussion with the following passages:

> Make haste to gather the medicinal herb and have it traverse the passes. Consume it, warmly nurture it. At this time, completely contract the genitals, firmly shut the gate of yang, cut off the external breath, and use the internal shen breath. Do not allow even a drop of leakage; you must have each and every breath completely return to the real, at each moment your shen must entirely follow these commands. Have this qi enter into the midst of shen, and have shen envelop qi's exterior. In time, the coming and going of the breath will suddenly cease. You will merely feel that there is a spark of numinous light existing vaguely atop the spiritual platform, as primordial qi will already have transformed into primordial shen.
>
> From this point let qi merge with oblivion and let shen concentrate in emptiness—as though existing and yet not, neither inside nor outside—in order to refine the ultimately empty and numinous shen.

The overarching principle at this stage is the same as before: one must regulate one's mental state and breathe even more subtly, in a manner that is effectively internal breathing. One's qi and shen must totally unite, with qi going into shen and shen enveloping qi. At a certain point, one will then feel as though shen and qi are indistinguishable—they will be in a state of unity. This unity of primordial shen and qi becomes a point of numinous light, within whose divine brightness there is energy. When this occurs, primordial qi has transformed into primordial shen.

In the beginning of this chapter we already noted that what happens during "refining qi, transforming shen" is not primordial qi turning into something called "primordial shen" that is different and separate from itself. What actually occurs is primordial qi returning to primordial shen, so that the two completely merge. After they have fully merged, what one has is a point of shen that is empty and nonexistent, yet numinous and radiant. At this juncture, the distinction-making later-heaven mind is absent. One is entirely in a state that is as though existent and yet as though nonexistent. This state is neither internal, nor external. It is at the extreme of emptiness, yet also at the extreme of numinosity.

■ ■ ■

Huang continues:

> Then do the work of rising, moving shen to the upper dantian. Using the wu wei fire of shen, do the seven-days' refining work of traversing the passes and consuming. Then the skill of the jade fluid will be complete. Henceforth, one will feel neither hunger nor cold, and the four seasons will all be as though springtime; there will be another heaven and earth over which presides, and one will possess the real self.

The subsequent stage of practice, in which shen is refined so that it returns to emptiness, requires further nurturing of shen. After primordial qi and shen have united, what one has is called "yang shen." Yang shen still needs to be fostered. This is done by using "shen fire"—which is empty, nonexistent, and based in non-doing—to dissolve the "seeds" of cognitive shen and bring yang shen to full maturity.

This stage of practice does not merely affect hsing. At the same time, in terms of ming cultivation, it produces an effect that is called "jade fluid returning the elixir." This obscure term means that, under the influence of "shen fire's" non-doing, the body's energies will further sublimate, even up to the point of giving the body special capabilities. For instance, one may cease to feel the discomforts of hunger or cold, and at all times will feel as pleasant as one does in springtime. This change indicates that a person's body has transcended the influence of the elements, and it is no longer subject to the external world, giving a significant degree of physical freedom.

The level of achievement described here is called having "real self." Implied in this term is that the "self" with which we usually identify is false. We are not really masters of our "selves," which are constantly changing and multiplying, leaving us fundamentally unsure of who we really are. However, when one reaches the stage in cultivation where one is the master over one's own body, one has found "real self." Of course, the authentic self is not merely that which controls the body. One must be master over both body and mind. To do so, one must dissolve the cognitive shen.

■ ■ ■

After refining shen and returning to emptiness, there remains another step, "returning to emptiness and merging with the Tao." This step revolves around nurturing the yang shen unto maturity. When it is fully mature, it will be no longer be threatened in any way by the activity of the cognitive shen. This process was already mentioned above, when we spoke about how cultivation is undertaken in order to transmute the seeds of habit, and about how one must learn to re-collect the mind whenever it goes bounding away. Eventually the cognitive shen turns into a person's "subtle, profound activity." This term, which means that one's mind simply responds in kind to whatever it comes into contact with, is associated with the highest achievement in inner alchemy cultivation. At the point when a person's mind behaves like this, one's yang shen is fully mature and capable of acting as its own master. No longer will one fall into confusion due to external circumstances; one will have constant sovereignty over body and mind.

Huang Yuanji's comments about this stage are extensive, but I will refrain from delving into them here. Instead, I will reiterate the differences between primordial shen and cognitive shen, because they play an extremely important role in Taoist alchemy.

Throughout the entire process of inner alchemy cultivation, primordial shen should play the primary role. In actual practice, it is the primordial shen that refines the elixir. Yet, it is still a reality that primordial shen and cognitive shen are not two separate things; these are just names for different functions of one and the same shen. One of these functions is prior heaven in nature, while the other is later heaven in nature.

Shen's later-heaven function is externally oriented and based upon the making of distinctions. As distinctions are made, grasping is born, and thus shen gets tangled up in things that lie beyond itself. This cascade is what "cognitive shen" refers to.

Prior-heaven shen is an aspect of mind that is awake and observant, but makes no distinctions. "Primordial shen" is thus a term for awake, observant, non-differentiating mind.

The process of internal alchemy cultivation requires that cognitive shen be transformed into primordial shen. Most people identify cognitive shen as their own self. Scarce are those who recognize the true master within, which Chan Buddhism calls a person's "original face."

Primordial shen and primordial qi are also in fact one and the same. Primordial shen cannot be found, because it is not a thing. It is merely a point of numinous, radiant awareness within primordial qi. Unlike cognitive shen, primordial shen does not plan and do. It is simply observant consciousness that just naturally exists.

If they are understood in these terms, it is clear that cognitive shen and primordial shen share the very same fundamental essence. It is only their functions that are different. When one's cognitive shen is in charge, the whole of one's mind scatters into the outside world, and primordial shen remains totally hidden and unapparent.

However, when primordial shen arises and comes to the fore, cognitive shen will be transformed by it. The two types of shen are defined by a relationship in which when one rises, the other falls, and when one fades, the other strengthens. The more successfully one practices inner alchemy, the higher one's state will be, meaning that one will experience ever-lengthening spans of time when primordial shen takes primacy, and ever-shortening periods when cognitive shen is in the commanding role.

In the end, it is necessary for cognitive shen to become nothing more than one of primordial shen's functions or capabilities. That means having a later-heaven shen that functions "subtly and profoundly," responding spontaneously and naturally to whatever one happens to encounter along one's path.

8

兩重天地

TWO HEAVENS AND TWO EARTHS

Humans, born of heaven and earth, ultimately come from the single qi of pri-mordial pure yang. This qi is the qi of great harmony. It is the limitless indi-visible that fills all space.

Humans are sculpted by yin and yang, and thus our bodies of blood and flesh are born. Although this yin and this yang come after taiji, they are still true yin and true yang, free of dreg or residue, and still close to the pri-mordial qi of the great harmony.

Once one is born, one's qi is constrained, and one is deluded by exter-nal objects and phenomena. All of the yin and yang in one's physical body transforms into the shen of cognition and perception; into the qi of breathing and movement; and into the jing of sex between husbands and wives. Then there is only yin but no yang. This qi cannot be used as a "medicinal ingre-dient," so how could it then become the elixir?

It is clear that later-heaven jing and qi are but dross; they are residual substances. Nevertheless, in cultivation one cannot but make use of them in order to enter the gate. But be that as it may, the formation of the elixir makes no use of them whatsoever. Thus, those who use that which has shape and form cannot create the grain of golden elixir that is empty and nonexistent.

If a person cultivates hsing by vainly refining his or her temperament, and, in the cultivation of ming, refines only his or her flesh-and-blood life, it cannot be said an elixir cannot be created. Yet, even if such a person does create an elixir, it will only be an illusory elixir, and he or she will plummet into the dens of foxes and into the ranks of snakes and rats. Unable to avoid angering the gods, struck down by thunderclaps, he or she will never again be able to obtain a human body. How is this not tragic?

Outstanding people fully recognize that the great way of the golden elixir is achieved via clear, numinous qi. But clear, numinous qi does not return to us of its own accord, so one must make use of the true yin and true yang within one's own body, and then one will be able to summon this qi to come and gather. When the ancients spoke of the "the homologous double eight substances," they were speaking of true yin and true yang.

It is especially important to know that primordial qi is fundamentally without any markers that can be searched for, and that it has no location that can be guessed at. How, then, does one seek it and glimpse it? Only by this: it is at the moment when the true yin and true yang in one's own body become active that primordial qi has entered the body. One must then seize and take charge of the numinous mercury and yin jing in one's own body—and allow them to naturally congeal into the elixir.

An ancient immortal thus said: "Those who cultivate the Tao must first know that there are two heavens and earths, and two yins and yangs. Only then can one begin the work."

What is that which is called "two heavens and earths?" None other than prior heaven and later heaven.

What is referred to by "two yins and yangs?" It is like this: when one is meditating, one must have something within the later-heaven physical body that can be relied upon as a starting point. Exhalations and inhalations are yin and yang. Yin and yang originate in the qi of oneness. When the qi of oneness dissipates, it becomes yin and yang. In and out breaths are of ordinary yin and ordinary yang.[10] So, when students meditate, they must first regulate the external breath,[11] in order to elicit the primordial breath of Realized Humans.

In the regulating of the external breath, in the beginning one must give priority to intention. Mencius said: "Will, it is the commander of qi." An ancient immortal said: "If one wishes to complete the cultivation of the return of nine, one must first refine the self and manage the heart." It is thus clear that rightening the heart and making one's intent sincere is the basis of cultivation.

To regulate breathing, one lets one's eyes observe the center of the dantian,[12] and lets the breath descend into yinqiao.[13] One lifts the qi of yinqiao so that it enters the yellow court;[14] then, one uses the breath to cause the yin jing in the purple palace[15] to descend so that it meets the dantian. All of this involves ordinary yin and ordinary yang.

After doing this for some time, yin jing and yang qi will blend together and congeal within the earthly cauldron of the dantian. Naturally, yin essence will transform into the essence of the jing of true yang, and ordinary qi will transform into the qi of true yin. Vigorous and flourishing, they will fill one's entire body. All of this involves true yin and true yang; primordial qi is not far off.

All of you should know that primordial qi is fundamentally formless and unconditioned. That which is vigorous and flourishing is true yin and true yang; it is not the universe's primordial qi. If one refers to true yin and true yang as though they were the universe's primordial qi, one has strayed far from the Tao.

Know this: when, from within the vigorous and flourishing, there comes that which is placid, tranquil, still, and serene, this marks the returning of primordial qi. It is not separate from yin and yang; yet, it does not mingle with yin and yang.

My teacher instructed us that, each time we sat to meditate, it was necessary to have an experience of peacefulness, naturalness, and contentment, as only in this way could we glimpse our original faces. We could not become fixated upon primordial qi and see it as some kind of object. This is the correct way to practice.

When my teacher transmitted these mysteries, it could be said that she fully revealed the profound essentials, as though she dug out her own heart and liver to put on display for her students. Students, you must really put this into practice. Be like Dong Zhongshu, who said: "Be straight upon your path and do not scheme for personal benefits; understand the way and do not fuss over gain and loss." This is the correct way to practice.

As for whether or not there will be results: do not expect results, and do not become elated or despondent because you gain or lose. This is how you approach the Way.

■ ■ ■

When cognitive shen—the later-heaven, thinking mind—makes distinctions, it does so because one side of a polarity is being chosen. We constantly seek after that which we find beautiful and reject that which we find ugly. If we choose the high, then we reject that which is low; if we choose the pretty, then we reject that which is unattractive. Wherever there is polarization, we usually pick one side and reject the other. Distinction-making is a part of this process.

We hold on to ideals, we aim for goals. Yet, in our lives in the world as well as in our interior mental states, we often find ourselves discontented. All of us are seeking after some sort of beatitude or perfection, but the reality is that in many aspects of our lives we feel anything but perfect satisfaction. If we look closely at this incongruity, we will find the source from which the later-heaven, distinction-making mind originates. If we hope to cultivate the Tao, and if we hope to find tranquility in our hearts, then we have to learn how to leave the habit of polarizing and choosing sides behind.

On this path, it is necessary to become aware of the greater whole. The whole includes both beauty and ugliness, both heights and depths. The whole transcends polarities, and yet, at the same time, it accommodates any and all polarities. We must thus develop the authentic contentment and placidity that comes not from seeking for perfection in the outside world, but from looking at things in an entirely new way. When we are able to see the whole and accept it for what it is, instead of always trying to find the "perfect choice" from polar opposites, our hearts will remain deeply contented. No longer will we chase after a heaven that is external to ourselves; instead, we will carry heaven within us. We will then go about our lives in the world without any sense lacking, as though the Pure Lands were already within us.

Buddhists are fond of saying "if the heart is pure, then the whole world is pure." Events on this planet never unfold as we will them to. Perfection always eludes us. If we strive for a perfect world, our disappointment will never end. Everything in our world is in a state of flux. All things are impermanent and prone to change. There is nothing that can remain in a fixed state so as to bring us permanent satisfaction. For this reason, true satisfaction only exists within our own minds. The prior-heaven, original, limpid state at the core of our own hearts is an internal Pure Land. When we maintain the prior-heaven state within our hearts as we engage with life, our minds are able to calmly operate in the present moment, and we feel profound contentment.

. . .

In the discourse featured in this chapter, Huang Yuanji speaks of "two heavens and two earths," but in simpler terms, what he means is that there are "two realms," one being the prior heaven, the other being the later heaven. These concepts have already appeared time and again since the beginning of this book, but we have yet to thoroughly unpack them, so this chapter focuses on examining them in detail.

Understanding the idea that there are "two heavens and two earths"—one pair representing prior heaven, and the other representing later heaven—is both key to comprehending the theories underlying Taoist alchemy as well as critical to success in actual inner alchemy practice. From "temperature and timing" to "medicinal ingredients," prior heaven and later heaven play a role in telling us what it is that we refine and what kinds of methods we use to do so. It is the teachings on prior heaven and later heaven that distinguish inner alchemy from other types of cultivation, as well as from the side doors that lead to crooked paths. The study of inner alchemy does not revolve merely around nurturing the health of the later-heaven physical body. Rather, its goals lie in the pursuit of the transcendent realm of spiritual immortals. This is a system that aims for a return to the eternal source of the Tao. It therefore requires practitioners to return to the prior-heaven realm, instead of simply tinkering with our later-heaven, flesh-and-blood bodies.

If one wishes to arrive at a state of transcendence, the requisite materials are prior-heaven jing, qi, and shen, not later-heaven jing, qi, and shen. Similarly, one must practice with methods that employ the observant function of primordial shen's "true intent," instead of trying to rely on the chaotic mental activity of the later-heaven mind. The mistaken approach can be seen in some qigong practices, where no skills for entering the prior-heaven state are developed, and instead students just busy themselves with their physical bodies, using intention and deluded notions to try and transform themselves. They circulate qi this way and that through their conception (ren) and governor (du) meridians, on the basis of little more than imagination and fantasy. Students of such qigong do not activate prior-heaven qi, and they possess none of the prior-heaven ingredients needed for alchemy; as a result, the fruits of their labors are confined to the later-heaven realm.

In a very literal sense, the line between prior heaven and later heaven is drawn at the moment when our lives as human beings begin. "Prior heaven" refers to that which we were before our lives began to take shape—before our parents were even born. As soon as our parents give us our physical lives, we enter "later heaven." Another way of saying this is that our existences are not limited to life in our physical bodies; we have prior-heaven origins in addition to our physical manifestation in later-heaven form. If there is no recognition of this prior-heaven source, Taoist alchemy's entire theoretical edifice collapses. Without this understanding, there is no logical basis for the idea of cultivating the Tao and achieving transcendence.

If our lives did not have prior-heaven origins, and we were solely the products of the mixing of our father's sperm with our mother's ova, then we would be nothing more than composites of matter. If that were the case, then there would be no basis for transcendence. In fact, any religion that seeks for transcendence recognizes that every human's existence has a prior-heaven foundation. For instance, Buddhism holds that buddha-nature is the prior-heaven "real life" that all people ultimately possess. Even though people's buddha-natures are contaminated and obscured by later-heaven factors, precisely because buddha-nature is the ever-present foundation of all life, it is therefore possible to transform the later-heaven mind, reveal its intrinsic nature, and become a buddha.

From a Taoist point of view, each person's original, prior-heaven life was in the form of an undivided union of primordial shen and primordial qi. Taoists hold that even after prior-heaven life has entered into the later-heaven realm, cultivation makes it possible to discover the traces of prior heaven that are hidden within later heaven, and then to use the prior heaven to transform later heaven, so that the two unite as one. That process is what leads to transcendence.

■ ■ ■

The Buddhist concept of "emptiness" can be helpful for understanding the distinction between prior heaven and later heaven. Buddhism teaches that all objects and phenomena are "essentially empty." This means that there are no things that exist in a set, unchanging way and that all things come into being as a result of dependent arising. According to Buddhism, even though all things are inherently empty, because we lack the clarity needed to recognize the way things really are, we tend to grasp on to objects and phenomena, treating them as though they are in fact eternal, as though they can be prevented from changing, and as though they somehow come into being independently of the confluence of prior causes and current conditions.

Our habitual grasping is a starting point in Buddhist cultivation. From within the habit of grasping, one awakens to the empty nature of all objects and phenomena, in order to break the tendency of treating things as though they exist permanently and independently. Before this habit is broken, all people occupy a state Buddhism calls "the unreality that precedes the realization of emptiness." In this state, we treat the seeming as the real. This state is also described as one in which we recognize objects and phenomena through "false names." The names that we give things are called "false" (or "provisional") because anything that we can affix a name to came into being through dependent arising and is therefore ephemeral. Nothing that exists has a set, permanent form, as the existence of all things is contingent upon dependent arising. This is not to imply that Buddhism views objects and phenomena as "fake" or "bad." Buddhism simply holds that, because all things come into existence solely because of dependent arising, it is inevitable that they will change and finally cease to exist. To fail to recognize this is to see things in a manner that is "false."

Put another way, Buddhism holds that before we recognize that all things are essentially empty, we lack the insight necessary to see that any labels we give to objects and phenomena are "false names," and thus we tend to cling to things as though the way we see them in our minds reflects the way they actually are. After a person recognizes that all things are at essence empty, things themselves do not change in any way. What does radically change is the person's way of conceptualizing objects and phenomena.

Arriving at the realization of emptiness does not alter objects and phenomena because, just as was always the case before a person had this realization, objects and phenomena are still what they are because of dependent arising. This realization, however, does change a person's state of mind. After realizing emptiness, a person still uses "false" or "provisional" names to identify things, but this habit is no longer a handicap, because it becomes a way of interacting with the world in a conventional manner. This habit is no longer based upon a fundamental misunderstanding of what things are. Thus, in addition to describing "the unreality that precedes the realization of emptiness," Buddhism also teaches of "the unreality that *follows* the realization of emptiness." In the former, typical "unreality," the very habit of naming objects and phenomena as though they existed permanently and independently is what keeps a person trapped in the cycle of birth and death. In the latter, enlightened "unreality," a person still labels objects and phenomena in the exact same "false" way but does so from the position of a bodhisattva knowingly performing marvelous works, not from the position of a deluded person.

Another way of saying "dependently arisen" is "constituted by elements." Attachment to the view that things have an independent nature and are not constituted by disparate elements is what leads a person to "see the seeming as though it were real." Letting go of this view allows a person to see the true nature of things. This is why Buddhists say, "the very same mind can open two entirely different doors."[16] Buddhas and ordinary people live in the same universe and see the exact same objects and phenomena. What distinguishes ordinary people from buddhas is that they cling to things as though they were "real" (meaning immutable), instead of recognizing them for what they really are. Ordinary people have not yet realized emptiness; buddhas already have.

We can use the above theories to better understand the prior-heaven and later-heaven states that inner alchemy emphasizes. The later-heaven state is much like what Buddhism calls "the unreality that precedes the realization of emptiness." This is the mental realm of clinging and attachment. Conversely, prior heaven is akin to the realm of one who sees things for what they are—essentially empty. Therefore, what Taoism describes as moving from later heaven to prior heaven is akin to what Buddhism calls "going from unreality to seeing the emptiness of all things."

The next step in internal alchemy, using prior heaven to transmute later heaven, equates to what Buddhism calls "returning from emptiness and seeing the relative truth of that which is transient, unreal, and illusory." We have already seen this idea described in another way, as "the unreality that follows the realization of emptiness." This is the realm occupied by bodhisattvas working efficaciously to help other sentient beings.

Finally, the stage in cultivation that Taoism describes as "prior heaven and later heaven merged as one" is akin to what Tientai Buddhism calls "meditation on the mean" or "seeing the absolute unity of all opposites." At this stage, emptiness and transient, unreal phenomena are completely merged and inseparable.

■ ■ ■

I must emphasize that in borrowing Buddhist terminology to explain the meaning of prior heaven and later heaven, I am not attempting a rigorous study in comparative religion. The goal here is only to help us better understand the theories of internal alchemy by borrowing the vocabulary of another tradition to describe them.

With that in mind, let us recall that emptiness is the foundation of Buddhist wisdom. In Buddhism, wisdom is a question of whether or not one has awakened to emptiness, as this awakening is what allows one to break the habit of clinging to the myriad objects and phenomena in life and the world as though they were absolutely real. Similarly, in Taoist inner alchemy, moving from later heaven to prior heaven is the foundation of wisdom. If one does not attain prior heaven, one remains spinning in circles eternally in the later-heaven realm.

When we discuss prior heaven and later heaven, we have to go a step further and address the difference between "the prior heaven of prior heaven" and "the prior heaven of later heaven." The former is the pristine prior-heaven state, while the latter is the prior-heaven condition that exists concealed within later heaven.

For example, in the previous chapter's discourse, Huang Yuanji spoke of refining primordial jing so that it transforms into primordial qi, while in this chapter's discourse he speaks of "the single qi of primordial pure yang." These types of qi are not exactly the same, but they are both referred to as "primordial qi" in Taoism, so if we do not clearly delineate them, it is possible to end up confused about how inner alchemy is supposed to be practiced. One may also end up wondering, "If primordial qi is universal, how could it be possible to gain or lose it? What is the point of practicing?"

The "prior heaven of prior heaven" is what we have previously seen described as "the single qi of primordial pure yang" or "the qi of empty nonexistence." Indeed, this universal qi cannot be increased or diminished; there is never any more or less of it. However, when the qi of prior heaven manifests in our later-heaven bodies, it does so as the primordial prior-heaven qi that is concealed within later heaven. In other words, it manifests as primordial qi that can be refined from within jing, and then further refined into shen. When we speak of primordial qi from this perspective, it actually is something that a person can have more or less of, inasmuch as it is a measure of the degree to which the qi of prior heaven is active in a person's own body, and of the effects it yields. An individual's primordial qi is not later-heaven qi, and yet it is not quite the same thing as the pristine "prior heaven of prior heaven" universal primordial qi.

The same point applies to primordial jing. The primordial jing that leads to transcendence is indistinguishable from primordial shen and primordial qi—its essence is that of the original source, and it is blended harmoniously with all else that is prior heaven by nature. On the other hand, the primordial jing that we speak of refining in internal alchemy is not entirely prior-heaven jing. It is not the later-heaven jing that allows for sexual reproduction, either. Rather, the primordial jing that is refined into qi is a manifestation of pristine prior-heaven qi within the later-heaven human body. It has to exist in this transitional state in order for the transmutation of primordial jing into primordial qi to be possible.

The crucial point in internal alchemy cultivation is to connect to the pristine prior-heaven qi of empty nonexistence, because this qi is an inexhaustible wellspring of energy. Once we connect to it, there will be reactions in our bodies that reflect changes brought about by primordial jing, qi, and shen. All of the practice we do has one ultimate goal, which is to return to the pure prior-heaven state. However, when a practitioner returns there after having used prior heaven to transmute later heaven, as well as having merged prior heaven and later heaven into one, then that state too will be different from what it was before one began practicing internal alchemy.

To understand this highly abstruse point, we can once again draw upon Buddhist ideas. Buddhism teaches that all people have always been buddhas all along; what this means is that at the prior-heaven level, all people possess buddha nature. In light of this teaching, one might ask, "if that is the case, then why is it necessary to cultivate in order to achieve buddhahood?" The answer is that, if one does not cultivate, one's buddha-nature will remain concealed in latency instead of expressing itself. Thus, what this Buddhist teaching is really saying is that buddhahood is a potential, metaphorically similar to a seed that is planted in all of us. We all have this seed, but we have not yet done what it takes to let it sprout and mature into a fully grown tree. When we study and practice in order to reach buddhahood or spiritual transcendence, what we are doing is allowing that latent potential become fully realized. So, while the prior-heaven realm itself is not subject to change, there is a major difference between having the latent seeds of prior-heaven potential concealed within ourselves, and returning to the prior-heaven state after these seeds have reached their full potential within us.

■ ■ ■

To understand the meaning of "two heavens and two earths," we also need to examine how yin and yang fit into the picture. At the purely "prior heaven of prior heaven" level, yin and yang have not yet separated, so there is nothing that can be labeled as yin or yang. However, following the evolution from prior heaven to later heaven, when taiji transforms into yin and yang, different layers of yin and yang begin to appear. One of these layers is called "ordinary yin and ordinary yang," which refers to yin and yang that are of a wholly later-heaven nature. Another is "true yin and true yang," which refers to the "prior heaven of later heaven" discussed above. (In some schools of Taoism there also exists another layer of prior-heaven yin and yang called "pure yin and pure yang," which are transcendent forms of yin and yang. However, internal alchemy theory only uses the term "pure yang" to refer to the pristine prior-heaven state.)

Yin-yang theory is an extremely important part of internal alchemy; the two words are used to delineate numerous different concepts. For instance, both shen and qi as well as prior heaven and later heaven are understood as yin and yang pairs or dualities. Yin and yang in fact define all of the specialized vocabulary and symbols used in inner alchemy writings.

In inner alchemy there is a principle referred to as "the mating of yin and yang," which means that yin and yang can merge together by engaging in intercourse. In previous chapters the principles of inner alchemy cultivation were introduced through the frameworks of prior heaven and later heaven, hsing and ming, jing-qi-shen, and so forth. If we use this chapter's yin-and-yang framework to conceptualize inner alchemy, we can say what happens in practice is that the mating of later-heaven yin and yang brings forth true yin and true yang (true yin and true yang are the "prior heaven of later heaven," or the prior-heaven energies in the human body). Then, at the next stage, the mating of true yin and true yang establishes a prior-heaven taiji state within later heaven. It is this taiji, "born" of intercourse between true yin and true yang, which finally allows a person to return to the *wuji* state, which is also called the "prior heaven of prior heaven."

■ ■ ■

In internal alchemy cultivation, there are different stages at which yin and yang mate, and each stage has its own implications. We can roughly identify three different levels at which yin and yang couple with one another in order to better understand alchemy.

The first of these levels involves the yin and yang of the human body. Our psyche and our physiology are a yin-yang pair; this is shen and qi. While practicing inner alchemy, when we concentrate shen and return its light to shine upon our own selves, it mates and unifies with the jing and qi within our bodies. This state represents ordinary yin and yang harmoniously merging into one; it is what allows true yin and true yang to appear.

The next stage involves the intercourse of true yin and true yang. This merger is what allows the prior-heaven state to manifest. The mating of true yin and true yang presents an opportunity—a convergence of qi—that gives rise to the portal of the mysterious pass. The final stage comes after the mysterious pass appears, when the mating of yin and yang allows us to fully experience the prior-heaven state. A human's existence starts with prior heaven and moves into later heaven; this transition is synonymous with going from taiji into yin and yang. Alchemical practice takes one in the opposite direction, from later heaven back to prior heaven. The final stage of yin and yang's intercourse therefore takes us from yin and yang back to taiji.

The highest yin-yang pair in internal alchemy is that of the universe and the individual. What this statement implies is that there is a yin and yang relationship between the "small universe" of a person's body and the "great universe" consisting of the earth below and the heavens above. The inner alchemy cultivation that takes place at the level of this yin-yang pair is called "the great elixir." Herein, the individual blends into the earth and the heavens, and at the same time, the heavens and the earth blend into the person. When the yin-yang pair comprising the "microcosm" of an individual human being and the "macrocosm" of the entire universe comes together, the result is called "heaven and human merged as one." When a human and the universe are truly merged in oneness, the dualities of yin and yang, self and other, or self and universe cease to be. This state is what Chuang-tzu described as "the sky, the earth, and I all being born at once; the ten thousand things and I all existing as one." This is when the ego disappears, as the individuated "I" dissolves into the vast ocean of the cosmos. In terms of Taoist alchemy, this experience amounts to "returning to emptiness to merge with the Tao." It represents entry into the highest level of intercourse between yin and yang.

■ ■ ■

Women and men are also a yin-yang pair at a certain level, so in Taoist alchemy as well as in esoteric Buddhism, there exist schools of "yin-yang dual cultivation" that employ partnered practices where a man and a woman cultivate together as yin and yang. This book will not go into detail on these teachings, but we can still briefly examine how the principles of yin and yang play a role in such practices.

For starters, partnered cultivation is not the same as what are commonly referred to as the "bedroom arts," because their goals do not lie in having a certain type of sex life or in performing the sexual acts themselves. Rather, they are based upon the principle of "starting with yin and yang to arrive at taiji." From within any given yin-yang pair, it is possible to find the moment of convergence where they merge into oneness, which means that it is possible to locate the prior-heaven taiji state that transcends yin and yang. Thus, this kind of practice uses the opportunity presented by the confluence of a woman and a man's yin and yang in order to return to true yin and true yang. Subsequently, the mating and merging of their true yin and true yang is used to take the practitioners further back into the taiji state.

No small number of classical writings on Taoist alchemy criticize the bedroom arts as being ways of chasing after sexual desire. Typically, sexual desire causes one's energies to dissipate outward. Since the scattering of energy is antithetical to the goals of inner alchemy, it is not hard to see why internal alchemists would reject the bedroom arts. The partnered cultivation internal alchemists speak of is fundamentally different from the study of sexual techniques. Their methods do not aim for sexual release; rather, they seek to use the intercourse of yin and yang to produce an opportunity for the prior-heaven state to manifest and for the practitioners to enter it.

■ ■ ■

To summarize the above, the words "yin and yang" can have different meanings that apply to different layers of existence, but any level of yin-yang pairing can lead from later heaven toward prior heaven. Any mating and merging of ordinary yin and yang can lead to true yin and yang, and the joining of true yin and yang in intercourse can allow the prior-heaven state to manifest. The ultimate goal is always to go from later heaven back to prior heaven.

Taoist alchemists will sometimes say that all of the secrets of alchemy are held within just two words, "yin" and "yang." All of the concepts such as "dragon and tiger," "lead and mercury," "shen and qi," and so on, are nothing more than ways of talking about yin and yang. Thus, once one fully comprehends the overarching principles of yin and yang, it becomes possible to answer many of the questions that arise when practicing inner alchemy.

Up till now, this book has touched upon terms such as "refining jing, transforming qi," "refining qi, transforming shen," and "refining shen, returning to emptiness." Inner alchemy is a step-by-step process, within which numerous changes occur. However, once we understand alchemy's principles, when we actually go and practice, we cannot hold the expected results in our minds. We cannot practice with the thought in mind, "first I'll do this thing, and then I'll go and do that." We can only *do* it. Practice is just like farming. One cannot sit and think about what the harvest might be like. One simply has go out and sow the seeds.

In Taoism we often say that it is best not to seek anything and best not to pine after particular goals. With the mentality that must be adopted when practicing inner alchemy, there is no attachment to, hope for, or expectation of results. A practitioner finds an appropriate method, learns its principles, and then practices with almost simple-minded sincerity. Results will come on their own, naturally. In internal alchemy, constantly thinking about obtaining a certain outcome almost always prevents one from actually getting it. This is because attachment to outcomes comes from the later-heaven mind, and it therefore interferes with one's practice by disrupting the very ingredients that lead to results. Thus, one must develop the type of wisdom in which one sees that there is nothing to obtain, nothing to do, and no need to seek results. It is only possible to return to the prior-heaven state if one has this type of mindset.

■ ■ ■

Now, let's explore some key points in Huang Yuanji's discourse.

In the first paragraph, Huang mentions "the single qi of primordial pure yang." This term is synonymous with "the qi of empty nonexistence" as well as "the qi of great harmony." This qi is the state from which universe originated; it fills the universe, such that there is nowhere it is not found. Humans originate in this qi, too. While still in its midst, we are slowly acted upon by yin and yang, until we are born in our later-heaven bodies of flesh and blood. This process takes us from prior heaven to later heaven, and from taiji to yin and yang.

In the very beginning of one's emergence from taiji to yin and yang, one is still composed of true yin and true yang. Being free of impurities, one is still close to the primordial qi of great harmony. However, the longer one lives in the later-heaven realm, the more one's later-heaven desires and temperament occlude one's original state, and the more one's prior-heaven qi transforms into later-heaven qi. This is how one's original true yin and true yang turn into ordinary yin and ordinary yang. This is also why primordial shen retreats into the background, and why the "later-heaven shen of cognition and perception" takes command in the foreground of our being. When cognitive shen, "the qi of breathing and movement," and "the jing of sex between husbands and wives" all dominate our lives, this means that later-heaven jing, qi, and shen are fully functional.

Later-heaven jing, qi, and shen are incapable of serving as the "medicinal ingredients" that are refined into the elixir. In internal alchemy, it is only prior-heaven jing, qi, and shen that can serve this purpose. This is why Huang Yuanji says that even if one manages to refine some kind of "elixir" using the later-heaven three treasures, it will ultimately be an "illusory elixir." Being something that lacks a foundation in reality, it will cause one to enter the side doors that lead on to sinister paths.

In Taoist internal alchemy, in order to refine the so-called elixir, it is critical to locate the serene, radiant qi of prior heaven. Primordial, prior-heaven qi is the foundation for alchemical practice. This qi responds when true yin and true yang join in intercourse within us.

The fact that the mating of true yin and true yang summons prior-heaven qi is an extremely important principle in alchemical cultivation. One of the implications of this teaching is that a person who is still incapable of directly experiencing prior-heaven qi can nevertheless begin practicing using later-heaven yin and yang.

Later-heaven yin and yang can be refined to yield true yin and true yang. Because true yin and true yang are quite close to prior heaven, when they respond to one another, a configuration of qi is created that resonates with prior-heaven qi and causes it to manifest. The only way to cause the formless, shapeless qi of prior heaven to respond within our later-heaven bodies is by experiencing it when true yin and true yang mate within us.

■ ■ ■

There are distinct levels at which inner alchemy is practiced. The type of training that brings one from later heaven to prior heaven one step at a time is known as the "gradual approach." There is also what is known as the "highest alchemical method," in which a practitioner starts at the very beginning with empty nonexistence. Starting with prior heaven is a viable path, but if a beginner is incapable of realizing the prior-heaven state, he or she will need to begin by practicing with later-heaven yin and yang. Later-heaven yin and yang is in and of itself a multilayered concept with numerous different meanings. Later-heaven breathing is one place in which later-heaven yin and yang are found, so it is possible to begin training in internal alchemy by training in bringing regularity to the breath.

When regulating later-heaven breathing, one lets the use of intent take center stage. Because the breath has no consciousness of its own, the first step toward regulating one's breathing is regulating one's mental activity. The qi associated with breathing plays a passive role, whereas intent plays an active role, and it "commands" the qi of breathing. Thus, regularity cannot be brought to the to the breath until regularity is brought to the mind.

Above, Huang Yuanji mentions "refining the self." This is work that starts with refining our hearts by evening out our mental activity. In other words, on a cultivation path that begins with later-heaven ordinary yin and ordinary yang, one of the very first tasks is to bring order to the activity in our later-heaven minds.

When one is actually practicing, one concentrates shen and turns the observant light of consciousness inward, so that it radiates upon the dantian; then one coordinates one's breathing with the mind's observance, so that mind and body, shen and qi, all meet within the dantian. This is one way of creating intercourse between ordinary yin and ordinary yang. When ordinary yin and yang mate and merge in this way, a change will occur within the dantian in which the "true yang essence" arises. The essence of true yang harmonizes with true yin qi. Shen and qi join in intercourse. In the midst of later heaven, prior-heaven transformations gradually begin to take place. The shorthand name for this stage of training is simply "true yin, true yang."

When the above changes take place, the primordial qi of the body will resonate with its close cousin, the universal "prior-heaven-of-prior-heaven" primordial qi. Prior-heaven-of-prior-heaven qi is, as Huang Yuanji says, "formless and unconditioned"—there is no method that can be used to search for it, nor is there any way to fathom it. The primordial qi that can be felt is that which is in one's own body, which responds to universal primordial qi. The "vigorous and flourishing" feeling that Huang Yuanji describes indeed reflects the flowing movement of one's own body's true qi, but as it is something that can be felt, it must not be mistaken for "prior-heaven-of-prior-heaven" qi.

Prior-heaven primordial qi and primordial shen are one. Thus, when a person is in a state of profound stillness, with no thinking whatsoever, primordial qi will return to that person of its own accord. This is a state that cannot be classified as yin or yang. It transcends the polarity of yin and yang, and yet, even so, it is totally inseparable from the workings of yin and yang. What this state reflects is the interrelationship of the prior-heaven and later-heaven realms.

When the processes described here are unfolding, one must remember not to get carried away by paying attention to the qi reactions taking place in one's body. None of the changes in the body, including those coming from the arousal of qi, indicate the presence of the original, pure, primordial qi of the universe. Rather, it is when primordial shen becomes active because one is in utter serenity and stillness that, by virtue of its own nature, the true primordial qi of the universe arrives. Then, primordial shen and primordial qi merge into oneness.

■ ■ ■

Regardless of what stage of cultivation one is working on, "regulating the mind" is the crux of practice, because it is the mind that leads whatever other factors are involved. Even if one is undertaking ming practices in order to transform the body, it is still the mind that is in charge. Moreover, it is only when one's heart returns to its fundamental aspect—when one is living in a state of uncontrived, natural peace and tranquility—that one will induce a response from the universe's primordial prior-heaven qi.

Universal primordial qi is not a thing or a substance. When the word "qi" is used in this context, its implications are entirely different from what they are when it appears as part of "shen and qi," the pair of opposites that describes the human mind and body. In fact, primordial qi and primordial shen are one and the same. They can be differentiated only inasmuch as the term "primordial shen" represents the uncanny, numinous consciousness of the universe's prior-heaven energy, whereas the term "primordial qi" represents the energetic foundation carrying this consciousness. Thus, the only possible way to correspond with the universe's primordial qi is by restoring one's primordial shen.

■ ■ ■

By clearly outlining prior heaven and later heaven as we have in this chapter, it is possible to see the difference between "the great, unsurpassed Way" of true internal alchemy, and typical later-heaven methods of promoting health. If a method or a system does not emphasize the prior-heaven state, does not teach how to cultivate the mind (for example, by illuminating the mind to reveal its nature), and does not teach one how to enter the state of pristine prior-heaven awareness, then no matter how hard one trains with the methods of that system, one will never go beyond spinning around in circles inside the human body. All of one's training and skill will unfold at the later-heaven level.

That which is later heaven is, by its very nature, limited. All things in the later-heaven realm have a beginning, and therefore they also have an end. Later-heaven training is not reciprocal with the authentic "great Way" of prior-heaven cultivation. Even if one's practice fills one with vitality and vigor from true qi, and even if one truly feels physical well-being, so long as one's practice is divorced from the prior-heaven state—meaning that when one trains, one's primordial shen does not take the lead—then none of the transformations that occur in one's body are indicative of the activity of pristine, prior-heaven universal qi.

Transformations that occur in the human body are ultimately later-heaven reactions. Because they have beginnings, they inevitably come to their ends. Therefore, in Taoist inner alchemy, all later-heaven, you wei cultivation methods—that is to say, all ming practices—serve only one purpose, which is to help the practitioner enter the prior-heaven state. Entry into this state is the only thing that counts as truly "going home." The jewel of inner alchemy can only be found in the prior-heaven realm, and thus, it is there that one's real goal must lie.

In order to emphasize the gravity involved in publicly revealing the subtlest and most essential teachings of Taoist alchemy, Huang Yuanji used an old Chinese idiom that likens this to a person cutting out his or her own heart and liver to show the world. What he means is that these discourses reveal internal alchemy's heart of hearts—they are far more than later-heaven practices bound by the limits of later-heaven existence.

Authentic training requires the involvement of primordial shen. But what leads primordial shen to respond to us? Huang Yuanji quotes Dong Zhongshu, a Confucian philosopher who lived during the Western Han dynasty, to answer this question. Dong said, "Be straight upon your path and do not scheme for personal benefits; understand the way and do not fuss over gain and loss." Huang's teaching is simply that we should reduce our later-heaven mind's tendencies to focus on making achievements, accruing benefits, avoiding losses, obtaining things, and having control.

Huang quotes Dong Zhongshu to remind us that we should not grasp at the effects and fruits of Taoist practice. The only way forward lies in finding an authentic path and then applying ourselves to the training. This means we have to deeply understand the principles underlying cultivation, and then just resolutely practice. In our hearts, we should harbor no expectations, no thoughts of gain or loss, nor any tendency to become elated or despondent over what happens next. When we make gains, we should not become overjoyed; when we face setbacks, we should not react with anxiety. Regardless of what kind of transformations occur in the body or in the mind, they should not disturb us. This is the only way to progress toward the state in which primordial shen is in command.

9

返本還原

GOING BACK TO THE ROOT, RETURNING TO THE SOURCE

The qi that is one spirals between heaven and earth, giving rise to the ten thousand things. But inside this unified qi, because there is intrinsic order, there arises differentiated qi. Because there is differentiated qi, there arise forms.[17] *It is from this that the infinite variety of things and the countless myriad changes come, and there is nothing that can limit them.*

The intrinsic order is taiji. Qi is yin and yang. Forms are of the five phases. Intrinsic order constitutes humans' original nature; qi constitutes humans' minds; form constitutes humans' bodies and sensory organs.

A human body and its sensory organs includes the ears, eyes, mouth, and nose; from these come seeing, hearing, speaking, movement, and all manner of behavior and expression. Moreover, all of our comings and goings, our social obligations, and our hundreds of daily activities arise pell-mell from the body and its organs. From them, too, come the burning of passion and desire, and then the birth of pretense and recklessness. In the end, our original, perfect brightness is obscured by objects and phenomena, and autonomy is lost.

It is not things that burden humans, but humans who burden themselves with things. How is this so?

After our original natures split away from the primordial qi of the universe, cognitive shen emerges and springs into activity. Cognitive shen does not know to turn inward and observe the interior, nor to gather itself in the land of nothing at all. Therefore, our minds are dragged about by passions, and passions are slaves to things. When one does not know to go back to the root and return to the source, the universal intrinsic order is obliterated.

Nevertheless, there has never been a person who did not have an original nature, a later-heaven mind, and passions and desires. So, why is it that sages make use of passion and desire to refine their minds and natures in order to become sages, while ordinary people let their minds and natures chase after passions and desires, and thus remain ordinary? Were sages bestowed with something we were not? No—the reason is that we do not know how to reverse course and to return.

Reversing course and returning is not a difficult task. Buddhists say, "Look back over your shoulder, and you will immediately see the shore." Confucians say, "Overcome thinking, and you become a sage." The entire path lies within just a single thought. So it is said, "Put down your butcher's knife, and you instantly become a buddha." How simple and easy! Confucius said: "If one's will is benevolent, there is no evil," and, "I wish for benevolence, and here benevolence is." Clearly, a single wanton thought is enough to make one lose one's true, natural nature. But a single thought that is fully awakened is unsurpassed bodhi.

What is required is no more than "cleansing the heart and stepping back to dwell within the obscure." Do not look upon the methods of cleansing the heart as though they were difficult, as if you had to climb a ten-thousand-story building. Actually, with one swing of your oar, you can arrive at the other shore.

Mencius said, "Great women and men are those who never lose the newborn innocence in their hearts." What is a heart that possesses the innocence of a newborn? Before its primordial unity separates, while it is still in the embrace of taiji, even though a newborn has ears, eyes, a mouth, and a nose, these organs do not cause the baby to drift into the contrivances of language and expression. It does not reject things it sees or hears, nor use words and actions to avoid those things. As for how it uses its consciousness, whether a newborn shows happiness or anger, sadness or joy, these all come naturally and spontaneously. When it comes time to laugh, a newborn laughs; when it comes time to cry, a newborn cries. Beforehand it was not thinking, afterward it will not remember. While in the moment, it acts only because that is its nature. Its heart is like a giant bell hanging in a temple. When struck, it rings; when the striking ceases, so does the ringing. Such a mind is wholly real, limpid and quiescent; to it, the ten thousand manifestations of nature are all empty. Such a heart can truly be called guileless and unaffected. If it acts, that is because it is natural to act; when it ceases to act, that is because it is natural to cease.

The above is the heart seal of sages. If a person is able to fully recover the newborn mind, even though he or she will not immediately arrive at unsurpassed, universal enlightenment, nevertheless, starting from darkness, light will gradually come, and in time it will be an enormous blaze that is integrated with emptiness and equivalent in function to the sun and the moon. This result, does it not come from the blending of shen and qi? The Heart Seal Classic states: "Maintain nothingness while keeping watch on that which exists; the two merge as though in a whirlwind." This is enough to show that the reason people cannot merge comes from their distinction-making minds.

When the ancients taught people how to cultivate hsing and refine ming, they required students to enter into primordial undifferentiation, their minds like those of hens brooding upon their eggs, indistinct and withdrawn, barely discernable, unknowing and undiscriminating. Only in this way can one obtain the warm, harmonious primordial qi of heaven and earth and then merge with it as one. This is how to hatch a chick that is just like its mother.

From the above, we can see that if a person wishes to practice inner alchemy, he or she must eliminate the sharply discerning mental habits of humans, and then naturally embrace the indistinct, traceless mind of Tao. When one accomplishes this, desires restrain themselves without one's needing to restrain them, and the intrinsic order maintains itself without one's needing to maintain it. How is this possible? It is so simply because before taiji separates—before the primal undifferentiation splits—that is the way primordial qi is.

You students still do not understand this qi, so I will try to approximate it in words. It is like this: when the sky is clear, and the sun is shining everywhere, and all things are out under the sun, you will not notice the sunlight growing brighter. You will only feel it when the light begins to diminish, at the cusp of the day's turn toward night, when there is an indistinct, foggy, unclear sensation, and you are unable to say where the daylight is going. This is the shade given by yin; it is the breathing of night and day; it is the moistening that comes from rain and dew. From these come the vitality that lets *things flourish. If there was only expansion and never any gathering back inward, then even heaven and earth would eventually exhaust themselves. There can only be this universe that has not ceased for ten thousand eons because yang rises, showing its capacity to grow and multiply limitlessly, while yin shelters things, harboring their qi of endless transformation. One opens, the other closes; one gathers, the other expands. The human body is heaven and earth in miniature, so how is it not the same?*

As for you students who are already weakened by age, for a long time your yang qi has been rising and leaking excessively, so henceforth, both night and day, you must "step back to dwell within the obscure" in order to increase your longevity and eliminate your illnesses. Otherwise, like spring flowers already in bloom, before long you will be wilting.

Taoism teaches to start cultivation by letting the "human mind" perish. It is thus said: "From that which exists, go toward that which does not." That which exists is the later-heaven mind of knowledge and sensations that are both chaotic and false. You must let this mind of knowledge and sensation perish. Then, while embracing the indistinct-but-brilliant real oneness, you can obtain the reality of wuji and taiji.

Next, Taoism teaches to search for the "mind of Tao." It is thus said, "From that which does not exist, an existence arises." When the portal of the mysterious pass opens, you must promptly gather without stopping for even an instant. Beginning like a wellspring of utterly pure water, this is where the real medicinal ingredients, temperature, and timing all lie. Starting here, you must gather and coalesce for a long period of time. This is what Mencius implied when he said "produce qi through the accumulation of righteous deeds."

From that point on, remain self-possessed. This is what Mencius instructed when he said "be nourished by rectitude and sustain no injury." If you continue like this, never ceasing day or night, how could your yang— which is like the faintest dawn light—fail to increase until it becomes so incredibly powerful and vast that it fills all between heaven and earth?

Be not like those modern students who mostly seek fast results; who expect success to be just around the corner; who train for a month or two without seeing progress, and then conclude that this is not the Tao. They either become too impatient to persist, or else they conclude that the greatest treasures of the highest heavens could not have been passed lightly into the hu-

man world, and lament that because they lacked destined affinity, they never found a real teacher to lift them out of suffering. The people who neglect to practice for these reasons are countless.

How many people realize that the phrase "building a foundation in one hundred days" and the method of "breastfeeding for three years"[18] apply to those whose shen is mature and harmonious, whose qi is abundant and flowing freely, whose self-centered desires have been eliminated, and who flow along with the intrinsic order of the universe. Now, place your hand over your heart and ask yourself, "Are my shen and qi wholly complete yet? Have I purified my desires and restored intrinsic order yet?" If you have not arrived at this stage, then how will you build the foundation?

Listen: the portal of the mysterious pass is present at all times, wherever you are. The key is but a flash of sudden, timely inspiration. As though you were grabbing hold of mist or clutching a cloud, obtain it from out of nothingness. Do not miss the moment. It is like Yan-tzu said: "Via the function of shen, notice things arising before they become evident." That is what we Taoists refer to when we say: "At the living time of zi when yang is born, it is shen that knows."[19]

If knowing comes prematurely, that is "future mind." If knowing comes belatedly, that is "past mind." If, when the mysterious pass is right before you, there is even a hint of thinking or planning, that is "present mind." These three minds are obstacles to the Way. That which clutches not at these three minds, and which is untainted by even a speck of dust, is called shen. What else could it be called? This is the real, unclouded medicinal ingredient, which naturally births the pure dharmakaya.

The vital point is that inner alchemy practice is no different from the natural transformations that take place between heaven and earth during the course of a year. No matter how extraordinary and manifold they may be, there is not one transformation in nature that was not charged with the yang that is born on the winter solstice.[20] If the Way of heaven and earth proceeds gradually, how, then, could humans—whose dust, muck, and pollution are already so thick that they are impossible to wash away in one go—not need to begin gradually, by starting with the subtle?

Since time immemorial, there has never been a vast, enlightened golden immortal who did not begin with the portal of the mysterious pass. They all

eventually realized their infinite dharmakayas by swiftly gathering and refin-
ing at the moment of the subtlest stirring of qi, accumulating until they were
complete.

However, when yang faintly begins to stir, most people are utterly indif-
ferent, and they let it disappear. They do not understand that a single spark
can cause a blaze that consumes a mountain, or that solitary drops of water
eventually fill a canal.

It is always up to each individual to fully understand this Way. Wher-
ever you find yourself, be vigilant and protect your progress. Month by month,
year by year, store up and accumulate. Nobody who has done this has failed
to achieve supreme bodhi.

This is perhaps the most difficult task that exists between heaven and
earth, but it is humans who make it difficult. The heavens do not restrain
mankind.

■ ■ ■

In the final two chapters of this book, I will not meticulously unpack Huang Yuanji's discourses. Instead I will focus on clarifying
the themes that have recurred throughout this book, while pointing
out the relevant issues Huang raises in the last of his lectures.

If we are "cultivating the Tao," what exactly is it we are doing?
People's reasons for cultivating are different, and so are their goals.
Some people have religious belief in their backgrounds, some are interested in the journey of transformation, and others are looking to
improve their health. But in the end, most people who are attracted to
Taoist cultivation are ultimately looking for a sort of spiritual home-
coming. Put another way, we are looking for the true meaning of life
and for final liberation. With regard to those two things, all religions
point in a similar direction. In the language of comparative religion,
the "ultimate concern" common to all religions is the search for a way
to bring real peace to the heart. Despite all of the dissimilarities in
various religions' vocabularies and theories, there are commonalities
they all share. Buddhists say, "phenomena may be infinite, but they
are all attributable to the mind." In the end, all religions bring us back
into our own hearts and minds.

Most of us lack the ability to peacefully settle our hearts and minds. Our hearts are homeless. Drifting like vagrants, we wander from one mental object to the next, chasing after this thing or that. In our lives, we constantly search for things outside ourselves, be they fame, profit, stature, or glory. We end up losing sight of ourselves amid the endless streams of ideas that crowd our minds.

At a certain point, we end up believing that we know and own lots of things, and we latch our minds on to our knowledge and possessions in order to reinforce our senses of self. But, in the end, ideas are incapable of bringing peace or liberation, because the heart can never obtain contentment from the objects of the mind. The things we believe we know and own are all too ephemeral and too prone to changing and disappearing to satisfy the heart. Sometimes we even achieve one of our goals or fulfill one of our fantasies, only to quickly become bored of whatever it was we sought, and then go off in search of something else, just as unsatisfied as ever. Other times, when we fail to realize our goals, we suffer on account of feeling unfulfilled.

We lose ourselves in the unending churn of events and objects outside of us. Buddhism talks about samsara, or "cyclic existence," the endless chain of transmigration we bring about by our chasing after the objects of our desires. In samsara, our mental objectification pulls us through different states of existence, leaving us incapable of deciding our own fates and unable to return the true sovereigns of our minds. The very objects we mentally fixate upon become the things to which we lose ourselves, and which make it impossible for the heart to find its way home, settle down, and truly live.

The heart's true home is not found in anything that can be possessed. In other words, peace will never come to us from anything we can claim to own. Nevertheless, given that we can possess things, this means that at the core of life there is something that does the possessing. The questions thus arise: Just who is it that possesses things? What is the real core of life? Who am *I*? These are the eternal questions lying at the heart of the world's religions.

To be a person whose heart has not found its true home is to be incapable of living a real life, because such a person does not know who he or she truly is. On the outside, such a person may have everything, from success and recognition to wealth and power, but these things are essentially no different from clothing draped over a person's true being. No "clothing" of this sort will ever be a source of everlasting riches; even if it brings a person happiness, impermanence guarantees that the happiness will be unreliable. And if this "clothing" should transfix the person who "wears" it, then, in the end, it will only lead to yet more worry and attachment.

■ ■ ■

The fundamental objective of all Taoist cultivation is the return to the true essence of the heart. Finding our "homes" means finding the central core of our lives. However, to use the word "finding" can be misleading, because it suggests that there is some "thing" or some target that can be located within us. Moreover, to speak of finding also carries the connotation that we are dissatisfied with ourselves.

Using terms like "searching" and "finding" suggests going somewhere to find something, but this search is not one that takes place beyond ourselves. Rather, we return to our hearts in order to conduct our searches, and paradoxically, we conduct them via "non-searching." "Non-searching" is the opposite of most seeking we do in our lives, because when things are sought, usually there is clinging or attachment involved. So, on the Taoist path, we have to put a stop to the typical sort of seeking, which is externally oriented and object-focused, and "search without searching."

There is another important question lying at the heart of internal alchemy: If this path is one of returning, where is it that we come back to? The answer is that we come back to the here and now. We come back to the present, which means coming back to the original state of life. The present is where our hearts' "homes" are, and it is in the present where the unadulterated, original state of mind can be found.

The only reason we "leave home" is that we constantly let our minds disperse into the external world. Thus, "returning" is a behavior that takes a course contrary to that followed by most people in the world. Returning means settling down peacefully in the here and now, so that the mind will no longer be fooled by the objects it conceives. To return is to strip the heart naked of its "clothing," and to let it be what it has actually been all along.

When the heart ceases searching for things outside itself, its vagrancy in the external world finally comes to an end. At last, the heart comes to rest within its own being. Instead of radiating outward, the light of its awareness shines back into its own interior, allowing the heart to know itself. When we experience this, we clearly understand who we are, and we awaken to our real nature, which is formless and unconditioned. To do this is to find the real self.

■ ■ ■

Finding the "home of the heart" is the basic point of cultivation. Terms we have encountered in this book like "illuminating the mind to reveal its nature," "primordial shen," and "the real protagonist in life" all point at the exact same thing. All of the Taoist methods like tranquil sitting, regulating shen, regulating the breath, and so forth, are also all meant to help us return to our hearts' homes.

If our minds are too chaotic, in the beginning we may need to find expedient methods that help us develop skill in bringing order to our mind-body states. But these methods only exist to help us return to the state of total tranquility, where there is no restlessness in the heart whatsoever. In other words, the methods only serve to help us return to our self-nature.

When we "come back" to the true nature of the self, worries and concerns are nowhere to be found. The heart occupies a state of freedom, fluidity, and unity with the Tao. In that state we experience beauty that cannot be expressed in words, as well as a sense of liberation that comes directly from the energy and power of the Tao.

Conversely, if we do not return to the home of the heart, and instead conduct our searches outside ourselves, what I just described will never be found. This is true even for those who search for the Tao within religious faith.

The original meaning of all religions lies in helping people to liberate their hearts—religions are meant to help people attain the "kingdom of heaven" within themselves. However, in reality, as religions develop over time, the rituals and dogmas that take shape within them often end up becoming the very things that pull the wool over their believers' eyes. It is all too easy to lose sight of religions' original intent and end up sidetracked in the midst of their ornate, even garish, trappings.

Many of us hope to meet some sort of "master" who can grant us liberation. Some of us hope that some sort of religious belief, article of faith, or doctrine will bring us freedom. Others among us lodge our hopes in a future incarnation or in some faraway realm. The truth is that all such ideas lead people astray, and the behaviors they lead to send us galloping directly away from the Tao. In fact, a genuinely religious mindset impels a person to trace backward through whatever has become formed and conditioned within a religion, in order to find the source from which these things emerged. People who have faith in a religion should trace so far back as to arrive at the state of mind of its founder at the time of the religion's conception.

■ ■ ■

The Green Pine Temple here in Hong Kong belongs to the Complete Reality school of Taoism. The original spirit of this tradition was embodied by its founder, Wang Chongyang. Wang Chongyang taught that to cultivate the Tao is to seek "complete reality." This work is not accomplished through any sort of external rituals, but through making jing, qi, and shen whole, which makes whole both one's life as well as the brightness of one's fundamental essence. Wang taught his students to transcend all external concerns such as success, fame, wealth, and rank, and instead to return to the home of the heart. In Taoism, this process is described by the phrase that serves as the title for this chapter: "Going back to the root, returning to the source."

To go back to the root and return to the source is to trace backward to where our lives originally came from—the Tao—in order to obtain harmony and liberation therein. Once our later-heaven lives take shape, the tendency of our jing, qi, and shen to dissipate outward takes us further and further away from the source. Going back to it liberates us.

There is a well-known phrase that expresses the underlying principles of internal alchemy: "Go with the current and remain mortal;

counter the current and transcend." This phrase alludes to the two directions that the universe's evolution unfolds in, as well as the two directions in which the skill we develop in cultivation can take us. This phrase's two main ideas, going with the current and going against the current, encompass Taoism's worldview, its understanding of individual life, and its basic theory of how to cultivate.

It is important to be aware that the notions of going with and against the current apply to specific contexts. If one is not clear about what these contexts are, there is a risk of developing a warped understanding of the teachings. For instance, Lao-tzu, one of Taoism's ancestral teachers, stated "the Tao follows its intrinsic nature." Given that the Tao was originally said to "follow its intrinsic nature," some scholars hold that internal alchemy amounts to a revolution in Taoist thought, in which the old teaching of following intrinsic nature was replaced with a new teaching, to "go against the current." However, scholars who think this way are operating on the basis of a major misunderstanding, because they are unclear about the frames of reference in which following the current and going against the current apply.

There is actually no contradiction between statements such as "go backward against the current to become an immortal" and "the Tao follows its intrinsic nature." Quite the opposite, the two teachings share the exact same essential meaning. The concept of "intrinsic nature" has two layers of meaning. One of these layers points to the realm of intrinsic nature realized by sages. This is the realm of wu wei, where one's essential nature is integrated with that of the Tao itself. But there is another context in which the term "intrinsic nature" is used, in this case to describe ordinary people doing whatever comes naturally to them. When used in this way, "intrinsic nature" refers to people's habituated characters; in this sense, "to follow nature" means to float along with the force of karma. If I was prone to getting drunk or taking drugs, I could very well ask, "aren't I just following my nature? Aren't I just going with the flow?" While that may be the case from a certain standpoint, this is not the type of "following intrinsic nature" that pertains to Taoist cultivation.

Just memorizing the lexicon of Taoist practice is not enough—one needs to directly experience its real meaning. Some people latch on to superficial meanings, believing until the end of their days that "the Tao follows its own nature" means having carte blanche to live a life of debauchery, because that's "just being natural." The truth is that one must have reached a very high stage in cultivation to be able to follow one's intrinsic nature. At this stage, all the pretense, scheming, and divisiveness of the later-heaven mind are gone. This is not a stage where one just goes along with spontaneously arising human desires; rather, it is the stage of flowing with the self-arising suchness of the Tao.

■ ■ ■

In order to better understand the worldview that internal alchemy draws upon, we can use "0" to symbolize the Tao. Emptiness and Tao are of the same plane, in the sense that the word "emptiness" can be used to suggest the Tao's character and properties. So, since zero can represent emptiness, we can use it to allude to the Tao.

In previous chapters we discussed the process of "refining jing, transforming qi," "refining qi, transforming shen," and "refining shen, returning to emptiness." This ordering represents "going against the current." It is the path of becoming "immortal" by returning to the emptiness ("0") of the Tao itself, where all the universe's myriad objects and phenomena have yet to take shape. The course of evolution followed by the universe goes in the opposite direction of inner alchemy. Thus, in this context, "going with the current" means following the direction in which the emptiness of the Tao gives birth to the ten thousand things.

"The unified qi of prior heaven" can be expressed with the number 1. There is not a massive difference between 0 and 1. Zero signifies a state of formless undifferentiation that holds in store the potential for infinite transformations. In Taoism, what emptiness refers to is formlessness containing infinite potential. One signifies the exact same thing that zero does in Taoism, but instead of describing its formlessness like zero does, one conceptualizes it as a single, holistic existence. The same relationship Taoist ontology describes with zero and one can be found in the Buddhist phrase, "the absolute void contains subtle, profound being." Taoism's "zero" is equivalent to Buddhism's "absolute void," while Buddhism's "subtle, profound being" is akin to the Taoist "one."

In this framework, "one" is also another way of saying unified prior-heaven qi. While unified prior-heaven qi is something that has no opposite, it contains the potential for all opposites, as well as for all transformations. Like a seed gradually cracking open, the one qi of prior heaven allows the emergence of two things: shen and qi. As emptiness transforms into substantiality, it passes through "one" and then evolves into the "two" of shen and qi. Shen is born through the transformations of emptiness, and qi is born from the transformations of shen. At the level of "two" are born the opposites of yin and yang. When shen and qi further differentiate, they become jing, qi, and shen, which are represented by "three." From this point onward, they continue to evolve into the myriad objects and phenomena with shape and form in the universe.

The above process is what Lao-tzu described as "Tao gives rise to the one, the one gives rise to the two, the two give rise to the three, and the three give rise to the ten thousand things." Using numbers, we can express it as 0 → 1 → 2 → 3 → 10,000.

Some readers may respond quizzically, "but is that *really* how the universe evolved?" Of course, what I just described is not meant to be read like an astrophysicist's description of the universe's genesis. It is only a vehicle to help us conceptualize the universe's evolution in a way that gives us a theoretical foundation for internal alchemy practice. This theoretical foundation can help us understand the rules governing the transformations that occur in life, as well as in Taoist practice. At the same time, the results of cultivation can serve to confirm this basic understanding of universal evolution. Internal alchemy does not seek confirmation using the instruments of scientific research, but through the inner experiences that come from training.

■ ■ ■

The above describes the universe's evolution as it "follows the current." "Going against the current" can therefore be expressed as 10,000 → 3 → 2 → 1 → 0. This entails starting from the point where all the "ten thousand things" have already taken form, and moving toward the "three," which represents the "medicinal ingredients" of inner alchemy practice: jing, qi, and shen. The process of refining jing and transforming qi takes a practitioner to the "two," which represents shen and qi. The refining of qi so that it transforms shen further reduces the "two" into "one" (the one can be described as primordial qi or as primordial shen—in fact, these two things are one and the same). Finally, refining shen to return to emptiness brings a person to "zero," which means returning to the Tao.

This kind of numerology serves to map out the direction a person should be taking in his or her cultivation. If one's course of practice involves ever-increasing complexity and proliferating mental activity, then the direction one's practice is going in is incorrect. Cultivation should "go against the current" of the universe's evolution from 0 to 10,000, which means that one should start with action and progress to nonaction, until one arrives at 0 and returns to the Tao. This is expressed in the phrase, "when not a single thought arises, the ten thousand things merge with the Tao."

The value of learning the above principles is that one can use them to check whether or not one's own practice is going in the right direction. If one's practice takes one toward a state of undifferentiation—what we can call "returning to zero"—then one's practice is going extremely well, and it could very well lead to marvelous results.

■ ■ ■

In the discourse at the beginning of this chapter, Huang Yuanji does not use the concepts of jing, qi, and shen. Instead, he discusses wuji, taiji, yin-yang, the five phases, and the ten thousand things. Just as is the case with the jing-qi-shen triad, the concepts Huang Yuanji presents in this discourse can also be mapped out using Taoist numerology. In this case, "zero" corresponds to wuji, while "one" corresponds to taiji (which Huang Yuanji also describes as "intrinsic order"). "Two" corresponds to the paired qi of yin and yang. "Three" represents further differentiation, to the plane where the five phases govern all objects and phenomena that have shape and form. From there, the "10,000" is born.

There is a confusing point in this chapter's opening discourse that is worth paying close attention to. Huang Yuanji uses the term "intrinsic order" to represent taiji, and he uses the word "qi" to represent yin and yang. When he does so, he is implying that the universe's evolution takes it from intrinsic order to qi. Thus, in his discourse above, Huang states, "inside this unified qi, because there is intrinsic order, there arises differentiated qi." The idea of intrinsic order giving rise to yin and yang qi is quite tricky to understand.

Because intrinsic order and unified qi are inseparable, all objects and phenomena are endowed with both of them, and neither factor can be said to come before the other. So, when Huang Yuanji says "because there is intrinsic order, there arises qi," the qi that he is speaking about cannot be something that exists at the same level as unified, prior-heaven qi. Put another way, the dualistic qi of yin and yang that is born of the intrinsic order in taiji is different from the unified, prior-heaven qi, even though both of them are called "qi."

Within taiji, intrinsic order and unified prior-heaven qi are both present in a yet-to-be-differentiated state. Although prior-heaven qi is present in taiji, Huang Yuanji uses the term "intrinsic order" almost as a synonym for taiji. Similarly, after yin and yang divide, even though both intrinsic order and prior-heaven qi are still present, Huang specifically uses the term "yin and yang" to describe the stage at which differentiated qi has emerged from taiji. We have to be careful here in order to properly understand Huang Yuanji's teaching.

■ ■ ■

When discussing going against or following the course of the universe's evolution, it is important to keep in mind that internal alchemy is not one of the natural sciences. Studying internal alchemy is not a way to research how the physical universe came into being, and more to the point, that is an issue of little interest to this discipline. Internal alchemy's cosmology provides a model that explains how cultivation affects one's life. In the end, "following the current" or "going against the current" are vital ideas only insomuch they apply to the direction Taoist practice takes us in our lives.

In terms of a person's life, "following the current" describes the process of going from prior heaven to later heaven. Most people habitually "follow" the external objects that our minds latch on to. Once we leave unconditioned, prior-heaven existence and are born into conditioned, later-heaven life, we are swept away by the world and its forms. Thoughts whose basis is in the physical body arise, and in time they produce later-heaven passions and desires, which lead to numberless delusions and divisions in the mind. These tendencies cause our energy as well as our thoughts to scatter outward, which in return results in body and mind disconnecting from one another. It is through these tendencies that primordial jing, qi, and shen are slowly depleted during our progression from childhood to adulthood and onward to old age and death. On the level of individual evolution, this is called "going along with the current."

In Taoist alchemy, to cultivate is to "go against the current," or to "return." This means putting an end to the outward dissipation of jing and shen, letting the body and mind once more join as one, and then letting one's self merge together with the universe. This process takes one gradually from later heaven back toward prior heaven. The entire curriculum of refining jing to transform qi, refining qi to transform shen, and refining shen into emptiness runs "countercurrent."

Always keep in mind that when inner alchemists speak of going with and against the current, they are not solely concerned with the evolutionary path of the universe, but with that of the individual, as well.

■ ■ ■

The information above gives us a theoretical basis for understanding what Taoists mean by "going back to the root and returning to the source." We will now take a look at two of the major approaches to actually accomplishing this task.

One of these approaches holds that returning to the Tao is not difficult at all, and that one can work on it all the time, wherever one might be. This line of thinking stems from the observation that we all came from the Tao, and indeed remain immersed in the Tao, so we in fact never actually left it. The Tao manifests within us as our prior-heaven life, which is one and the same with our prior-heaven nature. Prior-heaven fundamental nature, which is our true life, is blended into the Tao. Because of this, the energetic pivot that can take a person from later heaven back to prior heaven is always present;

the portal of the mysterious pass is capable of opening at any time. Given that this is so, a single thought is sufficient to trigger a sudden awakening that brings a person back to the Tao. This is why Huang Yuanji quotes Confucius's proclamation, "I wish for benevolence, and here benevolence is." A benevolent state of mind is never far off—as soon as we wish to arrive at that state of mind, then, well, there we are. The Tao is no further away than that.

A change that takes place in the space of a single thought can lead one from wandering lost in delusion to awakening. We already know that all thoughts are empty, as there is no such thing as a thought that can be grasped hold of. Thus, if one uses wisdom to observe thoughts, it is possible to return to the prior-heaven workings of the Tao.

On the basis of a similar recognition, Chan Buddhists say it is possible to become a buddha via sudden awakening. Why should awakening be difficult, they ask, when buddhahood is something you already possess? Buddhahood is your basic state, so there are no special conditions that need to be met before you can obtain it. Since buddhahood is your fundamental nature, the only thing you need to do is recognize it, discover it, and awaken to it.

In Buddhism there is a famous allegory about a beggar who has no idea that there is a priceless jewel sewn into the folds of his clothes. With no knowledge of the incredibly valuable jewel on his person, he unwittingly roams the streets asking for alms. This allegory describes all of us ordinary people; unaware of the priceless jewel we all carry inside us, we search endlessly in the outside world. We behave like beggars, despite the fact that we are all already the sovereigns of our own internal kingdoms. We are pitiable, but only because we never open the treasure chests we already carry within.

As humans, it is the norm for us to strive at all costs for grandeur and wealth, and for us to look enviously at those who enjoy great fame and success. But from the perspective of Taoist cultivation, so long as they fail to find contentment in their hearts and instead rely upon external objects and occurrences to bring them happiness, then even royalty and the leaders of nations are still just beggars. Externally they may be kings, but they are needy paupers on the inside. Conversely, a person who has truly awoken to the Way is an emperor within. Even if he or she lives in dire poverty, having already found the heart's home, he or she enjoys incredible wealth, and wants for nothing.

So, in terms of hsing cultivation, awakening is possible at any time and any place; when one awakens, it is possible to return to the source at that very moment. From this standpoint, it is equally possible for all people to awaken. Each person has the same opportunity—the only question is whether or not he or she manages to grab ahold of it. That is the main issue at the heart of "sudden awakening."

■ ■ ■

Whether Taoist cultivation is accomplished through sudden awakening or gradual practice is one of this tradition's perennial questions, and the various lineages have long debated it. Some in the sudden awakening camp go so far as to say that theirs is the only way; they claim that no matter how skillfully the gradualists practice, they are only adding and accumulating more "stuff," and they will never make it back to the Tao. Their calculus is that adding more of that which is limited (practices and methods) to that which is already limited (individual being) will never bring one to the unlimited (the Tao). They hold that, because the Tao is totality, the only way to reach it is via awakening. Those at the extreme of this view end up rejecting all of the "you wei" methods found in gradualist practice, as they believe that the "doing" of such methods is unnatural and therefore disconnected from the Tao.

However, at the other end of the spectrum are those who adhere to gradualist teachings. They hold that Taoist cultivation is a slow process requiring the accumulation of merit and skill, and they think it impossible that one could completely awaken to the Tao and obtain total liberation in one instant. Their understanding is that cultivation is a long-term affair, and over its course of its progression, periods of buildup give way to sudden breakthroughs. Those who take this viewpoint to its extreme reject the theory of sudden awakening. To them, the notion of reaching buddhahood through sudden enlightenment is untenable.

The reality is that there are reasonable points to be found on both sides of this debate, and that either camp may seem correct when viewed in a certain light, but wrong when viewed in another. This is because *both* of these mindsets fail to see the Tao in its entirety. From the standpoint of the workings of the Tao itself, sudden awakening and gradual practice are two inseparable aspects of a single thing. In philosophical terms, the relationship between sudden and gradual awakening is one of "quantitative change" and "qualitative change." "Quantitative change" represents the process of gradually cultivating, whereas "qualitative change" speaks to the process of sudden awakening. The key point is that if quantitative accumulation does not take place, then the conditions that are necessary for qualitative change to occur will be absent. At the same time, if a qualitative shift is never achieved, then quantitative accumulation ends up being meaningless. These two aspects of self-transformation have to be taken together and allowed to harmonize.

Just a moment ago we spoke about how awakening to the Tao is supposed to be very easy, because the span of a single thought is all that is needed to restore one's original nature. What that perspective emphasizes is the potential every person possesses for their prior-heaven nature to manifest itself. The unavoidable question this perspective leads to is, if all people share this potential, why don't any of them realize their potential and awaken to the Way? The answer lies in the fact that, at the later-heaven level, each individual is affected by the force of karma.

All living things, over the course of vast spans of time, accumulate innumerable impressions in their hearts. These impressions are stored like infinite seeds of future attachment in the storehouse of the mind. In Chinese there is a fascinating term, "the field of the mind," which portrays sentient beings' hearts as like rice paddies that gradually fill in until becoming mired with muck. For all of us, this muck is already so thick and deep that there is no way to remove it all at once, and thus gradual work is necessary. From this perspective, cultivating the Tao is not easy at all, and it is important not to get full of oneself or start thinking oneself somehow special. This teaching reminds us that *even if* one is enlightened, so long as later-heaven habitual qi remains—so long as polluted seeds remain hidden in the storehouse of consciousness—then true liberation is still a long way off.

This teaching explains why gradual practices are indispensable. If we wish to eliminate the deep-rooted habits and attachments in our lives so that we can set foot upon a new path, we have to clear the muck bogging down the "fields" of our hearts. The work required to embark upon a new path is arduous indeed.

■ ■ ■

Sudden awakenings and gradual practices need to be combined with each other. There are circumstances where one first engages in step-by-step cultivation and then has a sudden awakening, but there are also situations that work the other way around.

Placing step-by-step practice before sudden awakening is done so that people who have not yet illuminated the heart and glimpsed its nature will have a method that allows them to engage in cultivation. Practice lets people curb the force of karma and the qi of habit in their lives, and thereby helps them to break free of attachment. This work improves the quality of the seeds planted in one's "field of the heart." Cultivating in this way creates favorable conditions for illuminating the mind and realizing one's original nature.

Sudden awakening can occur before any gradual practice has taken place. This happens when a person awakens and finds the "home of the heart," thereby recognizing the ultimate nature of the mind is, and always has been, empty, numinous, and radiant. Such insight can serve as a starting point for cultivation. When a person who has already had this insight finds that mental distress, qi of habit, or the tendency to cling to objects or phenomena are arising within his or her heart, he or she should immediately shine the light of awareness upon whatever is arising, return to prior-heaven original nature, and remain firm in the knowledge that regardless of what vexations are active in the mind, they are unrelated to original nature itself. In this way, the practitioner will not be swept away by the activity of the mind. The point of cultivating *after* awakening is to transmute the qi of habit and to dispel the forces of karma that remain in one's "storehouse."

According to the teachings of Taoist internal alchemy, first awakening and then engaging in gradual practice involves "using prior heaven to transform later heaven." Gradual practice that takes place before awakening is "using later heaven to return to prior heaven." When prior heaven and later heaven are fully integrated, then so too are gradual practices and sudden awakenings. A person who can unite these two things will succeed in cultivating the Tao.

. . .

The prior-heaven realm must be awakened to, and the qi of habit in the later-heaven realm must be refined. These two tasks must be accomplished in an integrated manner.

Gradual practice is a process of cleansing the heart. It is sometimes described in Taoist literature as "letting the human heart die so that the heart of Tao can come to life." It was in reference to this process that Wang Chongyang called himself a "living dead man" and even named one of the places where he meditated "the Tomb of the Living Dead Man." "Living" meant that he was, of course, still alive, but what had "died" was his "human heart." This was another way of saying that he was no longer a captive of later-heaven, self-centered thinking.

In Taoist circles one sometimes hears the phrase, "If you don't want to die, then you'll have to perish." The meaning of this phrase is, "So you want not to die? You want to become a Taoist immortal? Well fine, that's simple—the only thing you'll have to do is get your later-heaven human mind to die!" Once the so-called human mind is gone, prior-heaven original nature comes to life; the "heart of Tao" is then active, and because it is eternal, one who has truly discovered it can be said not to die.

This teaching is another place where the concepts of going with or against the current apply. To go with the current is to follow the "human heart," which means having a mind that is prone to scattering itself outward as it attempts to clutch on to this or that object or phenomenon. To go against the current requires dismissing the human heart, so that one can return to one's prior-heaven nature.

However, it needs to be clearly stated that what "letting the human heart die so that the heart of Tao can come to life" really describes is a *result* of practice, not a *way* to practice. In terms of actual practice, the "human heart" and the "heart of Tao" are not two separate things that can be pitted against each other. One should not actually try to reject one's human mind while chasing after the "Tao mind." What these Taoist teachings describe is the awakening of wisdom, not an internal war waged against the ego. The task is to realize what the human mind is at its base, not to stubbornly struggle against it. The only correct way to "let the human mind perish" is to experientially realize that it is, by its very nature, empty. Suppressing, rejecting, or struggling with any aspect of one's mind is mistaken practice.

■ ■ ■

Taoists often liken the "heart of Tao" to the innocent mind of a newborn. In his discourse, Huang Yuanji teaches that it is the mark of a sage to have restored such a mind; he calls this the "heart seal of sages." In Chan Buddhism, there exists the idea that a person who has realized the Way can directly transmit it to others, by imprinting the "seal" of his or her mind onto students' minds. This does not mean that something within one person's heart can literally be delivered to another person's heart. Rather, it means that when a student "gets it," his or her mind bears the very same mark as the teacher's, that of "newborn innocence."

It is important to keep in mind that "the innocence of a newborn" is only a metaphor. The psychological state of a person awake to the Tao does not really have that much in common with the mind of an actual infant. That said, some characteristics of newborn babies' minds and enlightened people's minds are indeed quite similar. For example, they both react in a natural, spontaneous manner, unhindered by later-heaven tendencies like excessive distinction-making or attachment. However, there is a major difference between sages' and newborns' minds: even though babies' minds function in a very natural manner, they are not awake to their own nature. The only reason babies' minds do not make distinctions is that they have not yet had a chance to develop this habit; they act without thinking, but that is because their capacity for thought is unrealized. In contrast, a sage's mind is what comes after thinking and distinction-making finally cede control. Thought and distinction are things the sage has transcended, not things he or she has yet to develop.

"Primordial undifferentiation," or *hundun*, is a term that can be used to describe sages' minds, as well as those of infants. But the hundun of sages is "acquired," in the sense that sages first fully develop a later-heaven thinking mind before "going back to the root and returning to the source" in order to arrive once more at the prior-heaven state. Sages are thus fully conscious within primordial undifferentiation. They return to hundun after attaining liberation, whereas newborns are only there because their cognitive minds are still undeveloped.

The rather free-flowing discussion above summarizes the main themes of Huang Yuanji's lecture at the beginning of this chapter. There is no need to comb through each point he raised in his discourse, as most of the core concepts were touched upon in earlier chapters. I thus invite readers to plunge into Huang's lecture on their own.

10

天人相同

THE UNIVERSE AND THE
INDIVIDUAL, INTERCONNECTED

Students, when concentrating shen to nourish yourselves in tranquility, you yourselves must overpower and transmute the gloomy yin qi found between heaven and earth. Then, assuming the position of heaven and earth, nurturing the ten thousand things, repairing the deviations of heaven and earth and filling in the gaps in creation—these will not be difficult tasks.

Why is it that people see heaven and earth as incredibly vast, and believe that the powers of creation are controlled by the universe, yet conclude that humans pale in comparison? This is because they do not contemplate the "three forces" so often named by ancient sages and worthies: Heaven, Earth, and Humanity. They do not consider that, just as humans rely on the universe for life, the universe also relies upon humans to exist. If humans did not have a role in regulating creation and harmonizing yin and yang, then what need would heaven and earth have of us?

Thus is it said: "Humans are the heart of heaven and earth." If achieved humans did not set forth to take part in the origins of creation and assist with the transformations of heaven and earth, then heaven and earth would become undifferentiated chaos, and would not be capable of giving birth to and nurturing infinite beings.

Any ordinary, inconsequential fellow also "takes part and assists" in these things. They are not responsibilities that only lofty and extraordinary sages are capable of shouldering. How is that? The moment an ordinary person's heart is rectified, then the heart of heaven and earth is also rectified; the moment an ordinary person's qi flows smoothly, then the qi of heaven and earth also flows smoothly. Heaven, earth, and humans: while the point of absolute sincerity that interconnects them is extremely subtle, its activity lies in between each moment of stillness and movement, and in between each moment of speech and silence.

Thus, because the universe and humans are fundamentally interconnected via the very same qi, when I move, the universe stirs; when I am tranquil, the universe stills; when I am at peace, the universe settles; when I am righteous, the universe rightens. All of this originates in the profundity of breathing out and breathing in. It is not something so deep and distant as to be unreachable.

The only worry is being unwilling to reduce desires and maintain a tranquil mind in order to realize the lucidity, brightness, and vast spaciousness of the universe by oneself. If one can refrain from carelessness for the span of a single thought, then that thought puts heaven and earth in their places. If one can refrain from indiscriminate action for the span of a single breath, then that breath is the foundation of heaven and earth.

When one can do this to the level where it comes naturally, then the self is the universe, and the universe is the self. Not only this, one will encompass the heavens and earth, and transform and nurture heaven and earth. One will not be smelted by heaven and earth; rather, one will bring heaven and earth to completion.

When the sage said that the universe knows him, how could he merely have been speaking of the vast and silent external universe? In fact, it is but an instant of internal self-awareness that one connects to the subtleties of the universe.

In the Way of cultivating and refining, in the highest-order method of creating the elixir, one's shen enters into empty nonexistence, not attaching to form, not attaching to emptiness, instead forgetting both form and emptiness, until in due time one completely dissolves, and even the two words "empty" and "nonexistent" cease to be of use. This is what Chuang-tzu meant when he said "those whose shen is of the highest order take passage upon the light."

Shakyamuni Buddha used this method of recognizing the absolute void as subtle and profound being in order to achieve buddhahood. Few who fol-

lowed him have been able to understand this. Some spiritual know-it-alls claim that "the Buddha only cultivated hsing and did not cultivate ming." Little do they know that within this light is encompassed both shen and qi. Taiji is wuji. That which appears with no appearance, and has silence as its sound, is the root from which both shen and qi arise.

If one refines this light, there is nothing that is not brought to completion. How could it be anything like later-heaven shen and qi, which are split into yin and yang? For people in later times, this principle is difficult to understand, and they cannot be blamed for falling into one-sided cultivation of hsing.

As for mountain sprites and underwater goblins, even though they may be able to walk upon mist or fly through the sky, in the end their cultivation of the mind's nature is incomplete, so they fall onto the side of practicing mechanically, and ultimately they cannot avoid being wiped out by the course of nature. How do such beings cultivate? They do what Chuang-tzu alluded to when he said "those whose shen is of a lowly order take passage upon jing." This means using a shen that is neither clear nor bright and concentrating it in the aperture of later-heaven jing. In due time, when such training is successful, they too can enter samadhi, and they too can project their shen. But they ever remain as polluted and turbid ghosts; even if they can be said to have great longevity, they are still no more than ghosts clinging to corpses. They definitely do not have the numinous connection, and they lack benevolence, justness, virtue, and integrity. Though they may achieve unusual skills and fantastic abilities, they are no more than keen, clever ghosts.

All of you students: you ought to choose the highest-order method.

■ ■ ■

In any discussion of "cultivating the Tao," we can look at the principles of practice from a variety of different angles, but the essential point is always the same: a cultivator aims to go back to the root and return to the source. The goal is to return to the homeland of the heart, the Tao. As simple and straightforward as that goal may seem, identifying it invariably raises other questions: *Who* is it that goes back to the Tao? How does one get there? What is it that prevents us from already being there? Cultivators need to give serious thought to these questions.

In our typical states of mind as we go through life, we are seldom the masters of our own bodies and minds. Quite the opposite, we are slaves to them. I say this because, when it comes to most of what we do and say, we are not really in charge of ourselves; instead, we just act in response to whatever is going on in our external environments. Often, we *seem* to be in charge, saying and doing whatever we please, acting however we like. Even so, that does not mean that our decisions reflect our true selves. Yes, we do and say whatever we like, but we do so without awareness and clarity. This means our lives are essentially controlled from behind the scenes by long-established habitual patterns. We can go through our lives as little more than automatons, doing nothing but endlessly acting out our conditioned reflexes.

A person without awareness is like a robot that functions on the basis of programmed, automatic responses. Countless programs might be running at the same time in a person's "biological computer." Each one of a person's past actions, thoughts, and ideas is written into his or her mental programming, and this programming can function automatically, determining the way a person thinks, speaks, and behaves in the future.

Consider this question: When our thoughts race uncontrollably from morning to night, does that mean our "selves" are thinking? The answer is an emphatic no. Our endless torrents of chaotic mental activity come from the force of habit that builds up inside us over the long spans of our lifetimes. This is the karmic "programming" that compels us to behave reactively, including by causing us to think endlessly about this or that, without having any ability to stop our own thoughts.

When we want to stop our thoughts, we quickly find out that we lack the ability to prevent our minds from racing. Throughout the day, if we pay careful attention to ourselves, we soon realize that most of our behavior is enacted with very little consciousness. From the moment we get out of bed and start thinking about what we might do that day, our thoughts are already in constant flux. As soon as we come up with one idea, a new one follows on its heels and causes us to forget all about what we were just planning on doing. We might decide to head out to a café, but we end up passing a store that catches our attention, and that cup of coffee suddenly slips from mind, replaced by something else.

Thoughts flow endlessly through our minds, and we seem to have no say over them. When we are out walking, we are barely aware that we are doing so. True, our legs are taking us down the street, but as often as not, our minds are busy with something else altogether. It is the same when we eat—our mouths might be busy chewing on our food, but our minds have flown off somewhere far from the dinner table. All day long, the mind is filled with multitudes of thoughts and ideas zooming all over the place.

When we say "I want this, I want that," the "I" we are talking about almost always refers to nothing more than one of our infinite number of thoughts. So it is true that each of us possesses an "I," but close examination reveals that this "I" is not one thing, but actually a giant heap of "I's." These I's put on a dramatic performance that lasts for as long as we live. A thought can temporarily act in the role of protagonist, but there is no thought that really *is* the protagonist— thoughts just fleetingly take the stage one after another, in endless succession.

Think about the sweet things young lovers say to each other: "I will love you for a thousand years!" "That's not enough, you should love me forever and ever." "I will, I'll love you forever and ever after!" When somebody who really is in love with you says something like that, he or she is not lying to you. The person really does feel that way, because the "I" that has taken the stage to say those words is totally sincere. Unfortunately, that "I" is just a spokesperson, not somebody with the power to actually carry through with whatever is being promised. That "I" might even go so far as to sign a contract, but as life changes, so does the "I." After three months, or maybe even just three days, that "I" will leave the podium, and a new one will come to take its place. The new "I" might not remember the previous "I's" promises, and because of some small event or another, it might suddenly decide that dating you is insufferable. A love once meant to last a thousand years can begin crumbling after three short days, and before long conflict sets in. This is simply because the promises that come out of our mouths may only reflect one of our "I's," and not the entirety of our beings.

Our true beings almost never reveal themselves—all we witness is the rotating series of performances put on by our innumerable "I's." One moment we are happy, our hearts bubbling over with joy, but the next moment we can plunge right into the depths of anxiety and despair. Our thoughts, as well as our psychosomatic states, are constantly changing. Some might wonder: So is there a central, unifying "I" amid all of this? The answer is no! Most of us are no more than slaves to our surroundings, our internal worlds determined by the people around us. This is why a single word uttered by another person can strike a fatal blow to our hearts, troubling us so deeply that we literally cannot stop ourselves from thinking about it. A truly happy person would never get caught up in another person's words like this. It is only because we are not the sovereigns of our own beings that we end up getting buffeted by the things taking place in the world around us.

If it is true that our lives are a sequence of performances put on by a crowd of "I's," and that there is no integrated center in the midst of all of this, then where does happiness fit into the picture? After all, given the nature of our lives, even when we do experience happiness, not only is it fleeting, but the "I" who enjoys it is just the one that has temporarily taken center stage in our mind. That "I" plays its part, creating and enjoying a sense of happiness, and then it exits the stage. This is not the same as truly living life, with dignity and grace emanating from within one's real being.

This is why, at its core, Taoism teaches us how to become our own masters. The first step, naturally, is to find out what that actually means. We have to awaken to who it is we really are. This is done by illuminating the mind to see its nature, which is synonymous with finding one's prior-heaven "protagonist." If one does not realize what one is at one's core, then self-mastery is out of the question.

In the performance of life, the true center of the show remains ever hidden, always behind the curtains, never getting the chance to occupy the stage. Our first task, then, is to clearly see who the "protagonist" is, and to stop being fooled by all the "I's" playing bit parts. Once one finds the reality of one's being, one will clearly see the various short acts taking place on the stage in one's mind for what they are. One will cease to identify with them and cease to be attached to the stories they tell.

When a person who has realized what he or she really is thinks or emotes, he or she knows that whatever thoughts or emotions arise are no more than guests that have briefly taken the stage. There is no reason to reify them. Joy can disappear in the blink of an eye, and so too can frustration. Whatever arises is bound to change; since all thoughts and emotions are impermanent, none of them needs to be treated as particularly special. A person with this realization also knows that his or her true being is the only part of him- or herself that is actually capable of enjoying life in all its flavors. A person who has awakened and returned to the essence of his or her being sees through illusions and is no longer deluded by all the things taking place in the outside world. At all times, such a person recalls exactly what he or she really is. To accomplish this is to return one's to authentic, original nature; it is also to cease to be a slave to one's reactions to one's environment.

■ ■ ■

The first step in cultivation is learning how to maintain sovereignty over oneself while facing the outside world. Once one has this sovereignty, one ceases to be deluded by anything outside oneself, including fame, wealth, or any other possible marker of identity. One's surroundings and one's possessions will cease to seduce the mind. One will come to see these things as no more than tools to be used and no longer live one's life in service to them.

After achieving sovereignty relative to the external world, the next step in cultivation is to become sovereign over one's own body. This is a task that requires quite a high level of skill to achieve, because it requires transforming the habits ingrained in the body, as well as refining jing, qi, and shen. Being sovereign over one's body does not mean that one gains total, voluntary control over the body and its functions. Rather, it means that one is no longer disturbed by whatever is happening in the body. Thus, on days when one's body is in great shape, one is not beside oneself with joy, and on days when one is feeling under the weather, one's mood does not suffer as a result. One is able to clearly observe the state that the body is in and accept it. One no longer suffers on account of one's physical state, because one has ceased to identify as the body.

The third step in cultivation is to have sovereignty over one's emotions. Emotions are a subtle level of the physical body. The body, which cannot communicate with words, communicates via the emotions. Even a skilled cultivator still has emotions because the habits ingrained in the body have the force of accumulated karma behind them. However, a person who lives in accord with his or her true nature is able to sense and apprehend emotions without identifying with them. To achieve this means being able to perceive emotions as though they were just visitors passing through. Emotions are simply allowed to come and go, and one does not mistakenly see them as one's own self.

After this, one must learn to be the sovereign of one's thoughts. This indispensable step is central to further progress. "Thought" here refers to the ceaseless activity of the cognitive shen discussed in earlier chapters. It includes anything from thinking, making distinctions, calculating, and planning on through to comparing oneself to others, holding on to grudges, scheming, plotting, and so on and so forth. People who do not cultivate the Way tend to totally identify with thoughts—they treat their thoughts as though they were the seat of the self. Once one has illuminated the mind and glimpsed its nature, one awakens to the true nature of one's being, which is fundamentally formless and featureless. This yields the sovereignty that allows one to understand that the cognitive shen, with its capacity for mental activity, is a tool akin to a supercomputer. This tool then becomes something one can make use of, without it being an object of identity.

■ ■ ■

If one is the sovereign of one's thinking mind, then cognitive shen will "transmute," such that it behaves as a function of primordial shen. It is a mistake to think that a person who is awake to the Tao somehow loses his or her wits and becomes a nincompoop who cannot think or differentiate anything. Of course, Lao-tzu did say "those with great wisdom seem foolish," but he did not mean Taoist cultivation turns a person into an actual ignoramus. The key word here is "seems." Unlike many "smart" people, a skilled Taoist cultivator does not display a tendency to be calculating and engage in distinction-making, and thus may appear a bit like a simpleton. However, whereas a skilled cultivator may appear foolish while in fact having total sovereignty over his or her mind, a true fool has neither a sharp mind nor any awareness of his or her true nature.

Saying that a successful Taoist cultivator is the sovereign of his or her thoughts means that the thinking mind acts on his or her behalf. The cultivator no longer identifies with the thinking mind, but he or she clearly witnesses the mind's thought processes and its distinction-making, without getting dragged into those processes. When circumstances permit, he or she can then "shut down the computer," so to speak, which allows his or her prior-heaven, original nature to reveal itself. Letting the thinking mind shut down allows the cultivator to enter a state of complete naturalness, without distinction, without doing, free of the concepts of gain or loss, free of all anxiety and suffering, devoid of attachments, and undistracted by sensory phenomena. This is a liberated state, in which a cultivator returns to and merges with the Tao.

When a cultivator reemerges from that state, this is akin to going from the level of the Tao's "body" to the level of its "activity." Whenever circumstances require, a cultivator can reactivate the "computer" that is the thinking mind and use it to respond to whatever needs arise in the world. No matter how much the cultivator may use his or her mind, the mind will not become his or her "master," and the cultivator will never again spend endless days involuntarily influenced by the mind's unceasing motion.

All cultivators start as normal people, which means having the tendency to "live in the head." "Living in one's head" describes a state in which the habits of thinking and distinction-making are active, but the "sovereign" is nowhere to be found. Cultivators arrive at the "body" of the Tao when their true nature—which we can also call the "true self"—becomes manifest in a profound state of uncontrived tranquility. They go yet one step further—from the "body" of Tao to the "activity" of the Tao—when they are able to freely use their thinking minds while remaining unfettered by them.

Using Buddhist terminology, this is the point at which cultivation loses any escapist character, and one "enters the world"—one can no longer be accused of following a Hinayana interpretation of the Buddha's teachings, because one is now walking on the Mahayana path, capable of acting as a bodhisattva. A beginning cultivator works for self-awakening; a bodhisattva works to awaken others. As normal people, most of our thoughts revolve around the ego, so we use our minds to plan and calculate in a self-centered manner. Our plans to bring benefit to ourselves are often made at the expense of others. Conversely, the minds of people who understand the Way work on behalf of other beings. Because they already have freedom, there is nothing else that they seek.

People who are truly liberated brim with the radiance of aliveness, overflow with goodwill for others, and deeply celebrate life. They avidly share the state of awakeness with everybody else, bringing the redolence of their achievement with them when they mingle with humanity, letting their cultivation path be one of "awakening the self while awakening others." In Buddhist terms, to fully achieve this is to reach a state of completion—buddhahood itself. Buddhism teaches that one who merely attains self-awakening by finding the "sovereign" within and ending his or her own personal suffering will remain at the level of an arhat.[21] Going beyond that to liberate all other beings is what brings a cultivator full circle, taking him or her through bodhisattvahood and on to buddhahood.

■ ■ ■

Although there has been little mention of "merit" in these ten discourses, Taoism's teaching regarding rendering service unto others is no different from Buddhism's. The lion's share of this book's discussions is devoted to "self-awakening," but we must keep it in mind that, in the end, the goals of cultivation are not self-centered. The aims of cultivation are so broad in scope that they encompass the entire universe and all of the beings in it. This is because, when one truly understands the Tao, one realizes that no living thing is an independent entity and, moreover, that there is no such thing as individual liberation. Our personal liberation is not important; what is important is the entire world and all of its occupants. Liberation is only meaningful when it is shared by all. Each person is totally interconnected with the world at large, because each of us is of one body and one essence with the Tao. Failing to see this means treating the self as a separate entity, trying to stake out a personal claim on a piece of the universe, and then getting locked into contention with others. That is precisely what keeps people attached to their egos.

The truth is that each and every living being is as though a wave atop the vast ocean that is the universe. Each individual life is totally integrated with the entirety of this endless sea, and thus we both emerge from the ocean of the Tao while also remaining a part of it. This is why Taoism says that "the universe and the individual are interconnected." This term does not mean that there is no difference whatsoever between each person and the universe as a whole. Rather, there is interconnection, such that in terms of what we are at essence, we are completely blended into the greater universe, but in terms of how we take form as beings, we are still unique. Examining the various levels of existence that make up our being, we see that the differences between us and the Tao are greatest at the levels where we have concrete, discrete form. However, as we move away from those levels, observing the increasingly unformed and inapparent aspects of our beings, we find that they are more and more interconnected with the Tao, until they eventually become indistinguishable from it.

All of us are interconnected and integrated with each other and the Tao, but at the later-heaven level, each of us creates our own world, and in so doing we separate ourselves from the Tao. All of us, in a certain sense, live in our own universes. On the surface, we all go about our lives underneath the same big blue sky, and we might even be neighbors in the same city, but internally each of us perceives an entirely different world.

Within each of our hearts lie our own worlds, of which we are the creators. Some of us create our own Pure Lands, and others create polluted garbage dumps. Being simultaneously the creators of the worlds within as well as members of the greater universe that we all share, each of us bears a certain responsibility as we play our parts in the universe's creation and transformation.

There are two aspects to the role we play in the universe's development. One of these is energetic. One of the ways in which we are connected to and communicate with the universe is through the single qi common to all things. The connection and communication that takes place through qi is impossible to see, but it exists, operating through waves and vibrations to link all things and all occurrences. The other aspect of our role in the universe exists at the level of mind. Whenever we give rise to a thought, we emit a psychic wave. Its ripples emanate near and far, dispersing throughout the entire universe. For this reason, as we purify our hearts, we contribute to the purification of the entire universe. On the other hand, whenever we enter into filthy or frustrated mental states, we also exert our influence on the entire energy field of the universe.

We can use a simple analogy to understand how each individual human is interconnected with the single qi that fills the universe. In chapter 4 we spoke about three types of "food" that sustain us in our lives, the most important of which is air. All of us need to breathe, and if we are all occupying the same classroom, we do so together. The air that I breathe out and the air that you breathe out mingle together in the classroom—once that happens, it is impossible to say which portion of the air came from me, and which portion came from you. Within the space of our hypothetical classroom, our shared breathing of the same air brings us into communion. Taking a broader view, our breaths permeate the entire world—each and every breath that anybody takes is interconnected with everybody else's breaths. There can exist no living being who is independent and beyond influence. If I somehow taint or poison the air as I breathe it out, it can directly harm you. On the other hand, if I somehow purify the air as I breathe it out, it will be of benefit to all those who breathe it in.

The above example describes how we are interconnected at a fairly gross level. At a subtler level, human bodies are energetic, and the energetic field of each person's body affects everybody else's. Sometimes we enter an unfamiliar environment and it feels "just right"— this feeling reflects that place's unique qi field. Each of us contributes our own body's qi field to the collective qi field of the universe. Thus, on those occasions when we sit to meditate and enter into profundity, not only do we purify our own bodies and minds, we also take part in purifying the world as a whole. By that same token, when we commit grievous crimes against living things or any other heinous deeds, the ramifications of such actions affect not just our lives alone but the lives of all beings in the world.

Vast calamities are thus built of countless small disasters; the crises and catastrophes of our world are born of the collective karma of all living things. This is why Huang Yuanji teaches that we must all play an active role in purifying the universe we inhabit. By rebuilding the individual worlds unique to each of our lives, we simultaneously take part in reconstructing the entire universe. That we each have a role in the universe's evolution is an objective fact. Whether we are aware of it or not, all of us influence the world, while also being influenced by it. These influences of course vary greatly. Some are overwhelming, some negligible; some are positive, some negative.

■ ■ ■

At a deeper level than energy, our thoughts are also interconnected with our world. It is easy to see that our emotional and mental states affect our own physiological conditions, but states of mind also interact with the world beyond our bodies, both informationally and energetically. To students of Taoist cultivation, this point is what allows us to consciously take part in the universe's transformation and evolution. Instead of just being passively influenced by the world around us, it is up to us receive its influence in an active, engaged manner. Once a cultivator finds the core of his or her being and reconnects with the Tao, he or she begins to evolve in an active manner. A Taoist practitioner's personal evolution therefore pushes the universe to become more harmonious.

The meaningfulness of Taoist cultivation deepens considerably when one understands interconnectedness. A cultivator starts by transforming his or her own mental and physical condition and in so doing creates changes that ripple out to other people and to the universe. The harmony cultivated in a person's own body and mind affects the society he or she lives in, humanity at large, and the universe as a whole. The mentality informing our Taoist practice needs this kind of broadness of scope in order for us to ascend to the lofty heights cultivation can bring us to.

Buddhism teaches that it is necessary for Buddhists to produce "bodhichitta," the mindset that leads a person to seek awakening, in order to be able to help others do the same. In the language of Taoist alchemy, "merit" plays the same role. Merit is understood by Taoists as being so crucial that, if a Taoist practitioner wonders why he or she seems to not be making any progress on the path, the answer is often that he or she has failed to accumulate merit. A person who has not accomplished meritorious deeds will not be subtly aided by the universe as he or she attempts to cultivate the Tao. Moreover, if he or she already has a history of doing foul deeds, the karmic ramifications of these acts will influence cultivation in a negative manner.

When a person performs acts of kindness, these deeds are like offerings to the universe that help to purify it. The universe is just, and to those who build merit through selfless deeds it returns support in subtle ways. Taoist practice thus integrates all aspects of our existence. One is not "cultivating" only at those times when one sits to meditate in silence. One starts with refining and purifying one's own body, mind, behavior, and speech, but this work extends outward, becoming a part of the universe's evolution.

Building merit pertains to something called "simultaneously cultivating felicity and wisdom." A person might possess the type of wisdom necessary to embark on cultivating the Tao, but nevertheless find him- or herself in straitened circumstances that make it very difficult to actually practice. Conditions like these reflect that, in the past, this person did not make substantial contributions to the universe and to human society, and thus enjoys relatively scanty karmic rewards in the present. The more a person acts out of kindness and selflessness to benefit society and the universe, the more those acts result in a kind of reciprocation that creates the external conditions necessary for cultivation. This can be as simple as actually having free time to set aside for meditation and having access to a suitable place in which to do so.

There is an interrelationship between the cultivation of wisdom within ourselves and having felicitous conditions around us. Similarly, the work of seeking self-awakening and the work of helping to awaken others are inextricably linked. None of the factors determining progress on the Taoist path exist in isolation.

■ ■ ■

"The universe and the individual, interconnected."

In just a few words, the name of this chapter reveals the foundational principles that guide Taoist cultivation, as well as the ultimate goal. In the end, we have to transcend the limitations of the ego in order to return to the Tao. We transcend the self in order to locate the boundless life that exists in integration with all things. Inexhaustible, endless, and limitless, this life is like an ocean. To return to it is to no longer be just one wave atop its surface, but to be the limitless sea in its entirety.

Huang Yuanji mentions the "highest-order method for creating the elixir." It is this method that lets one return to the state of living as this vast ocean. By directly refining shen so that it returns to emptiness, one connects to the Tao. One does not need to start with "lower-order" methods and make step-by-step progress before practicing with the "highest-order" method. Rather, one can begin training with the highest-order method from the very outset.

Why is it possible to begin with the highest-order practice? The answer to this question can be found in the discussion of "sudden awakening" in chapter 9. We are all fundamentally already interconnected with the Tao—it is only because of our minds' habits of making distinctions and becoming attached to things that we separate ourselves from it. Thus, when we awaken with a single thought, returning the light of awareness to its source, we can demolish all of our attachment to the small, limited self, and instantaneously submerge in the great ocean of being.

There is no need to contrive a state of interconnectedness with the Tao. The only things preventing us from being connected to it are our own attachments. Our attachments turn into our own obstructions, occluding our real nature. When the obstructions are eliminated, reality opens up, and we awaken.

The Tao is limitlessness. It is limitless time and limitless space. Limitless time is eternity; it is the absence of even the appearance of time, and the transcendence of changes in time. Limitless space is the transcendence of the concepts of big and small. When space has no limits, there is no coming and no going, no beginning and no end. Our fundamental prior-heaven natures exist in a state marked by these traitless traits. None of the limitations inherent in later-heaven existence apply to prior-heaven nature. What we are at the prior-heaven level is oceanically boundless consciousness and immeasurable energy. Thus, starting from what we in essence already are, we can refine shen to return to emptiness, going straight back to a state of union with the Tao.

When the "highest-order method for creating the elixir" is practiced successfully, our prior-heaven, primordial shen connects to and merges with the emptiness of the Tao. In this state, primordial shen completes the processes of refining jing to transform qi and refining qi to transform shen of its own accord. With this type of practice, the work is accomplished by starting directly with fundamental essence itself. In order for this approach to work, however, one must first have direct insight into the essential nature of one's being. If one lacks such insight, then it is still necessary to search within the later heaven for that which is of prior heaven. This means starting out by using gradualist practices to move toward an awakening that reveals fundamental nature.

■ ■ ■

To practice the "highest-order method for creating the elixir" one needs a starting point, and that point lies in direct comprehension of one's essential nature, which originates in the Tao. Having this, one must then be capable of reverting to one's original nature, anytime and anywhere. If one's mind becomes distressed or one starts to cling to things, one has to be able to use awareness to see through what is happening, so that one can revert to one's nature right away.

The practice of directly returning to the Tao is very similar to the practice of Chan Buddhism. The true practice of Buddhism starts with what one already is. Buddhist practice can thus encompass both hsing and ming; this is because it works at the level where hsing and ming are still united as one, when they have yet to separate. Huang Yuanji refers to this type of Buddhist practice as "recognizing the absolute void as the incomprehensible entity."

At a certain point in China's history, some Buddhists began to declare that Buddhism focuses solely on the cultivation of hsing, while Taoism focuses solely on ming practices. This kind of thinking stemmed from the mistaken thinking of certain Buddhists. They used the imaginary limits created by this distinction to criticize Taoists for being attached to ming practices, while praising Buddhism for being focused on hsing. Huang Yuanji makes a point of saying that this kind of thinking is mistaken—authentic Taoism and authentic Buddhism *both* simultaneously cultivate the mind's nature as well as the essence of life. To think that one can practice with either just hsing or just ming is tantamount to imagining that one can sever the Tao into two pieces, one representing its "body," and the other its "activity." This is impossible.

When one experiences true emptiness, one finds that it contains something that is real and yet incomprehensible. An experience of an emptiness that is not imbued with this "subtle, profound being" reflects only insensate oblivion. In the ultimate state of true emptiness—where the reification of self, objects, and phenomena have totally disappeared—one simultaneously experiences reality from the point of view of emptiness *and* from the point of view of phenomena. In Taoist terms, this is the state of taiji, or of the Tao itself. Such an all-encompassing experience naturally includes both hsing and ming.

■ ■ ■

In earlier chapters I briefly described a few different ways to get started with Taoist meditation practice. As a small parting gift as we reach the end of the final chapter, I will introduce a way to start practicing the "highest-order method" described by Huang Yuanji.

This is a method of "observing the Tao." Regardless of whether or not one has actually awoken to the Tao, and regardless of whether or not one has actually illuminated one's heart and glimpsed its nature, one can start by "simulating" the Tao, so to speak. This means that one starts by intentionally "imagining" the Tao in order to create a sense of it. This practice is the epitome of an "expedient means"—it starts with artifice, but that artifice eventually helps to ferry one toward the real.

Here is the way to "visualize" the Tao:

Step one: Look upon time as limitless. See that the Tao has neither beginning nor end, as it is beyond time. Whether you think about humanity or the earth itself, those are things that exist in time. Even if their time is measured in billions or trillions of years, their time still has its limits. But the Tao is beyond all concepts of time. It never began, nor will it ever end. It is eternal, but to enter into its eternity is to go someplace "timeless." So the first step is to look upon time so that you see the eternity that transcends time and all of its markers.

(Buddhism's *Avatamsaka Sutra* describes the same concept of time, expressed in the line, "Amid all of the ten times, from time immemorial up through to the present, in all perpetuity, there is no time that is other than the present thought."[22] To "observe" the endless, unlimited time of the Tao is to eliminate your attachment to time. Not only does this type of observance remove the distinctions between past, present, and future, it also eliminates all concepts related to time, as well as the habit of making calculations on the basis of them. When you return to the eternal present moment, there are no distinctions. There is simply peaceful abiding. Within timeless time, there is no gain, and there is no loss. How could there be?)

Step two: Look upon space as limitless. See that the Tao has no edges and no borders, as it is beyond space. The paths that our lives unfold along exist within a limited space. We go from point A to point B, with everything we do defined by the markers of space that create distinctions between large and small, coming and going. However, none of the markers of space apply to the Tao. It is free of all boundaries and not defined by the concept of size. Thus, look upon space as unbounded and unlimited; see it as though it were not spatial. Seeing space in this way breaks the attachments to spatial concepts, allowing you to return to the eternal here and now. The here and now encompasses the entire universe. That is why in his commentary on the *Avatamsaka Sutra* Li Tongxuan said, "In the vast, unlimited world, there is not even a hair's breadth of distance between you and me."

Step three: Look upon the Tao as an integrated totality, inclusive of all things. All things exist within the Tao, including our bodies, including our thoughts, including even this practice itself. The wholeness of the Tao puts it beyond verbal expression and conceptualization. In order to try to conceptualize the Tao or describe it in words, we have to act as though we were somehow positioned outside the Tao, while in actuality whatever ideas we come up with and whatever words we might say are themselves a part of the Tao. So, you must experience the ineffability and incomprehensibility of the Tao.

The Tao is an integrated whole, where nothing is separate from anything else. Within the totality of the Tao, there is no gain, nor any loss. There is no coming to life, nor is there any loss of life. There is no increase, nor is there any decrease. This is because, from its own standpoint, concepts like gain and loss or increase and decrease do not suffice to describe the Tao. When we speak of gain and loss, we can only do so in reference to something that is limited. From the perspective of the limitless Tao, nothing is ever gained or lost, and nothing is ever added or subtracted. This is what the *Heart Sutra* expresses with the lines, "No birth, no death; no defilement, no purity; no increasing, no decreasing."

When you look upon the Tao as a holistic entity, your mental habits of making distinctions or worrying about gain and loss disappear. All markers of difference are shattered. Your body and your mind are both in and of the Tao. You see that this is true of others' bodies and minds, not to mention each star and planet and everything else in the universe. Our galaxy and an infinity of galaxies beyond ours all occupy the same Tao. In the Tao, there are no spatial limitations whatsoever.

■ ■ ■

Above are the three steps for "visualizing" the Tao. When practicing using these three steps, you may find yourself coming to a stop within the state of integrated wholeness, which cannot be expressed in words, and in which the mind makes none of the distinctions that separate you from the Tao. Simply observe the Tao as borderless, endless, inexhaustible, impossible to lose or gain, and beyond increase or decrease. When you notice thoughts or worries arise, just return to gazing upon the Tao as I described above. This method of observing will allow you to merge with the Tao.

It is very likely that if you try to "observe the Tao" according to these instructions, you will find that you do not really "merge as one with the Tao." However, this practice is an expedient that can eventually bring about real results. How will you know when you have truly joined as one with the Tao? At that time, even the act of "visualizing" disappears, and the practice becomes completely wu wei—it is accomplished through non-doing. All phenomena will then become quiescent, falling peacefully into place, being just as they always were all along. The entire world and all within it will enter into harmonious union. This is great liberation. It is the home to which we return.

Author's Postscript

In the first lunar month of 2009, I accepted an invitation to deliver a series of five evening lectures at the Hong Kong Taoist College. As I had recently published an annotated version of Huang Yuanji's *The Oral Record of the Hall of Joyous Teaching*, the organizers asked me to base my lectures on this text. Of course, there would be no way to thoroughly examine Huang Yuanji's monumental book on Taoist alchemy in just five short evenings, so I decided to choose ten chapters from the *Oral Record* and use them as a basis to broadly introduce the thinking behind internal alchemy. During each evening lecture I presented two of Huang's original discourses, each followed with a discussion of the points Huang raised. These ten discussions became the ten chapters of this book.

I attempted to explain Huang Yuanji's classic work by unpacking both its overall esoteric meaning as well as many of the specific things Huang said while he was teaching. My hope was to organically combine a broad-ranging explanation of Taoist thought with an analysis of what is written in *The Oral Record of the Hall of Joyous Teaching*. My thinking was that a close reading of Huang Yuanji's words would bring the essence of the principles of Taoist cultivation to light. However, I did not limit the contents of my lectures to Huang Yuanji's teachings, and instead used his words as starting points to present a plain-language summary of internal alchemy's theories and practices. At the same time, I blended my own experiences and insights from years of practice into each discussion. Thus, this book is far more than a line-by-line explanation of the *Oral Record*. Instead, it is an effort to reveal internal alchemy's theoretical framework, as well as the profound knowledge that lies hidden within the subtle language Taoists often use to express themselves.

My original plan was to first discuss the overall meaning of each of Huang Yuanji's discourses, and then present a line-by-line explanation of the original text. However, I soon realized that there was not enough time to stick to this approach. While trying to go through each sentence in the first discourse, I ended up using almost the entire evening, leaving little time for the second discourse. This left me with no choice but to let go of my plan to meticulously comb through the text, in order to preserve my wish to comprehensively explain Taoist alchemy. For this reason, only chapter 1 contains a line-by-line analysis of the original discourse, while in later chapters I only analyze certain important passages from Huang's teachings. In the last two chapters, I eschewed textual analysis altogether. This is also why the chapters differ in length—those where I focused on the specifics of Huang Yuanji's wording tend to be longer.

So, the chapters of this book progress from discussing all of Huang Yuanji's words, to only discussing key passages, before finally leaving the discourses behind altogether. This means that broad discussion of his teaching's underlying esoteric meanings gradually replaces a sharply focused textual analysis, which I think is an excellent progression. A semblance of balance and order grew from my change of plans as the evenings progressed, and several students expressed that they found the final two lectures the most enjoyable, because freeing ourselves from the particulars of the text allowed the discussion to really flow with shen and qi. Perhaps this was because I was no longer racing against the clock and was therefore able to take it easy and share genuine insights from my practice.

This series of lectures was a bit like an experiment, in which I tested out a new way of trying to speak about the Tao. This was the first time I lectured on this topic outside an academic setting, speaking in public to Taoism enthusiasts from all walks of life. Although the lectures and the format were far from perfect, I still feel the results of this experiment were incredibly meaningful, especially since it was my first attempt at using a classic text to "preach" the Tao.

I did not prepare notes before my lectures, and instead just followed my train of thought wherever it took me. I had the recordings of the lectures transcribed, not only so that those of us who were present could return to them to refresh our memories, but also in order to share the material widely with the reading public. It has long been a sincere wish of mine to exit the ivory tower of academia and use the fruits of my research and my own practice to provide service to the broader public, especially by sharing what wisdom and experience I have gained while seeking to understand the mysteries of our universe. It brings me great pleasure to have had the chance to realize this goal.

I must offer thanks to Lei Wing-Ming, chairman of the Hong Kong Taoist College at Green Pine Temple, whose invitation gave me the opportunity deliver the lectures that became this book. I also extend my gratitude to three students of the Hong Kong Taoist College: Fong Suk-Faan (she transcribed chapters 1, 7, and 8), Wai Yuk-Ming (he transcribed chapters 3 and 4 as well as part of chapter 2), and Lei Naam-Jung (he transcribed chapters 9 and 10). Additionally, I thank Qiao Qi of Shanxi Province for his transcription of chapters 5 and 6. I am especially grateful for the work of Yao Huifang of Beijing, who, in addition to transcribing part of chapter 2, proofread and edited the transcripts of all ten lectures. Her meticulous, conscientious work ensured that the transcripts accurately reflect the original lectures. Once the hard work of transcription was complete, I made a few editorial changes to the transcripts, and the book became what you now hold in your hands.

I am also grateful to all those who helped in the publishing process. I thank Tang Yijie and Li Yi for their strong backing, Dong Wei of the Central Compilation and Translation Press for his meticulous editing, and my many friends in the Taoist community for showing enthusiastic interest in this book. I thank Zhu Tieyu, chairman of Xinshan Taoist Studies Cultural Promotion, LLC, in Henan Province, for his support—it is wonderful to have a friend in the entrepreneurial world so dedicated to promoting the study of Taoism and traditional culture.

The mysterious science of Taoist internal alchemy has never been easily understood or practiced. Because inner alchemy ties into the somatic sciences and the mysteries of the universe and life itself, most scholars look at the study of this field as an undertaking best to be avoided, as it is incredibly difficult to obtain a real understanding. I devoted years of my life to reading thousands of volumes devoted to inner alchemy, including those found in the *Taoist Canon* and those found elsewhere. I have also explored internal alchemy through first-hand training for many years. This approach has given me a strong theoretical foundation alongside a wealth of practical experience. It is only by thus familiarizing myself with Taoism that I was able to lecture on *The Oral Record of the Hall of Joyous Teaching*, using my own knowledge and experience of inner alchemy's methods to explain Huang Yuanji's teachings in an accessible manner. I hope that this book will serve as a useful reference that helps others to deepen their research into internal alchemy. May it also light the way for all of us who seek to directly experience the wisdom contained in traditional Taoist cultivation.

This is my first book based on lecture transcripts, and to an extent it represents a new direction for my work. I intend to spend more of my time helping to satisfy the spiritual needs of the general public, especially by letting traditional wisdom serve modern people through public lectures devoted to explaining the classics of Confucianism, Buddhism, and Taoism. As I tread the never-ending path of Taoist cultivation, I hope to scatter seeds of truth that will grow to help others purify their hearts—so that they too will spread kindness to all those they come into contact with. I offer great gratitude and good wishes to all of the people that this book brought me into contact with. May it bring new beginnings to everyone who reads it!

—GE GUOLONG 戈國龍
Written in the Observing-the-Return Studio
Geng-yin year (2010), Summer

Glossary

BODHI 菩提: This Buddhist term refers to awakening/enlightenment/ realization.

BODY AND ACTIVITY 體用: see "substance and function."

COGNITIVE SHEN 識神: Refers to mental activity based upon distinction-making, thought, learned information, desire, and planning. "Cognitive shen" is a term for normal human mental activity, as opposed to the activity of the mind when a deep level of tranquility and clarity has been reached during practice.

DE 德: This character often appears in English as "virtue" or "integrity." At a more surficial level, de corresponds to acts of "goodness." At a deeper level, it comes from living in natural accordance with the Tao. It is sometimes written as *te*.

DHARMAKAYA 法身: Literally meaning "truth body" or "reality body," the dharmakaya is one of the "three bodies" (*trikaya*) in Mahayana Buddhism; it is the unmanifest and inconceivable "form" of buddhas. In internal alchemy, its meaning is closely synonymous with Tao. It is the "true" or "prior-heaven" body.

ELIXIR (*dan*) 丹: The character 丹 originally referred to cinnabar, but its usage in Taoist internal alchemy is distinct from its use in mineral and metallurgical alchemy. It represents the unification of the yin/ yang, extant/nonexistent, and prior-heaven/later-heaven factors comprising one's being. One explanation for reading the character 丹 is as a graphical unity of 日 (the sun, representing yang) and 月 (the moon, representing yin). The 一 (one) running through it represents this unity, while the 丶 (understood as a single dot, but stylized into a slightly elongated brushstroke in writing) in the center symbolizes the state of being born of this unity.

EMPTINESS: In this book, "emptiness" is used to translate two different Chinese characters. The most common is 虛, a character that figures prominently in Taoism. 虛 is a reference to the intangible and unmanifest nothingness from which all things arise and within which all things presently exist. The word "emptiness" is also often used to translate 空, a character used in Chinese Buddhism to translate the Sanskrit *sunyata*. The concept of sunyata explains that all objects and phenomena are "empty of" permanence and independent existence. Neither 虛 nor 空 is meant to utterly negate the reality we live in, nor point the way to nihilistic oblivion. In internal alchemy, although the two terms are not entirely interchangeable, their meaning is closely intertwined.

FIVE PHASES or FIVE ELEMENTS 五行: This term describes an ancient symbolic system that uses images of metal, wood, water, fire, and earth to explain how various phenomena come into being and interact with each other. The five phases are often arranged in a circular fashion, but internal alchemy makes use of an arrangement that treats "earth" 土 as the center around which the other four phases revolve. In this arrangement of the phases, earth, which is subtly integrated and ever present within the other four phases, symbolizes emptiness (both that of the Tao and that of a practitioner's mind). The emptiness that "earth" represents is reached by quieting the mind and allowing the mysterious pass to be active.

HEART 心: In both classical and modern Chinese, the words for "heart" and "mind" are written with the same character. Because these terms can often be used quite interchangeably, and also because the word "heart" has implications such as "central," "core," "authentic," "sensing," "intuiting," and "true self" in both English and Chinese, "heart" is frequently used to translate 心 throughout this book. However, when 心 is being used to discuss mental activity or the nature of the mind, it is translated as "mind."

HSING (Pinyin: *xing*) 性: This term is generally synonymous with "original nature," "buddha nature," "true mind," "prior-heaven mind," and "primordial shen." All of these terms describe the aspect of our beings that is not born and does not die, is inapparent, and is beyond limitation. Because hsing is used extensively in Buddhist teachings, it is often associated with the mind. However, hsing is not simply something "mental," in that its being is not predicated in any way upon the activity of the human mind.

HUNDUN 混沌、渾沌: Meaning something akin to "primordial undifferentiation," hundun can be thought of both as a primordial state from which all things emerged, as well as a state that can be returned to in meditation.

IMMORTAL 仙: Sometimes translated as "transcendent" or Romanized as "hsien" or "xian," this term refers both to humans who have reached the highest levels of Taoist cultivation (including through methods other than internal alchemy), as well as to divine beings that have always existed in close harmony with the Tao and never incarnated in the physical realm. In the context of inner alchemy, the goal of "immortality" should not be interpreted as an attempt to permanently stave off the aging and death of the physical body—scarce few of the founding sages of this tradition are said to have sought or attained such a result even in legends, and the deaths of most early masters are openly discussed in hagiographies, even if those hagiographies also include stories of their reappearances in visions or in temporarily assumed physical form following death. While it is true that a tiny fraction of internal alchemy practitioners *do* claim permanent physical existence as their goal, generally speaking the notion of immortality points figuratively toward the recovery of that which was never born and therefore does not die—that is, the nature of the Tao itself within the individual.

INSENSATE OBLIVION 頑空: This term describes a state of stupor or torpor that can be reached in meditation. Internal alchemists warn against mistaking this state for true tranquility; true tranquility only quiets the mind's churn of thoughts and emotions, not its capacity for observant awareness.

INTRINSIC ORDER 理: A term of particular interest to neo-Confucian thinkers during the Song dynasty, it was absorbed into Taoist internal alchemists' theoretical frameworks as well. This term refers to the laws, patterns, rhythms, and relationships underlying all things. Intrinsic order is usually seen as deriving from or reflecting the Tao.

JING 精: On a later-heaven level, jing can broadly refer to the physical body, to physical vitality, or more narrowly to the various fluid "essences" of the body (when the word "jing" is used in classical Chinese medicine, it generally refers to these things). On a prior-heaven level, jing can refer to the fundamental force of life, and is closely related to ming.

LATER HEAVEN 後天: This term refers to all that exists in the manifest, apparent world we all experience after leaving the womb. This world is governed by duality, time, and space. It is not "elsewhere" from the prior-heaven world, but for most of our lives (especially after early childhood) we experience it as though it were.

MIND 心: See "heart."

MING 命: This word implies life, both in the senses of destiny or life path, as well as in the sense of biological life. It therefore implies health, vigor, and energy. At a deeper level, it refers to the fundamental "spark of life" underlying one's existence as a living being. This latter aspect of ming is of a prior-heaven nature; when it is united with hsing, the elixir is created, and a return to the Tao becomes possible.

NONEXISTENT 無: This term refers to that which is inapparent, unmanifest, unknowable, ineffable, and intangible—yet real, ever present, and interwoven with all that "exists." It is closely related to the Taoist term "emptiness" (虛).

PRIMORDIAL 元: That which is "primordial" are those aspects of our beings that have not lost their prior-heaven nature.

PRIOR HEAVEN 先天: This term refers to the state prior to the "later-heaven" world of form, duality, and impermanence. From the standpoint of typical human experience, that which is prior heaven in nature is "empty" and "nonexistent." Thus, the period of life spent as an unborn child in the womb—with no thoughts, no sense of self or other, and no sense of place or time—is often described as prior heaven. However, even though they are generally beyond our awareness, the prior-heaven elements of our individual beings (as well as the universe at large) are immanent and ever present. The goal of internal alchemy is to recover one's prior-heaven nature and join with that of the universe.

QI 氣: This character's meaning is similar to "energy," but only in the sense that in English the word "energy" has a wide variety of colloquial and literary usages that describe all manner of phenomena. Qi does not merely refer to energy that can zap things or charge them up, but to things that can be felt and sensed. In the same way in which a locale, a piece of art, an activity, or a person might all be described as having a certain type of "energy," qi can describe a vast variety of things, and indeed the character is a part of countless compound words in Chinese. In internal alchemy, especially at the later-heaven level, qi does describe the body and mind's energy levels. At the prior-heaven level, qi describes the subtle aliveness of being itself, which is not exclusive to any particular individual or object, but rather suffuses and links all things, including that which is "nonexistent." The character 炁, which has the same pronunciation as 氣, is mentioned once in the book. This rare character is usually used to describe the prior-heaven field of qi that is, in essence, one with the Tao.

SHEN 神: This word is close in meaning to consciousness, spirit, and mind. At the later-heaven level, shen is called "cognitive shen." At the prior-heaven level, shen is called "primordial shen," and is effectively synonymous with hsing.

SUBSTANCE AND FUNCTION 體用: This pair of terms has been in use in Chinese philosophy for close to two millennia and remains widely used to this day. "Substance" refers to the "body" or "being" of a given subject, whereas "function" refers to its activity, its dynamic manifestations, its effects, and its ways. As these two terms refer to different aspects of a single subject, substance and function may be very different (for instance, substance may be intangible, but function observable), but they are inseparable aspects of the same whole. Due to the far-reaching influence of Wang Bi's (226–249) commentary on Lao-tzu, it is often said that the "Tao" and "de" are terms describing the substance (the so-called Tao) and function (de) of one and the same thing. In some contexts in this book I translate this term as "body" and "activity."

TAIJI 太極: Sometimes the word "taiji" is used in a way that means "yin and yang together," and therefore the widely recognized yin-yang symbol is sometimes referred to as the "taiji symbol." However, other understandings treat taiji as a state that exists prior to the separation of yin and yang. In these cases, taiji is usually depicted as a circle with a dot in its center, instead of as a yin-yang symbol. The circle with a dot at its center can be interpreted as implying that the energies of yin and yang are still entirely merged and indistinct in oneness. This dot is similar in meaning to the one found in the character for "elixir," 丹.

TAO (pinyin: Dao) 道: Often translated as "the Way," from its very first mention in Lao-tzu's *Tao Te Ching*, we are told that the Tao is ineffable, mysterious, incomprehensible, and unnameable. The Tao underlies all that exists, as well as all that which—from a human perspective—is "nonexistent." It is our origin, our return, and that which we cannot and indeed never have left.

TAOIST CANON 道藏: Enormous canons of Taoist texts were compiled several times during China's dynastic history. The Tang dynasty (618–907) canon contained over three-thousand fascicles, while the Song dynasty (960–1279) canon surpassed five-thousand fascicles. The Tang dynasty canon was lost to the fires of war, while the Song dynasty canon was destroyed on imperial order during the Yuan dynasty (1279–1368). The surviving collection entitled *Taoist Canon* was compiled during the Zhengtong reign period of the Ming dynasty (1368–1644) and expanded during the Wanli period.

TATHATA 如如, 真如: Sometimes translated as "thusness" or "suchness," this Buddhist term describes the mind that rests in the reality of the truth of things as they are.

TRUE INTENT 真意: This term describes a state reached in meditation. The cultivation of clarity and stillness will lead to deep tranquility and equipoise, and then to a state that can be described as "hundun." Being in this state allows the "mechanisms" of internal alchemy to unfold spontaneously and naturally, guided in a wu wei manner by true intent instead of being guided by thought or later-heaven intention.

TRUE MIND 真心: The meaning of this term is essentially synonymous with "hsing" and "tathata."

TRUE QI 真氣: When used in Taoist writings, this term refers to prior-heaven qi. It may refer to prior-heaven qi that lies in latent potential and constitutes "ming." It may also refer to prior-heaven qi that has become active within the human body as a result of inner alchemy practice. The uses of this term in Chinese medicine have different implications.

TRUE YANG 真陽: True yang is prior-heaven, primordial yang. It is the "true qi" of "ming." It is "yang within yin," symbolically represented as the prior-heaven yang line hidden within the two post-heaven yin lines of the kan/water trigram, ☵.

TRUE YIN 真陰: True yin is prior-heaven, primordial yin. It is the "true mind" of "hsing." It is "yin within yang," symbolically represented as the prior-heaven yin line hidden within the two post-heaven yang lines of the li/fire trigram, ☲.

WUJI 無極: This term refers to the non-dual, the non-polarized, and the infinite. It is sometimes framed as the stage preceding "taiji" in the universe's genesis, while other times it is understood as being a trait of reality that exists alongside the potential for duality within taiji, as well as the fully manifested duality of later-heaven existence.

WU WEI 無爲: Sometimes translated as "non-doing," "nonaction," or "doing nothing," wu wei describes the experience of activity that seems to initiate and accomplish itself, rather than activity that comes about due to thinking, planning, controlling, emoting, and so forth. Additionally, wu wei activity seems to take place "just because"—it is natural, spontaneous activity that need not have an explicable reason or purpose. For example, while eating a meal may be described as "you wei," the digestion of food, the distribution of its nutrients throughout the body, and the delivery of its by-products to their exits is entirely wu wei. Just as indigestion would be the inevitable result of trying to intentionally manage and control the body's ability to digest food, much of the work in internal alchemy is accomplished by getting out of wu wei's way. Similarly, were one able to ask one's stomach, "why do you digest," the stomach—whose behavior is wu wei—could only laugh quizzically and reply, that's just what I do.

YANG SHEN 陽神: In the context of yang shen, the character "yang" refers to that which is wholly "real" or "true," and therefore of a prior-heaven nature. In internal alchemy, the term "yang shen" is therefore sometimes used to refer to "primordial shen," which all humans are intrinsically endowed with, even if it is effectively dormant. Yang shen can also refer to the nature of shen in a person who has completed the path of internal alchemy. The mysteries of fully realized yang shen are beyond comprehension; miraculous tales surround this level of accomplishment, and it is often close to impossible to discern whether their meaning is literal, figurative, or a mix of the two.

YIN-YANG 陰陽: "Yin" and "yang" are words used throughout classical Chinese thought to describe any and all manner of dualities. The notions of "yin within yang" and "yang within yin" add subtlety and layering to the understanding of any pair of factors, by pointing to the way in which opposites contain the seeds of one another, and give rise to one another. Of particular interest to internal alchemists are the dualities of existence and nonexistence, prior heaven and later heaven, hsing and ming, and shen and jing-qi, all of which can be expressed using the symbolism of yin and yang.

YOU WEI 有爲: The opposite of wu wei, you wei refers to "doing" and implies an act being undertaken with intentionality and purpose. There is always a "reason" for you wei activity.

Notes

1. Here, the Sanskrit "dharma," when written with a lowercase *d*, is akin to the word "phenomenon." When written with an uppercase *D*, it refers to the teachings of Buddhism.

2. The "river chariot" has somewhat different meanings in different internal alchemy texts and practice lineages. It can refer to true yang qi itself, or to the movement of this yang qi through the body through the "governor meridian" running up the center of the back of the body, and the "conception meridian" running down the center of the front of the body.

3. The "six directions" refer to the four cardinal directions in addition to above and below; this term means "everywhere and all places."

4. The "broomcorn millet pearl" is a euphemism, often used in inner alchemy texts, for the result of the merging of prior-heaven shen and qi, or hsing and ming.

5. In the context of inner alchemy, dragon and tiger represent the prior-heaven essences (i.e., the central lines) in the two trigrams of *kan* and *li* (☵ and ☲, respectively), which Huang Yuanji discusses below. In this context, the number eight also represents both of those inner lines. Saying "double eight" is equivalent to saying "two times eight taels," which would be "a whole catty." (This is very similar to saying "two times eight ounces," which equals "a whole pound.") The importance of this allusion lies not with taels, catties, or the numbers eight and sixteen, but with the idea of combining the two "halves" of true yin and true yang to create something "whole."

6. The trigram li, ☲, has a yin line at the center of two yang lines. The yin line symbolizes the primordial tranquility of mind. Its

location, "hidden" between two yang lines, implies that this tranquility is of a prior-heaven nature, and therefore seldom realized in daily life. The trigram kan, ☵, has at its center a single yang line that symbolizes the primordial qi that is the essence of life. It too is "hidden," and must be made active and accessible through internal alchemy so that it can be "gathered."

7. This statement comes from an interpretation of the numerology of the "River Diagram," which is connected to the five phase-elements. In the "River Diagram," the number one is associated with water.

8. This term can be differentially interpreted, depending on whether one is reading this text as a "highest-order alchemical text" or a "middle-grade alchemical text." The former approach to practice makes use solely of prior-heaven factors; the latter involves later-heaven factors, including the physical body. When discussed in "highest order" teachings, the "earth cauldron" refers abstractly to the "center," which is also synonymous with the "heart of heaven." To gather medicine into the earth cauldron is, then, to return the mind to the mysterious pass and reside there naturally. Conversely, if "earth cauldron" is read as a "middle grade" alchemical instruction, it may refer to the so-called lower dantian in the abdomen.

9. Written here with a capital Q, Qi refers to the character 炁. Written with a lowercase q, qi refers to the character 氣.

10. Here, "ordinary" contrasts with the word "true" used above. In this context, "ordinary" is a synonym for "later heaven," and "true" is a synonym for "prior heaven."

11. "External breath" refers to the normal breathing of air.

12. This instruction, if interpreted as a "highest order" internal alchemy teaching, may refer to the mysterious pass; if interpreted as a "middle grade" teaching, may refer to one of the dantian locations of the body. Actual transmission from a teacher is crucial.

13. Yinqiao, from 陰蹺, is often understood as synonymous with the perineum region, the lowest point on the trunk of the body.

14. "Yellow court," from 黃庭, is variously defined in Taoist practices. One location is the upper dantian, located in the head.

15. The "purple palace," from 絳宮, usually refers to the middle dantian region.

16. This phrase, found in the *Treatise on the Awakening of Faith in Mahayana*, implies that all beings—from ordinary mortals through to buddhas—have the exact same type of mind. Because buddhas understand the actual nature of phenomena, they open the door to liberation; because ordinary beings "mistake the seeming for the real," they open the door to endless transmigration through the cycle of birth and death.

17. Huang Yuanji uses the same word, "qi," in the same sentence in two different ways. The "single qi" refers to universal prior-heaven qi; the second qi he mentions is that which has already separated into yin and yang. The relationship between them is one of prior heaven and later heaven.

18. These two terms refer to periods of training in some approaches to internal alchemy. The first, based on a metaphor that compares cultivation to building a structure, takes place near the beginning of training (some schools place it at the very beginning, but Huang Yuanji clearly thinks that it is beyond the reach of most beginners). The second, based on a metaphor that compares cultivation to nurturing a baby, takes place at very advanced stages in practice.

19. The two-hour period of zi goes from 23:00 until 01:00. This is midnight, when yin at its apex naturally gives rise to yang and the potential for morning is born. "Living zi" borrows from this concept to describe any moment in inner alchemy practice when yin, at its apex, births yang. It does not reflect an actual time of day.

20. The winter solstice is the calendrical equivalent of zi, or midnight; the exact same metaphors that are built around the "time of zi" can be built around the winter solstice, where the yang of spring is born from the yin of winter.

21. This teaching reflects the typical Mahayana Buddhist use of the word "arhat." Theravada Buddhist teachings differ.

22. This line comes not from the sutra itself, but from the foreword to Li Tongxuan's (635–730) *New Treatise on the Avatamsaka Sutra* (新華嚴經論). The "ten times" refer to the past of the past, the present moment in the past, and the future of the past; the past

of the present, the present moment in the present, and the future of the present; the past of the future, the present moment in the future, and the future of the future; and the thought in the present moment. This rather ornate example of Buddhist philosophy may simply be understood here as meaning "all time."